Constraints on Language Acquisition: Studies of Atypical Children

Constraints on Language Acquisition: Studies of Atypical Children

Edited by

Helen Tager-Flusberg
University of Massachusetts

LEA LAWRENCE ERLBAUM ASSOCIATES, PUBLISHERS
1994   Hillsdale, New Jersey   Hove and London

Lawrence Erlbaum Associates, Inc., Publishers
365 Broadway
Hillsdale, New Jersey 07642

Library of Congress Cataloging-in-Publication Data
Constraints on language acquition : studies of atypical children /
edited by Helen Tager-Flusberg.
    p. cm.
Includes bibliographical references and index.
ISBN 0-8058-0667-9
1. Language acquisition. 2. Handicapped children – Language.
I. Tager-Flusberg, Helen.
[DNLM: 1. Handicapped. 2. Language Development. 3. Language
Development Disorders. WS 105.5.C8 C756]
P118.C673 1994
401'.93 – dc20
DNLM/DLC
for Library of Congress   92-48969
                                                               CIP

Books published by Lawrence Erlbaum Associates are printed on acid-free
paper, and their bindings are chosen for strength and durability.

Printed in the United States of America
10 9 8 7 6 5 4 3 2 1

Contents

v

Preface

The idea for this volume grew out of a day-long symposium that I was invited to organize for the 1986 Boston University Conference on Language Development. The symposium brought together researchers studying language acquisition in very different groups of children — blind, deaf, brain injured, mentally retarded, and autistic. What we shared was an interest in grammatical development in children who faced severe obstacles to acquiring language. Despite the differences in our populations and methodological approaches, several common themes emerged from the presentations. First, the acquisition of grammar is a remarkably constrained process, though it may be impacted in certain predictable ways when linguistic input is highly impoverished. Second, grammar may be spared and even flourish in individuals whose cognitive or social functioning is otherwise severely impaired. And third, following on from these two themes, studies of children who are "experiments in nature" offer support for a modularity approach to language, while they illustrate some of the ways in which language connects with and even fosters aspects of cognitive and social development. These themes form the core around which this volume is organized, in order to illuminate the complex ways in which biological and linguistic constraints interact with other forms of knowledge and with different kinds of crucial experiences, which is the central goal of the book.

Eric Lenneberg was among the first in recent times to approach the study of language acquisition by investigating children with sensory, neurological, or cognitive impairments, and we owe him a significant intellectual debt. I was introduced to his work by Rick Cromer when I was still an undergraduate at University College London. Rick, who was working at the MRC unit affiliated with University College, had just formulated his version of the cognition hypothesis, sparking my own interests in language acquisition in children with autism. At the time of his sudden death, which occurred while this book was in progress, Rick was in the midst of his studies of DH, an adolescent girl with remarkable language abilities, who poses a serious challenge to any simple theory about the relationship between language and cognition. It is most unfortunate that Rick was not able to continue his unique work with DH and others like her, but I am grateful that he was able to complete his last and most detailed description of DH for this volume.

ACKNOWLEDGMENTS

Some of the preparation of this volume was undertaken while I was a Fellow at the Bunting Institute at Radcliffe College. I also received funding from National Institutes of Health (1RO1 HD 18833; 1RO1 DC 01234) during different phases of this project. I would like to acknowledge my gratitude to the organizers of the Boston University Conference on Language Development for their invitation to organize the original symposium. Finally, a very special note of thanks to Jason Barker and Kate Sullivan for their much needed assistance in the final stages of pulling this volume together; and to Judi Amsel, Kathryn Scornavacca, Robin Weisberg, and Debbie Ruel at Lawrence Erlbaum Associates for all their help, patience, and persistence.

Helen Tager-Flusberg

1 Contributions to the Field of Language Acquisition From Research on Atypical Children

Helen Tager-Flusberg
University of Massachusetts

After decades of research, most scholars generally agree that language acquisition is a complex and multifaceted process that involves the interaction of innate biologically based mechanisms devoted to language, other non linguistic cognitive and social mechanisms, linguistic input, and information about the social and physical world. Theoretical work in the field of language acquisition now needs to focus in greater depth and detail on some specific aspects of this general model, which is the main goal of this book.

The particular questions that are raised by contributors to this volume include:

- What kinds of constraints operate on the process of language development?
- Which aspects of the acquisition process depend on language-specific mechanisms?
- Are there critical brain structures necessary for the acquisition of language?
- What role do cognitive and social mechanisms play in language development?
- How critical is perceptual input about the physical and social world?
- What is the specific role played by linguistic input in the child's construction of a linguistic system?

These are just a few issues that must be considered in any detailed theory of language development, and the chapters in this volume provide us with some new insights into one of the most remarkable accomplishments achieved by almost all children.

In this volume these questions are addressed from the perspective of children who come to the task of acquiring language with major hurdles to overcome. Each chapter focuses either on an individual case, or studies of groups of children with different handicapping conditions, that in theory might adversely affect the acquisition of language. These conditions include deafness (chapter 2, de Villiers, de Villiers, & Hoban) and blindness (chapter 9, Peters), which significantly reduce the child's access to linguistic input and perceptual input respectively; mental retardation (chapter 5, Fowler, Gelman, & Gleitman; chapter 6, Cromer; and chapter 7, Rondal), in which the child's cognitive abilities are compromised; autism (chapter 8, Tager-Flusberg), which involves a major impairment in social functioning; and children with prenatal or perinatal brain damage involving the left hemisphere (chapter 3, Levy, Amir, & Shalev; and chapter 4, Feldman), generally considered to be the biological locus of language functions.

Why should the kinds of issues addressed here be investigated in studies of atypical children rather than relying exclusively on normally developing children? In normal children the period from birth to 5 is one in which all aspects of development, neurological, motor, social, affective, cognitive, as well language take place simultaneously. Given the very rapid developmental changes that occur in normal children across all domains during the critical years it is hard to unravel the contributions each makes to the others because they are so highly correlated and thus confounded. The child with some form of handicap provides a kind of natural experiment where one (or more) factor may be partialled out and therefore its influence can be more directly investigated. For example, in high-functioning children with autism whose primary deficits are in social functioning but who do not have mental retardation, one can selectively investigate the influence of social factors on the process of language development (see chapter 8, Tager-Flusberg). Although most children with mental retardation show delays in all aspects of development (chapter 5, Fowler et al.), there are some individual cases (see chapter 7, Rondal), or indeed syndromes (see chapter 6, Cromer) where language may be selectively spared. These examples provide particular and original insights into the relationship between language and cognition. Thus different kinds of impairments — neurological, developmental, or sensory — provide unique opportunities for investigating the influence of individual factors on the process of language development. By bringing together in one volume a wide range of studies that focus on a variety of atypical populations we can make some progress in piecing together the contributions made by a broad range of factors on the acquisition of language.

Many of the questions that are examined in this volume were first introduced into the newly emerging field of developmental psycholinguistics in the 1960s by Eric Lenneberg. From the beginning, Lenneberg pioneered the study of atypical populations to address fundamental questions about the nature of language acquisition. In his seminal work, published 25 years ago, Lenneberg, (1967) proposed the biological theory of language acquisition, arguing that language was a maturational process, similar to motor development, and that there was a critical period between about 18 months and puberty during which a first language can be acquired. Central to Lenneberg's view was the idea that language develops so rapidly and with such ease during the preschool years as a result of maturational processes that are specific to the domain of language. Lenneberg marshalled evidence for his proposals about domain specificity and the critical period hypothesis from studies of several atypical populations including children with focal brain damage in the left hemisphere, deaf children, and children with mental retardation. Although some of Lenneberg's hypotheses and, more importantly, the empirical evidence he cited have since been criticized, his work had an enormous impact on the field and continues to influence major research in this area, especially theoretically motivated studies of different populations of children.

Lenneberg's theoretical and empirical research was, like other research in developmental psycholinguistics conducted in that era, heavily influenced by the advances made in linguistic theory, especially the work of Chomsky (1957, 1965). Chomsky's principles provided the overall theoretical framework for Lenneberg's ideas. By the 1970s the scope of interest in the field broadened as more developmental psychologists became engaged in the study of language development. Initially there was a strong emphasis on cognitive development, deriving from Piaget's theory, and many researchers began exploring whether language could be accounted for by more general nonspecialized cognitive developmental processes (e.g., Cromer, 1974; Sinclair-de Zwart, 1969). Within a few years, researchers added to the cognitive view of language development the idea that the foundations of language lay in the social interactions between infants and their mothers (e.g., Bruner, 1975; Lock, 1980; Snow, 1979). On this view all aspects of language and discourse, including syntactic categories and rules, could be discovered in the formats of mother–infant interaction or were derived from specialized linguistic input provided by mothers. At this point the notion that language might be an independent cognitive system fell into disfavor. There was also less interest during this period in exploring the biological basis of language. Although much research was stimulated by the cognitive and the social–interactionist accounts of language development, some serious problems with both theories were soon recognized (for critical reviews see e.g., Cromer, 1988; Shatz, 1982).

Partly because of the criticisms leveled against the alternative theories of the 1970s, by the next decade the idea that language is an independent cognitive system with a distinct biological substrate regained recognition and now emerged as a topic for empirical investigation in all areas of psycholinguistic research. Advances in linguistic theory, especially the introduction of the Government-Binding framework and the theory of parameters (cf. Chomsky, 1981), also stimulated acquisition research that was, once again, based on linguistic approaches (e.g., Hyams, 1986; Lust, 1986; Roeper & Williams, 1987).

The research on language acquisition in atypical children included in this book grew out of the changes that have occurred within the broader field of language acquisition in recent years. Unlike many descriptive studies of language development in blind, deaf, brain-damaged, mentally retarded, or autistic children, the studies discussed in each of the following chapters were designed to address some basic theoretical questions. In turn, each contributor also discusses how the study of atypical children provides important information and makes a significant contribution to our understanding of the process of normal language development. Several important issues can be identified as major themes in this book.

Traditionally, studies of atypical children have focused on the question of whether language develops in a normal but delayed way, or whether language development is truly "deviant," which would suggest that there are alternative ways of acquiring language. The notion of deviant language development in children who are, for example autistic or mentally retarded, might imply that deficits in social or cognitive development lead children to find alternative routes to acquiring language. On the other hand, if language development looks very similar across groups of children — normally developing, mentally retarded, autistic, blind, deaf, or brain-damaged — then this suggests that there are some fundamental constraints on the process of language acquisition that are independent of broader cognitive or social developments. These constraints may be inherent to the linguistic system, they may be an aspect of the biological basis for language acquisition, or both.

Every chapter in this volume addresses this issue and the consistent finding across studies of a wide range of children and populations is that at least grammatical development proceeds in a remarkably similar way (see especially chapters 4, 5, and 8 by Feldman, Fowler et al., and Tager-Flusberg). Thus, there is little evidence that syntax, when it is acquired, is deviant in any of the groups that are represented in this volume (although they may show significant delays and not reach the same endpoint as normally developing children), despite the popular view of language disorders in clinical literature on the topic. These studies show that grammatical development follows an essentially normal pathway in atypical children, pointing to constraints in the linguistic system and the biological substrate for language.

In addition, however, research on oral deaf children who do not have access to some aspects of the linguistic input (chapter 2, de Villiers, de Villiers, & Hoban) suggests that constructing a grammar does critically depend on access to certain specific information in the input. Without access to information about particular forms, especially functional categories, oral deaf children cannot progress beyond an early stage in grammatical development, with their language resembling that of very young children. Although the idea that children will not acquire language without access to linguistic input is not controversial, the more significant issue concerns exactly what role input plays in acquiring different aspects of language. This question is taken up in some detail in the chapter by de Villiers, de Villiers, and Hoban whose research on oral deaf children leads to important new conclusions about the nature of the language problems encountered by these children, and suggests the critical role that unambiguous input plays in constructing a grammatical system.

Another major issue that is addressed in this volume is the relationship between brain maturation and language acquisition. According to Lenneberg's (1967) critical period hypothesis, because the brains of young children before they reach puberty are in a state of relative plasticity, any damage sustained to the left hemisphere will result in the right hemisphere assuming the language function, without loss of functional potential. The evidence that Lenneberg cited in support of his view has since been re-evaluated and criticized. Nevertheless, questions about how the brain is organized for acquiring language remain an important area of controversy, and are the main focus of two chapters in this volume. Both Levy, Amir, and Shalev (chapter 3) and Feldman (chapter 4) conducted longitudinal studies of young children who suffered pre- or perinatal damage to the left hemispheres of their brain. Levy and her colleagues document the lesion in their single case study, the result of a congenital infarct, in the regions of the left hemisphere that are considered important for language. Because their subject was acquiring Hebrew as a first language, a language rich in inflectional morphology, he provides significant new data on the issue of how damage to the left hemisphere may affect acquisition. Thus, their study provides a unique view on the influence of brain damage on morphological and syntactic development. Feldman presents data from a larger group of six children, with a variety of documented focal lesions.

Both studies document the fact that children with damage to the left hemisphere acquire language following normal developmental patterns, however, for all the children studied there are some important differences. Feldman notes that the children she studied were delayed in the onset of language, although once they began, the rate of development was within normal limits, even for the children who sustained damage in the left hemisphere. Levy and her colleagues also found a delay in onset and, because they performed a fine-grained analysis of morphological develop-ment, they were able to document that their subject had a higher than normal error rate. Thus, there do seem to be some relatively subtle effects of brain damage on the onset of language acquisition that was not anticipated by Lenneberg, but perhaps the most significant findings from these studies are that left hemisphere damage in the pre- or perinatal period does not lead to specific deficits in acquiring grammar.

At an individual level there may also be some important question of how the brain is organized to perceive and produce speech. In an intriguing study, Rondal (chapter 7) presents the case of a Down syndrome woman with highly developed language abilities, which is very unusual for this population (see chapter 5 by Fowler et al.). Rondal suggests that one explanation for why his subject achieved such high level language abilities is because her brain is organized for language in fundamentally different ways than other individuals with Down syndrome.

The case presented by Rondal raises another issue regarding the modu-larity of language. The recent literature includes a number of studies of atypical children that address the question of whether language constitutes a modular system, and if so, how this should be defined (e.g., Curtiss, 1982; Thal, Bates, & Bellugi, 1989; Yamada 1990). Striking evidence for the fact that language is independent of other cognitive systems comes from the detailed case study of a young woman (DH) with spina bifida and hydrocephaly presented in the chapter by Cromer (chapter 6). The subject Cromer describes has particularly excellent language skills despite that fact that she is severely retarded in all other cognitive domains, with the exception of social cognition. Her case is unusual because DH not only has intact grammatical abilities, she also has excellent pragmatic skills. In contrast, other cases where language is excellent compared to cognition (e.g., Yamada, 1990) tend not to have excellent pragmatic abilities. How can we interpret the abilities of DH? Does the entire language system, including grammar and pragmatics, constitute a unified module, or can we identify a number of modular systems relevant to language that interact? By looking at a range of cases and syndromes, the most likely explanation is that DH has two spared functions: language and social cognition (as measured by theory of mind tasks) which together account for her excellent language and pragmatic abilities (see also chapter 8 by Tager-Flusberg).

Levy and her colleagues also take up the issue of modularity and provide an interesting new way of defining an autonomous system. They argue that autonomous systems are most easily acquired and less vulnerable to brain damage, as evidenced by their case study. This is consistent with some of the ideas proposed by Newport (1991), who, on the basis of her studies of the critical period hypothesis using second language learners, argues that autonomous systems such as grammar are easiest to learn when other cognitive systems are relatively immature and therefore less likely to "interfere" in development.

Although there is strong evidence to suggests that certain aspects of language, for example syntax and morphology are autonomous, cognitive and social factors do play a role in acquiring language, most especially aspects of semantics and pragmatics. For example, Tager-Flusberg's research on autistic children (chapter 8) demonstrates the significance of social factors in acquiring aspects of pragmatic ability, but not grammatical knowledge. And Peters (chapter 9) presents a case study of visually impaired child to illustrate how language development interacts with, and fosters social and cognitive development.

Each of the chapters in this volume provides some insight on how an innate language-specific biological substrate interacts with cognitive and social factors, as well as with external information, to support the child's construction of a linguistic system. Studies of atypical children offer a singular contribution to this enterprise by allowing us to see the specific influences of each component, and in turn, they shed new light on how all children are able to acquire language so effortlessly and during such a brief period in development.

REFERENCES

Bruner, J. S. (1975). From communication to language: A psychological perspective. *Cognition, 3*, 255–287.

Chomsky, N. (1957). *Syntactic structures*. The Hague: Mouton.

Chomsky, N. (1965). *Aspects of the theory of syntax*. Cambridge, MA: MIT Press.

Chomsky, N. (1981). *Lectures on government and binding*. Dordrecht: Forls.

Cromer, R. (1974). The development of language and cognition: The cognition hypothesis. In B. Foss (Ed.), *New perspectives in child development* (pp. 184–252). London: Penguin.

Cromer, R. (1988). The cognition hypothesis revisited. In F. Kessel (Ed.), *The development of language and language researchers: Essays in honor of Roger Brown* (pp. 223–248). Hillsdale, NJ: Lawrence Erlbaum Associates.

Curtiss, S. (1982). Developmental dissociations of language and cognition. In L. Obler & L. Menn (Eds.), *Exceptional language and linguistics* (pp. 285–312). New York: Academic Press.

Hyams, N. (1986). *Language acquisition and the theory of parameters*. Dordrecht: Reidel.

Lenneberg, E. (1967). *Biological foundations of language*. New York: Wiley.

Lock, A. (Ed.). (1980). *The guided reinvention of language*. London: Academic Press.

Lust, B. (Ed.), (1986). *Studies in the acquisition of anaphora, Vol. 1*. Dordrecht: Reidel.

Newport, E. (1991). Contrasting concepts of the critical period for language. In S. Carey & R. Gelman (Eds.), *The epigenesis of mind: Essays on biology and cognition* (pp. 111–130). Hillsdale, NJ: Lawrence Erlbaum Associates.

Roeper, T., & Williams, E. (Eds.). (1987). *Parameter setting*. Dordrecht: Reidel.

Shatz, M. (1982). On mechanisms of language acquisition: Can features of the communicative environment account for development? In L. Gleitman & E. Wanner (Eds.), *Language acquisition: The state of the art* (pp. 102–127). New York: Cambridge University Press.

Sinclair-deZwart, H. (1969). Developmental psycholinguistics. In D. Elkind & J. Flavell (Eds.), *Studies in cognitive development* (pp. 175–208). New York: Holt, Rinehart & Winston.

Snow, C. E. (1979). The role of social interaction in language acquisition. In W. A. Collins (Ed.), *Children's language and communication* (pp.157–182). Hillsdale, NJ: Lawrence Erlbaum Associates.

Thal, D., Bates, E., & Bellugi, U. (1989). Language and cognition in two children with Williams syndrome. *Journal of Speech and Hearing Research, 32,* 489–500.

Yamada, J. E. (1990). *Laura: A case for the modularity of language.* Cambridge, MA: Bradford Books, MIT Press.

2 The Central Problem of Functional Categories in the English Syntax of Oral Deaf Children

Jill de Villiers
Peter de Villiers
Smith College

Esme Hoban

The relationship between developments in syntactic theory and the study of language acquisition in language-delayed children is a reciprocal one. Current models of grammar provide us with a theoretical underpinning for generalizations about the patterns of acquisition and disability in syntax observed in language-delayed groups. In addition, we gain a better understanding of how handicapping conditions that lead to variations or distortions in the input to the child might or might not affect syntactic acquisition.

On the other hand, detailed studies of syntactic acquisition in particular language-delayed groups can provide tests of the implications of specific models of syntactic development. For example, most theories agree that first language acquisition is a function of several factors that interact in complex ways, though the weight placed on each of these factors at different points in normal acquisition varies from theory to theory. Among these are (a) the grammatical structure of the language itself, (b) possible innate language acquisition mechanisms or biases, (c) biological or cognitive maturational factors, and (d) the nature of the language input to the child and the social context in which it takes place. In the normally developing preschooler, the effects of each of these factors on the pattern and process of syntax acquisition are difficult, and often impossible, to tease apart.

Orally taught deaf children, however, provide an interesting test of the contribution of some of these variables. Such children are much older and intellectually more mature at the point at which they acquire much of the grammar of English. In fact, when acquiring more complex forms such as relative clauses (if they are acquired at all), many deaf students are past the age of puberty that has been held by some to be the end of a critical or sensitive period for the normal acquisition of a first language. Secondly, oral deaf children often master complex syntactic constructions in both their spoken and written English at about the same time, from formal language instruction rather than from immersion in natural discourse, and with written text serving as a major source of input for these forms. Consequently, the nature of the input and the language-acquisition context is quite different from that of normally hearing children acquiring English as a first language.

Much of our recent research investigates parallels and differences between oral deaf children (and adolescents) and normally hearing preschoolers in their mastery of several major grammatical processes in English. To the extent that parallel patterns are found, they reflect constraints of the structure of the language itself or inherent language acquisition processes that all children bring to the task of acquiring a first language. Differences in the pattern of acquisition might be traced to (a) the effects of variations in the context in which language is acquired, (b) differences in cognitive maturity, or (c) aspects of the language (such as stress and intonational patterns) to which the deaf students have, at best, only limited access.

In this chapter, we discuss what current linguistic theories of the syntax of English can tell us about the differential difficulty of particular syntactic structures for deaf students. We also use a variety of empirical descriptions of deaf children's English acquisition to support a particular view of grammatical processes. We take seriously a model of grammar put forth in recent years that makes a fundamental distinction between lexical categories (e.g., Noun Phrase, [NP], Verb Phrase, [VP], Prepositional Phrase, [PP]) and functional categories (e.g., I = INFLECTION and C = COMPLE-MENTIZER). These are defined in detail.

In describing this model, we owe a debt to Radford (1988), who set forth a detailed proposal about the nature of young children's early sentences, arguing that they lack the functional categories at the start. In what follows, we argue that a serious delay in the acquisition of functional categories would result in just the kinds of impairments that are reported for deaf children acquiring English as their first language. Although rich data exist on the English acquisition of deaf children, there is no comprehensive theory to date to account for the characteristics of that language. By laying out such a theory, we hope that future research can be tested against it and that further advances can then be made in the theory and practice of English language instruction for deaf students.

THE SYNTACTIC MODEL

First, an introduction to the model of grammar being assumed. In X-bar (X′) theory (Chomsky, 1986; Radford, 1988; Stowell, 1981), the proposal is made that all grammatical categories have the same canonical form, with a specifier, a head (of the same type as the phrase), and complement(s):

(1)   X″
      /   \
Specifier X′
         / \
        X   complement(s)
      (head)

For instance, a noun phrase (NP) might be structured as follows:

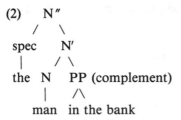

(2)   N″
      /   \
   spec   N′
    | / \
   the   N   PP (complement)
         | /\
        man in the bank

The head of the phrase "selects" its complements, to allow for lexical variation with respect to which complements can occur with which nouns or verbs.

As a consequence of this proposal, the simple sentence (alias S in earlier grammars) is conceived as a phrase with the subject as the specifier, and I (for inflection) as the head:

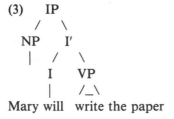

(3)   IP
      /   \
    NP   I′
     | / \
     I   VP
     | /_\
Mary will write the paper

The new form of the standard sentence is then called an IP (Inflection Phrase), and the I (for INFLECTION, sometimes called INFL) is the key constituent of that phrase. If it is a finite sentence, it contains the modal (e.g., *will*), or a form of tense; if it is nonfinite it contains an infinitive particle such as *to*. In X′ theory, the head is also what selects the complements of the phrase; hence, the I subcategorizes for a VP. The final function of the I constituent is that it provides for the nominative case of the subject. An additional importance of I to the overall grammar under some analyses is that it is claimed that verbs move into I from the VP in order to take tense markings. That is, in a sentence with no modals:

(4) John goes home regularly.

what is the mechanism by which "go" receives the tense marking? Originally, the proposal was for a transformation of "affix hopping," by which means the tense affix hopped from the auxiliary component onto the verb (e.g., Chomsky, 1981). In Koopman's recent proposal (1984), the verb migrates into I to achieve that marking. This analysis is disputed, but evidence for the movement of the verb is most convincing in the case of the two main verbs *have* and *be*, that in many respects behave like their auxiliary counterparts, especially with respect to properties like negation:

(5) Jill isn't afraid.
   *Jill gon't downtown.   [The asterisk is a convention to indicate that the sentence is ungrammatical].

Hence in the revised framework, a hitherto scattered and seemingly unimportant set of functional elements — modals, infinitive *to*, and tense — become central to the grammar of sentences. The mechanisms for tense assignment and nominative case assignment, as well as the use of modals, are all functions of I. I is called a functional category, in contrast to NP, VP, PP, and AP, which are lexical categories, headed by lexical forms: noun, verb, preposition/postposition, adjective/adverb.

Are there other functional categories? In modern treatments, IP is part of a larger constituent called CP (Complement Phrase), of which the head is a complementizer:

```
(6)   CP
     /  \
    C    IP
        /  \
      NP    I'
           /  \
          I    VP
```

In earlier grammars, this maximal projection was called an S-bar. What is C (sometimes called COMP for COMPLEMENTIZER)? In embedded sentences it is the constituent for complementizers such as *that, whether, if,* and so on:

(7) I believe [*that* he is coming].

(8) I wonder [*if* he will come].

In main clauses, the C constituent is held to be obligatorily empty in English except in the case of questions. In yes/no questions, the C serves as the landing site for auxiliary movement (now called "I-to-C movement"):

(9) Can he come early?

and as the landing site for wh-question movement:

(10) What should I bring?

The fact that both auxiliaries and wh-questions move to the CP suggests it has further internal structure, in other words that the wh-word actually moves to the specifier position of CP and the auxiliary into the head of CP:

(11)

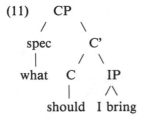

Hence, C is another functional category with key roles in the grammar of English. Question formation is dependent on the mastery of CP structure, as are all embeddings of sentences either as complements or as relative clauses, in which a CP is embedded within an NP:

(12) I saw the man [who you like].

The relative pronoun in such a structure is akin to the moved wh-word in a wh-question in many respects, in that it stands for the head of the relative clause within the embedded sentence, but has moved to the front roughly as in a wh-question, leaving a trace:

(13) I saw the man$_i$ who$_i$ you asked me about t$_i$.

The final importance of the CP lies in its role in long distance movement of wh-questions (Chomsky, 1986). How can a question word move from a site in a lower clause in English? Take the following as an example:

(14) How did he say that he would do it?

Under one reading of the sentence, the answer could be:

(15) With a penknife.

In other words, the "how" is considered to be an adjunct of the second verb, from the lower clause in the tree structure:

(16) How did he say that he would do it t?

But how can the wh-word move across clauses to the front of the sentence? Movement is supposed to be clause bound. The usual proposal is that the movement of wh-words is "cyclic," in that it takes place in a series of moves, each one respecting the single clause requirement. The wh-word moves by "cycling" through the medial CP node before moving to the initial specifier of CP.

(17) [$_{cp}$ How did he say[$_{cp}$ that he would do it t]]

Strong evidence for this proposal comes from consideration of cases where the specifier position of the medial CP is already filled with a wh-word:

(18) How did he say what he would do?

Suddenly, the "with a penknife" answer is bizarre, and one must answer instead "grudgingly" or "with a whisper"—that is, the "how" must come from the upper clause with a trace after *say*. That it is crucially the position of the lower question word in CP that blocks a long distance interpretation is proved by sentences with a wh-question in situ in the lower clause, in which it has not moved forward into the medial CP:

(19) How did he say he would do what?

Now the "how" question can once again refer to the verb "do" from the lower clause since the medial specifier-of-CP node is empty.

These illustrations of the theory demonstrate the significance of both of the functional categories I and C to the full working grammar of English in the adult language.

WHY ARE FUNCTIONAL CATEGORIES IMPORTANT FOR ACQUISITION?

Let us examine the distinction between lexical and functional categories, and why the distinction might be of importance for acquisition theories.

Abney (1987) proposed that functional categories are different from lexical categories in several critical ways:

1. They constitute closed classes. Our lexicons add new verbs and nouns, but not new tenses or new complementizers.
2. They are often morphologically and phonologically dependent. They are generally unstressed, often clitics or affixes, or even phonologically null.
3. They permit only one complement, unlike lexical categories, which can permit several. That complement is generally not an argument; that is, it does not contribute essential semantic information.
4. They lack "descriptive content." Unlike the lexical categories, functional categories seem to contribute less basic semantic information, perhaps the sort that gets omitted in a telegram.

Others (e.g., Fukui, 1986; Lebeaux, 1988) argued that a major source of cross-linguistic variation lies in differences in the functional categories, with lexical categories being universal in form. In fact, this is the source of the prediction that the functional categories should be late in acquisition for normal hearing children, as they require specific input to "set" the parameters for the language being learned (Lebeaux, 1988; Radford, 1988). It is exposure to the functional elements in English (tenses, complementizers, and possibly articles) that will allow the construction of the appropriate functional categories IP, CP (and maybe DP[1], the DETERMINER system) for that language.

Before that input evidence is assimilated, Radford argued that young children's grammars have only the lexical categories: NP, VP, PP, AP. In his 1988 paper, he argued that children's early sentences have the structure of adult "small clauses," namely they lack IP and CP, and consist of the structure:

(20)   S
         /   \
      NP   XP = VP,AP,PP.

As evidence, he sets forth multiple examples that show the lack of modals and tense in early sentences, the lack of complementizers and movement of auxiliaries, and the lack of nominative case:

(21) Me have biscuit.
     Sausage bit hot.

---

[1]To achieve strict parallelism, a functional category called DP for Determiner phrase is sometimes claimed to head the noun phrase (Fukui & Speas, 1985). Its existence is not so fully accepted so we have chosen to ignore it here.

Teddy drink.
Him gone.

Notice that these types of structures appear in adult English as the complements of certain verbs (usually verbs of perception):

(22) He watched [me have a biscuit].
I found [the sausage a bit hot].
I saw [Teddy drink].
I found [him gone].

In these embedded small clauses, there can be no tense or modal auxiliary:

(23) *I watched him went home.

nor complementizer:

(24) *I watched that him went home.

and the subject is in the accusative case (probably controlled from the top verb):

(25) *I watched he go home.

but they never appear as matrix sentences in the adult language.

THE CASE EXAMINED WITH RESPECT TO DEAF CHILDREN ACQUIRING ENGLISH

A general theoretical proposal about the distinctive characteristics of the English spoken and written by deaf children has not been forthcoming, although Quigley and his associates (Quigley & King, 1980), as well as others, argued that it is grammatically structured rather than completely free of rules. In what follows, we take seriously the notion that most deaf children lack sufficient exposure to critical features of the input English language to formulate functional categories. The reasons for their impoverished input are several, but most critically, the nature of the speech they hear/lipread will differentially lack unstressed grammatical elements such as tense markers, inflections, relative pronouns, and other functional elements needed to build the functional categories of English. Written English will supply those forms once schooling begins, but it is possible that deaf children begin by parsing written English with their existing and impoverished grammar, filtering out the features they do not yet have grammars to accommodate.

The proposal that deaf children have special difficulty with functional elements is by no means novel with us (Kretschmer & Kretschmer, 1978; Quigley & Paul, 1984), but most earlier analyses of this notion have focused on difficulties with "function" words or closed class items. What is new is the claim that a fully articulated grammar of English depends on these elements as "triggers"; that is, that they serve as crucial data for building a fully articulated grammar of English. The broad functional categories of grammar as defined by Radford and others (INFL, COMP, and perhaps the DETERMINER system) are all part of those aspects of English that are more dependent on the input and hence more "fragile" in cases of impoverished input language and delayed acquisition.

The review that follows weaves together existing data on the nature of English grammar in deaf children with new data of our own collected over the last several years. Our data come from a variety of tasks used with profoundly deaf (more than 90dB hearing loss), orally educated deaf children who have had little exposure to formal Sign (either ASL or Signed English), and attend an oral school for the deaf. Almost all of these children come from families in which they are the only deaf member and have hearing parents who speak English. We include data from large-scale studies of the written and "through the air" English syntax of deaf students from total communication (TC) programs (such as those from Quigley, Wilbur, Power, Montanelli, & Steinkamp, 1976; and Engen & Engen, 1983), where there are close parallels between the findings from oral and TC students, and no evidence that the English data are affected by the students' formal exposure to Signed English forms or their informal exposure to ASL.

We will discuss the evidence for the functional categories of IP and CP in turn, assessing the degree to which the characteristics of English used by the subjects fit the hypothesis already discussed about the general impairment of these systems in deafness.[2]

The I-system:

A failure to build an appropriate structure containing an IP category would have several consequences for grammar:

---

[2]Although there are some descriptions about the relative difficulty of a variety of determiner forms in deaf students (e.g., definite and indefinite articles [de Villiers & de Villiers, 1986]), a similar analysis of the acquisition of the DP system by deaf children is not appropriate until the case is better resolved for the status of that system in linguistic theory.

1. Auxiliaries would be missing or improperly analyzed (as part of VP, perhaps).
2. Tense marking would be severely compromised because tense is considered part of I.
3. The main verb may not be considered obligatory because it is the head of IP (I) that subcategorizes for the verb.

In 1969, Quigley's analysis of written samples from deaf children revealed that there were four aspects of the verb system that deaf children found particularly difficult. They included (a) the use of auxiliary verbs, (b) the use of tense markers, (c) the use of copulas, and (d) the obligatory nature of verbs.

Auxiliaries

Auxiliary verbs begin to be mastered quite early by young hearing children, typically in Stage III of Brown's MLU (Mean Length of Utterance) stages (MLU 2.5–3.0). Deaf students continue to have difficulty with auxiliary use even when they are producing long coordinated utterances and their MLU far exceeds 3 morphemes per utterance. In a follow-up study to Quigley's 1969 work, Quigley, Montanelli, and Wilbur (1976) asked deaf students to judge the acceptability of sentences containing missing auxiliaries, and found that "Sentences with a missing auxiliary verb . . . were the most difficult for deaf students to judge; they correctly judged such sentences ungrammatical only 45% of the time"(p. 541). Similarly, sentences that failed to provide do-support with negation (e.g., "The boy no go to school.") were judged as ungrammatical only 41% of the time by deaf 10-year-olds.

De Villiers (1988) reported the results of an elicited production task used to collect a sample of spoken wh-question forms *what, where, why, how,* and *when*) from oral deaf subjects aged 6 to 14 years (Williamson, 1985). Compared with normally-hearing 3- to 5-year-olds, the deaf students made far fewer pragmatic errors (i.e., answering rather than asking, or asking a question that was not specific enough to get the information required for the task), but they made many more syntactic errors (see Table 2.1).

The majority of their syntactic errors lay in the omission of an auxiliary form from the sentence, with 82.4% of their syntactic errors falling into that class, and only 1% into "aux placement errors." In fact, 65% of all the wh-questions produced by the deaf students lacked an auxiliary verb. In contrast, the normally-hearing preschoolers had relatively more trouble with auxiliary movement, with 31.5% of their syntactic errors being of the aux-placement type (though the absolute frequency of this error was still

TABLE 2.1
Percent of Wh-Questions for Which Correct Auxiliary was Provided

	What	*Where*	*Why*	*How*	*When*
Normally Hearing (3-5 years) (*n* = 26)	91%	96%	91%	89%	88%
Profoundly Deaf (6-14 years) (*n* = 26)	49%	36%	32%	34%	34%

very low, only some 3% of all the wh-questions they produced). (see Table 2.2).

Tense

Tense marking appears in hearing children as early as age 2, and is mastered in the order: present progressive *-ing*, then past tense (irregular and then regular *-ed*), and still later the third person present singular *-s* (Brown, 1973, de Villiers & de Villiers, 1973). Acquisition of the past tense is characterized by an exhaustively documented period of overgeneralization of the regular rule to irregular verbs (e.g., *comed*, *bringed*, *falled*) (Brown, 1973; Bybee & Slobin, 1982; Kuczaj, 1977).

In contrast, deaf children frequently omit the tense marker in written sentences describing a present or past event (Quigley, 1969). In judgments of grammaticality of written English, deaf children also fail to recognize omissions of the tense marking as ungrammatical (60% correct across all ages 10–18 (Quigley, Montanelli & Wilbur, 1976), this being especially true in multiclause sentences (e.g., "Yesterday a girl pushed Mary and she cry."—only 39% correct across all ages). In that study, the nature of the tense marking (past, future, or present progressive) appeared to make little difference.

Baumberger (1986; see also Baumberger, de Villiers, & de Villiers, 1986) set out to test the Bybee and Slobin (1982) phonological predictions about overgeneralization of the regular past tense to irregular forms by eliciting past tense use from oral deaf students and normally-hearing preschoolers in

TABLE 2.2
Number and Percent of Syntactic Error Types

	Normally Hearing	*Profoundly Deaf*
No AUX	27 (50%)	338 (82.4%)
AUX Placement Errors	17 (31.5%)	5 (1.2%)
Number and Tense Agreement	8 (14.8%)	52 (12.7%)
Redundant NP Copying	2 (3.7%)	15 (3.7%)

a range of phonological contexts. She used both an elicited production task (see Berko, 1958) and a task in which the children described sequences of actions they had just observed on videotaped silent cartoon clips. However, the major finding was that the regular past tense was so poorly used by the deaf students as to virtually never overgeneralize to the irregular contexts (see Table 2.3).

Written production of irregular past tense forms by a larger group of oral deaf children aged 9 to 14 that overlapped somewhat with Baumberger's subjects was considerably better (79.9% correct) in a task in which they produced short paragraphs to describe everyday incidents depicted in a sequence of three pictures. Nevertheless, their production of regular past tense was still erratic in the written mode (57.2% correct), with the predominant error being omission of any tense marker. Overgeneralizations to irregulars were vanishingly rare (Magner, de Villiers, Hoban, & von Schlegel, 1988).

Optional VP

Radford (1988) pointed out that early child speech is characterized by an optional VP, which follows from the hypothesis that, in adult speech, it is the I component which subcategorizes for a VP and makes it obligatory. By age 3, however, most hearing children always produce utterances that contain verbs unless discourse ellipsis allows an incomplete sentence. In contrast, deaf children are reported to omit the verb quite frequently in writing English (Quigley, 1969). In Quigley, Montanelli, and Wilbur (1976), 10-year-old deaf children correctly judged sentences with deleted verbs as ungrammatical between 60 and 70% of the time. However, when the students rewrote the sentences they judged to be ungrammatical, some 33% of them did not insert a main verb, suggesting that the verb was still not considered obligatory in their grammars.

In summary, deaf children's syntax has the characteristics of a grammar

TABLE 2.3
Elicited Past-Tense Production

	Normally Hearing (n = 19, 4:0–5:6 yrs)	Profoundly Deaf (n = 21, 6:4–13:4 yrs)
Correct Usage		
Irregular Past	45%	38%
Regular Past	90%	34%
Errors on Irregulars		
Unmarking	10%	75%
Present Progressive	14%	8%
Overgeneralized -ed	56%	8%

deficient in the functional category of I, in that auxiliaries, tense, and the obligatory nature of the main verb are all poorly controlled. It may be too strong to say that there is no I component at all, because all of these features are present some of the time. It may be more accurate to say that this aspect of the grammar has not yet been firmly established, and that deaf children show evidence for many years of allowing a default structure that fails to include I.

The C-system

What would be expected if children had a grammar that did not contain the component C and the corresponding CP category? One might expect that several consequences would follow:

1. Sentence embeddings that involve complementizers (e.g., complement constructions and relative clauses) should be differentially difficult, in contrast to conjunction or adjunction.
2. Auxiliaries should be unable to move to initial position because they are hypothesized to move into C.
3. Wh-question words should be unable to move into the specifier position of CP.
4. Long-distance movement (i.e., cyclic movement) should be impossible, as the wh-word must move through a medial specifier-of-CP position.

Complements

Limber (1973) demonstrated the early use of sentence complements by hearing children. Before age 3, infinitival and *that* complements make their appearance, though sometimes these are unmarked. Nevertheless, certain complement-taking verbs (*ask, tell, promise*) are not mastered until quite a bit later (Chomsky, 1969). Bloom, Takeff, and Lahey (1984) provided evidence that young children master the complement system by learning the subcategorizations for particular verbs—important because the complement system in English is notoriously verb specific. Their study confirms that children acquire some complements in the preschool years.

Quigley, Wilbur, and Montanelli (1976), using the Test of Syntactic Abilities (TSA) to study the grammatical judgments of deaf students concluded, "Of the three recursive processes in English, the TSA has shown complementation to be the most difficult. This difficulty is reflected in the chance level of performance of all but the oldest deaf students on the subtest (of complementation)" (p. 455). Their subjects were equally poor at judging the syntactic accuracy of object and subject complement construc-tions. "Poss-ing" constructions were easier than "for-to" complements, and the nature of the verb — active, stative, or perception — also made a differ-ence. Upon examination of these items from the perspective of current grammars, it is apparent that many of the easier forms (stative and perception verbs with "ing" complements) would now be called "small clause" structures. Small clauses are hypothesized to lack CP, and be subcategorized and take case from the main clause verb (Radford, 1988). Under such an analysis, it would be expected that the deaf children's grammars of English could accommodate them more readily. In fact, in a picture-cued sentence elicitation task we are currently using with deaf students aged 8 to 15, sentences of the form "The girl saw the man break(ing) the window" are much easier for the children to produce than forms like "The boy asked his mother if he could go outside."

It is probably the case that deaf children have an understanding of recursion from an early age, and their communications must require embedding of propositions. Even Goldin-Meadow's (1982) young oral deaf subjects produced gestural sequences that could be considered to express the meaning of sentence embeddings, though not conventionally. It is the expression of that recursion by conventional, formal, means that seems particularly impaired in deaf children's English grammar.

Auxiliary Movement

Auxiliary movement is predicted to be difficult on the assumption that C is either absent or underspecified, yet this is only predicted under the assumption that I exists first! The present theory is in too embryonic a state to suggest an ordering of acquisition of the functional categories of English in either hearing or deaf children. Is there any evidence of failure of AUX-movement?

As mentioned, de Villiers (1988) reported data from a wh-question production task showing that AUX was usually omitted by 6- to 14-year-old deaf subjects rather than supplied in an unmoved position. Quigley, Wilbur, and Montanelli (1974) found yes/no questions to be understood only 58% of the time at age 10 by deaf students, and to be judged appropriately only about 50% of the time at that age (66% across all ages 10 through 18). Wh-questions involving aux were more difficult still: Only 45% were understood or judged correctly at age 10, with an average of 58% across the age range studied. Tag questions were the most difficult of all. One phenomenon reported in this study is not in keeping with the most specific prediction made by the theory being advanced. If the CP node were present but underarticulated, one would predict that aux-inversion might be possible for yes/no questions but not for wh-questions, as there would be no "room" in CP for both elements. Such a prediction accommodates the data from hearing children's development quite handily (see Weinberg, 1990, for a discussion). But Quigley et al. reported judgments of grammaticality for sentences with aux-inversion to be easier for deaf *and* hearing subjects in wh-questions than in yes/no questions. This may arise from the pragmatic difficulty of judging the grammatical appropriateness of uninverted written yes/no questions in the absence of any referential context, when the only cue to the sentence being a question is the question mark at the end.

Speculation in this domain is rather hampered by not yet having an articulated theory of the ordering of development of functional categories, to determine whether IP develops before CP.

Wh-movement.   Wh-movement involves movement of the wh-word into the specifier position of the CP node, hence it should theoretically be impossible with a grammar that lacks CP. However, the wh-question may appear in a "topic" position in the front of the sentence, rather than via grammatical wh-movement into CP. What is the difference? In English, wh-words move obligatorily into the CP except under certain discourse circumstances, in which case they are left in situ as echo questions:

(26) You said what?

In other languages, such as Chinese and Japanese, the usual position for the wh-word is in situ, so in the normal form of the question the wh-word would be unmoved. However, wh-words do appear at the front of sentences in these languages in so-called topicalized questions, in which the wh-word is considered to occupy a "topic" position at the front of the sentence, not in CP. These questions are subject to similar discourse constraints that characterize echo questions in English. It has been suggested by Roeper, Akiyama, Mallis, and Rooth (1985) and de Villiers, Roeper, and Vainikka (1990) that the first wh-questions of young children may, in fact, not involve the wh-movement rule, but rather, topicalization. Roeper et al. (1985) argued that the wh-word is in these cases coindexed with a "small pro" in the in situ position, which may or may not be overtly expressed in the form of a pronoun copy.

Finally, there is controversy over whether young children's subject sentences involve movement at all. The subject wh-question:

(27) Who ate this?

has the wh-word superficially in the same position as the subject,

(28) John ate this.

unlike the object question:

(26) What did you eat t?

Thus it is possible that subject questions could appear in the absence of either movement into CP or topicalization: Object questions obligatorily involve either one or the other.

Turning to the evidence on deaf children, it is clear that they produce wh-questions with the wh-word in initial position. Quigley et al. (1974) found what they referred to as "verb–object" movement (i.e., movement of the wh-word to the beginning of the sentence) to be easier for their subjects than AUX movement.

Williamson (1985) tested both hearing preschoolers and deaf subjects aged 6 through 14 in her elicited question procedure (see de Villiers, 1988). Both groups almost invariably asked the right question to get at the information needed for the task, showing that they grasped the semantics and pragmatics of the situation, and the wh-word was almost always produced in sentence-initial position (though only the deaf students produced any in situ echo question forms in this task [2.7% of trials]). However, the deaf subjects made many more attempts that were grammatically incorrect, primarily, as described, in omitting the auxiliary (65% of trials; see Table 2.1). With the auxiliary omitted, the wh-word could simply be appended to the beginning of the sentence in topic position. So these sentences could well involve topicalization rather than movement of the wh-word into the specifier position of the CP. Unfortunately, Williams did not elicit subject questions, so we do not know if they would be easier for the deaf students because they can perhaps be produced without applying any movement rule.

Quigley et al. (1974) studied deaf children's judgments of written wh-questions, and reported that *who* as the subject was significantly easier than *who* as an object. Furthermore, they explicitly tested deaf children's judgments of questions containing copies, as in:

(29) Who did the boy see him?

in which the site of the moved question word is occupied by a pronoun or NP copy. Quigley's data on written productions (1969) showed this to be a prevalent syntactic error. Over 60% of these deviant structures were accepted as syntactically correct by deaf 10-year-olds, declining to 37% by age 18. These errors suggest that some deaf students may form wh-questions by simply appending the wh-word to the beginning of the sentence.

Hence, there are significant hints in the existing literature that for many of these children wh-questions may be formed by a process other than grammatical movement to the specifier position of CP. This conclusion is reinforced by new data discussed on long-distance movement. First, however, let us consider the data on another grammatical form in English that requires CP and wh-movement: the relative clause structure.

Relative Clause Structures. The first attempts at relative clauses in normal hearing children appear in the speech of 2-year-olds, but children make mistakes in understanding them until at least age 6. There is some controversy over the grammars of relativization in young children. Elicited production techniques developed by Crain and his associates (Crain, McKee, & Emiliani, 1990; Hamburger & Crain, 1982) suggested that if the appropriate discourse circumstances are met, children can produce relative clauses from an early age. However, researchers who focus on comprehension are less impressed. Tavakolian (1981) argued that children parse relatives as if they were conjoined structures rather than embedded forms, misunderstanding for example:

(30) The dog bit the cat that hit the rat.

as

(31) The dog bit the cat and hit the rat.

Lebeaux (1988, 1990) used this phenomenon and others to argue that children's "default" analysis of structures is as adjuncts, attached to S without embedding. How would that be manifest in production?

Labelle (1989, 1990) argued that in the case of French children acquiring relative clauses, the structures may not involve movement until quite late in development (over age 6). Her subjects frequently used resumptive nouns or pronouns in their relative clauses, in the place where an empty category would normally be found in the structure. Hence, these sentences involved no movement, but instead the head noun and the resumptive pronoun were coindexed:

(32) The boy$_i$ who the man saw him$_i$.

Quigley, Smith, and Wilbur (1974) presented evidence from deaf subjects aged 10 through 18 on a comprehension task involving written relative clause structures. They studied the processing of relative clause sentences; how deaf children judged the appropriateness of relative clause sentences with respect to two single propositions; and whether they accepted sentences containing "copies" or resumptive pronouns. First, deaf children were very poor at understanding the meanings of the sentences with relative clauses; they had more difficulty with medial relatives than final relatives, and more difficulty with relative pronouns serving as objects of the subordinate clause than with those serving as subjects. In judging the correct embedding of clauses, deaf subjects improved only slightly with age, from 47% correct judgments at 11 to only 56% at 18. Finally, Quigley's subjects accepted the relative clause forms with copies 62% of the time at age 10:

(33) The man saw the boy who the boy kicked the ball.

Quigley, Wilbur, and Montanelli (1974) showed a graph of the acceptance of the relative clauses with copies against the graph of the acceptance of copying in wh-questions: The two are extraordinarily parallel; clearly the processes are identical, and change in concert with each other.

Engen and Engen (1983) reported comparable data on picture-choice comprehension of medial and final relatives produced in simultaneous signed and spoken English. Again, medial relatives were much more difficult than final relatives, with correct responses on medials being less than 50% and showing little improvement across the age range from 6 to 18 years in a large group of deaf students. The dominant error pattern on the medial relatives was one in which the children regarded the object of the relative clause as the subject of the main clause action, thus wrongly interpreting:

(34) The boy who is talking to the man is sitting in the car.

as meaning that the man was sitting in the car.

Are there production data on relative clauses in deaf subjects? Quigley (1969) presented data demonstrating that the copying phenomenon was frequent in deaf subjects from 10- through 18-year-olds. De Villiers (1988) described an elicited spoken production procedure with orally taught deaf children aged 11 through 18. The referential communication task required the children to verbally pick out one referent from other similar referents for a listener who could not see the depicted events. The distinctive characteristic of the referent to be specified was an action that they were performing or that was being performed on them. This procedure success-fully elicits full relative clauses of several types from normal hearing children aged 4 to 6, and examples of the targets are provided in Table 2.4. De Villiers concluded that relative clauses are acquired very late by oral deaf children, but that the overall pattern of difficulty they show is similar in kind to that shown by normally-hearing children of a much younger age. This conclusion is warranted mostly by the difficulty ordering shown in Table 2.4.

The percentages of relative clause attempts in the various categories

TABLE 2.4
Relative Clause Production

Clause Type	Group	
	Normally Hearing[a]	*Profoundly Deaf*[b]
Percentage of trials eliciting target form[c]		
SS	63.3	40.7
SO	10	2.8
OO	16.7	9.2
OS	30	22.2
Percentage of each type regardless of target		
SS	71.2	63.7
SO	5.1	2.9
OO	8.5	8.9
OS	15.3	24.4
Percentage of target trials on which a relative clause was produced		
Before prompt	64.6	47.9
After prompt	71.1	55.9

Note. From "Assessing English Syntax in Hearing-Impaired Children: Elicited Production in Pragmatically Motivated Situations" by P. A. de Villiers 1988, in "Communication Assessment of Hearing - Impaired Children: From Conversation to Classroom, *Journal of the Academy of Rehabilitative Audiology*: *Monograph Supplement, 21*, p. 65.

[a] n = 20, age = 5-6 years.

[b] n = 36, age = 11-18 years.

[c] The target form is the grammatical form that the picture was designed to elicit and that adult native English speakers most often produced for that picture.

Sample targets in order of difficulty:

SS The cowboy who brushed the horse is washing the cow.

OS The policeman is grabbing the man who broke the window.

OO The farmer is kicking the pumpkin that the raccoon licked.

SO The cat that the boy brushed is chasing the mouse.

suggest delayed acquisition but patterning like that of normally hearing children. However, the specific types of sentences produced by the two groups of children call this simple analysis into question, as a detailed perusal of the transcripts of the study attests. The primary "error" that young normally-hearing children make is in not providing a specifying expression that picks out the referent for the listener in the referential communication task. However, when prompted with the question: "Which X?," they readily provide a well-formed, truncated, relative clause, for example,

(35) Experimenter: Which cowboy?
    Child: The cowboy who brushed the horse.

The deaf subjects, on the other hand, provide more initial, unprompted attempts at specification of the noun phrase, that is, they understand better the pragmatics of the communication task and what it requires of them. However, they often failed to use relative clause constructions to do so, even after prompting, using instead two separate sentences or conjoined forms.

When deaf children did attempt a relative clause structure, the sentences they produced during these attempts were sometimes very peculiar. We divided the attempted relative clauses into several kinds: *correct*, *"stylistically different,"* and *deviant*. In the stylistically different category, there are three types: (a) topicalization to the front, (b) topicalization to the end, and (c) extraposition. Examples of each of these are provided in Table 2.5.

Note that the topicalization forms create redundancy:

> (36) The girl that petted the dog, her father is feeding the dog the food.

And the extraposition of relatives often results in a sentence that doesn't sound quite right:

> (37) The boy empty pail who was washing the car.

Nevertheless, these are all variants of well-formed relatives in English, and at least the first two are produced, if rarely, by hearing preschoolers in the task. The percentage of attempts that are stylistically different is around 18% for the deaf subjects, with a standard deviation of 23%, so there is considerable variability.

As Table 2.5 shows, the deviant category contains several types of error: redundancy introduced by resumptive pronouns, mistakes in the relative pronoun, relativizing the "wrong" noun phrase (i.e., the character in the pictures that did not need to be specified for the listener), and serious mistakes in the thematic structure. These errors make up over 25% of the attempts on average, again with a high standard deviation of 26%.

Hence, the oral deaf subjects in this study are not simply delayed in their acquisition of relative clause structures, but their grammars are incomplete in ways that do not seem typical of hearing children. Deaf children recognize the necessity for specification in this task but frequently fail to articulate what they mean.

Are these the kinds of errors in production that might be expected from grammars that contain no CP or a deficient development of the CP system? As argued in the case of wh-movement, the resumptive pronoun errors would be predicted if the wh-word (relative pronoun) were in the topic position, coindexed with a pronoun copy in the normal location. That the topic position is a possibility in these children's grammars is made obvious by the frequent use of topicalization for the relative clause as a whole. The

TABLE 2.5
Attempts at Relative Clause Structures by Deaf Children

Stylistically Different Examples

Topicalization to the front:	*Target Sentences:*
The fan that blows the shirt, the woman catches it, shirt.	The woman is catching the shirt that the fan blew.
The girl that petted the dog, her father is feeding the dog the food.	The girl is petting the dog that the man fed.
The baby that's feeding the bird, his mother is holding him.	The mother is holding the baby who is feeding the bird.
Topicalization to the End:	*Target Sentences:*
The nurse was calling the telephone, the nurse that was feeding him.	The nurse who was feeding the man is talking on the phone.
A nurse talking on the telephone, the nurse feeding the boy.	The nurse who was feeding the man is talking on the phone.
The old lady is trying to put the shirt back, the one the fan blew.	The woman is catching the shirt that the fan blew.
Extraposition:	*Target Sentences:*
The boy empty pail who was washing the car.	The boy who washed the car emptied the pail.
The baby is playing with the rabbit that the mother holds.	The baby who the mother is holding is patting the rabbit.
The man gave the dog food which pat the girl	The girl is petting the dog that the mad fed.
The nurse answers a call who was feeding the boy.	The nurse who was feeding the man is talking on the phone.
Redundancy:	*Target Sentences:*
The man$_i$ wash the cow that before the man$_i$ brushed the horse.	The man who brushed the horse is washing the cow.
The girl caught the soccer ball$_i$ which the boy kick the ball$_i$.	The girl caught the soccer ball that the boy kicked.
Another baby was alone and another one$_i$, the girl is caring over baby$_i$ that the baby$_i$ kissed the rabbit.	The baby who the mother is holding is patting the rabbit.
That the girl pet the dog$_i$ that the man gave him$_i$ food.	The girl is petting the dog that the mad fed.
Relative Pronoun Errors:	*Target Sentences:*
The mother was holding the baby watch bird.	The mother is holding the baby who is feeding the bird.
One the baby is feeding the bird is the mother is carrying on him.	The mother is holding the baby who is feeding the bird.
The mother hold the clothes what the fan blow the air.	The woman is catching the shirt that the fan blew.
Wrong NP Relativized/garbled Thematic Structure:	*Target Sentences:*
The girl that holds the baby, kiss the rabbit.	The baby who the mother is holding is patting the rabbit.
One boy who kick the ball, the girl catch.	The girl caught the soccer ball that the boy kicked.
A baker itches his nose, the car that hit him.	The car hit the baker who was scratching his nose.
The girl who was petting the dog was eating a dog food.	The girl is petting the dog that the man fed.

relative pronoun errors, ungrammatical deletion, and frequent case errors when case is produced are in keeping with a lack of analysis of CP. Other errors, such as relativizing the wrong NP, are not related to the proposal in any simple fashion and may reflect only the deaf students' great difficulty with relativization as a grammatical procedure. It remains to be seen whether the difficulty is mirrored in the speech of normal hearing children at a much younger age. Labelle's (1990) data on French children suggests a reanalysis may be warranted of the existing English data on early relativization.

In many ways, the hypothesis that functional categories are acquired late if acquired at all makes the same predictions about deaf students' English that a simpler hypothesis makes, namely that function words and morphemes are learned late (Kretschmer & Kretschmer, 1978; Quigley & Paul, 1984). However, this proposal goes beyond that hypothesis by arguing in addition that deaf students' difficulties with complex sentence-forming syntax in English also arises from a failure to develop appropriate functional categories. The behavior of long distance (LD) movement of questions provides the best evidence that CP is not well established in the English of deaf children.

LONG-DISTANCE MOVEMENT

Although no previous data existed on the LD movement of wh-questions in deaf children, the following describes a new study designed to provide some initial evidence. A battery of 30 stories with associated questions was developed to test the comprehension of a variety of different structures involving wh-movement. The structures and stories had all been used in previous research with 3-to 6-year-old normal hearing children (de Villiers, Roeper, & Vainikka, 1990; Roeper & de Villiers, 1991), and hence substantial information existed about the course and process of normal development. The focus of these structures was on two separate properties of wh-questions: (a) long distance movement, and (b) bound variable readings. What follows is a brief reminder of the linguistic issues involved in long distance wh-movement; the bound variable questions have to do with a different issue that we will not discuss in this chapter.

The Linguistics of Long-Distance Movement

Wh-questions are hypothesized to involve a movement rule in which the wh-word moves from its site in the canonical sentence to the front of the sentence, where it occupies a position in the CP node:

(38) What did you see t?

The echo question provides an illustration of the wh-word left in situ, though the echo question is used for distinct discourse purposes:

(39) You saw what?

The wh-word can move from a considerable distance away, and is argued in many grammatical treatments to undergo cyclic movement in which it passes through the CP nodes for the embedded sentences:

(40) Who did Mary claim John saw t?

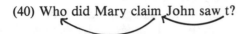

(41) Who did John claim Mary saw Jane hug t?

Some verbs subcategorize to allow an embedded question, and in such cases a question word occupies the medial CP node as the complementizer:

(42) John asked who Mary liked.

However, if a question word originates in the lower clause of an embedded question, theoretically, it cannot undergo cyclic movement because its landing site is already occupied:

(43) a) John asked who Mary saw how?
     b) *How$_i$ did John ask who Mary saw t$_i$?

Hence long distance movement is ruled out in such cases. This analysis predicts, then, that sentences of this sort should be interpreted as involving short distance movement. In 43b, a short distance interpretation:

(44) How$_i$ did John ask t$_i$ who Mary saw?

is just fine, where *how* is an adjunct of *ask*, not *saw*. But the long distance interpretation is blocked.

One further complication is necessary to this (still oversimplified!) story. Long-distance movement rules interact with the distinction between verb adjuncts and arguments. Questions such as *who* and *what* occupy the argument positions of the verb and hence can be connected to their traces (or their traces "licensed") directly by the lexicon. Adjunct questions, such as *why*, *where*, *when*, and *how*, do not fill argument positions and hence can only be connected to their traces via CP-to-CP movement. Compare the sentences:

(45) a) Who did Mary ask how to paint?
     b) When did Mary ask how to paint?

Most adults agree, whatever their first preference, that 45a is ambiguous in a way that 45b is not. In 45a, *who* can question either *ask* or *paint*, but in 45b, *how* can only connect with *ask*. This difference reflects the additional way in which the argument question's trace can be licensed.

What happens with LD movement if the sentence contains no CP node? Small clause structures are treated in some grammars as having no CP node yet still containing two clauses:

(46) John saw him running.

With some reluctance, most adults find the long-distance movement of a wh-question possible from such structures, regardless of the argument/adjunct distinction:

(47) How$_i$ did Jim see him running t$_i$?
(e.g., "with bare feet").

(48) Who$_i$ did Jim see him painting t$_i$?
(e.g., "Whistler's mother")

It is thought that the adjunct in such a case can move across the clause boundary because the main verb is dictating the case of the subject in the lower clause, (notice it is *him*, not *he*), thus "opening up" the boundary (see Roeper & de Villiers, 1991).

On the other hand, the adjunct cannot be moved from within a superficially similar structure involving a nominalization:

(49) How$_i$ did John see his running t$_i$*?

Now the answer "with bare feet" is not allowed, but an answer such a "by going to the track meet" is fine. In contrast with the adjunct forms, argument questions can move long distance from within such a nominalized structure, though probably not in preference to the short-distance interpretation:

(50) Who$_i$ did John show his copying t$_i$?
(possible answer: "the singer on TV".)

Hence the acquisition of complex wh-questions involves a considerable degree of linguistic sophistication, and is only now being studied in normally-hearing children. Most of the past literature on wh-acquisition has focused on the learning of the individual wh-words, and on auxiliary movement in questions. But clearly the more complex phenomena just described are deserving of thorough study in both normally-hearing and deaf children as they involve:

1. The acquisition of long distance movement.
2. The acquisition of cyclic movement.
3. The distinction between adjuncts and arguments.
4. The acquisition of subcategorization frames for verbs and their complements.
5. Case marking across clause boundaries.
6. Learning the requirements and restrictions on wh-traces.
7. The development of the CP node.

Previous Results With Normally-Hearing Children

In previous work with preschool normal-hearing children, 4- to 6-year-olds have been shown to respect the basic distinctions described. In all cases, stories that allowed ambiguous questions were read to the children and accompanied by illustrations. A sample can be seen in Fig. 2.1. For example, take the short story:

> (51) Once there was a boy who loved climbing trees in the forest. One afternoon he slipped and fell to the ground. He picked himself up and went home. That night when he had a bath, he saw a big bruise on his arm. He said to his Dad, "I must have hurt myself when I fell this afternoon."

Now comes the question:

> (52) When did the boy say he hurt himself?

Notice there are two possible answers, either to when he *said* it, or to when he *hurt* himself. That is, the "when" question could be connected to the "say" or to "hurt."

But now consider a variant containing a medial question:

> (53) When did the boy say how he hurt himself?

The reader should now find the answer "in the afternoon" decidedly awkward. Suddenly, the ambiguity is gone, and only one answer, the short

Once there was a boy who loved climbing trees in the forest.

One afternoon he slipped and fell to the ground. He picked himself up and went home.

That night when he had a bath he noticed a big bruise on his arm. He said to his Dad, "I must have hurt myself when I fell this afternoon"

FIG. 2.1.   Sample pictured story for question task.

distance answer to "say," seems right. This fact has been known for several years about the adult language (Chomsky, 1986), but do children see the subtle difference? Table 2.6 shows their preferences for interpretation of the various structures discussed.

Notice that the children allow LD movement of the question when there

TABLE 2.6
Preschool Children's Long-Distance Interpretations of
Questions

     Argument   O medial
a. *Who* did the boy _____ ask to call _____ ?
             68%   32%

     Adjunct   O medial
b. *When* did the boy say _____ he hurt himself_____ ?
             50%   44%

     Adjunct   Adjunct medial
c. *When* did the clown say _____ *how* he caught the ball _____ ?
             48%   6%

     Argument   Argument medial
d. *Who* did the girl ask _____ *what* to feed _____ ?
             70%   2%

     Adjunct   Argument medial
e. *How* did the girl ask _____ *who* to paint_____ ?
             23%   8%

     Argument   Adjunct medial
f. *Who* did the boy ask _____ *how* to help _____ ?
             63%   30%

Note: The data are from de Villiers, Roeper, and Vainikka, 1990.

is no medial question word in a sentence with a complement (a and b) but disallow it when the medial CP is filled (c, d, and e). They also show a systematic difference between adjunct (e.g., *how*) and argument (e.g., *who*) movement (compare e and f). In this respect their behavior is like adults tested on the same structures. In fact, only rare 3-year-old children answer "in the afternoon" to 53 (equivalent to c in Table 2.6). They seem already to know the constraint that adjunct question words may not "move" over another question word: a constraint that is embedded in universal grammar. Recent studies (see papers in Maxfield & Plunkett, 1991) explored children's knowledge of this constraint in German, French, Spanish, and Greek, and have found strikingly similar results from young children exposed to the translations of 52 and 53.

Not all of their responses were compatible with adult grammar, however. For instance, they sometimes answered the medial question rather than the initial question, a mistake never made by adults. The full results and an interpretation of the error are discussed in detail in de Villiers, Roeper, and Vainikka (1990).

In a second series of studies, young children and adults were tested on the small clause cases and nominalizations described in examples 47 through 50. These results are shown in Table 2.7.

Notice again that adult subjects show an adjunct-argument asymmetry in the case of the nominalizations but allow long-distance movement of both from small clauses. Children did not allow movement of the adjunct from

TABLE 2.7
Long-Distance Interpretations in Small Clauses
and Nominalizations

Argument	Small clause	
g. Who did the sister show _____ him copying _____ ?		
Preschool (n = 16)	25%	62%
Adult (n = 12)	12%	83%
Argument	Nominalization	
h. Who did the sister show _____ his copying _____ ?		
Preschool	53%	25%
Adult	54%	37%
Adjunct	Small Clause	
i. How did the mother see _____ him riding _____ ?		
Preschool	81%	18%
Adult	54%	45%
Adjunct	Nominalization	
j. How did the mother see _____ his riding _____ ?		
Preschool	88%	12%
Adult	91%	1%

Note: The data are from Roeper and de Villiers, 1991.

the small clause, but very readily considered the argument question to have moved long distance. In the case of the nominalizations, the children are unlikely to allow LD movement of either arguments or adjuncts. Nevertheless, it is clear that these young children do differentiate the small clauses from the nominalizations, despite the superficial resemblance between the structures.

Long-Distance Movement in Deaf Students

On the basis of the previous studies by de Villiers and Roeper, we constructed a battery of 30 stories and questions that could be read by deaf students, normally-hearing third graders, and adults. The part of the battery that concerns LD movement is shown in Table 2.8.

Sentences a through j followed stories that contained two possible answers for the wh-question: one appropriate given a long distance interpretation, and one for a short distance interpretation of the question. The stories were administered in a booklet, each page of which contained an illustrated story, with the words beneath the appropriate picture. A question followed at the bottom of each page with a space for the written answer (see Fig. 2.1). The booklet was divided into halves, with the second part a repeat of the same structures with different examples. The adult subjects completed the task in a single session; the children were given the two parts of the booklet on two different occasions less than a week apart.

TABLE 2.8
Battery of Wh-Questions

a. Argument questions with O medial:
Who did the boy ask to call?
Who did the girl ask to help?
b. Argument questions with argument -wh medial:
Who did the boy ask what to bring?
Who did the girl ask what to make?
c. Argument questions with adjunct -wh medial:
Who did the boy ask how to help?
Who did she ask how to paint?
d. Adjunct questions with O medial:
How did the dog say his bone was gone?
When did the girl say she ripped her dress?
e. Adjunct questions with argument -wh medial:
How did the mother learn what to bake:
How did Rover learn what to catch?
f. Adjunct questions with adjunct -wh medial:
When did the boy say how he got a bruise?
When did the clown say how he caught the ball?
g. Argument questions with nominalization:
Who did the sister show his patting?
Who did the woman show his hugging?
h. Argument questions with small clause:
Who did the mother show him watching?
Who did the sister show him copying?
i. Adjunct questions with nominalization:
How did the mother see his riding?
How did the father see their mixing?
j. Adjunct questions with small clause:
How did the mother show him reading?
How did the friends see him dancing?

The Subjects

The subjects were 52 deaf children ranging in age from 11 to 19, all attending an oral school for the deaf, 20 normally-hearing children in the third grade of a small private school, and 20 adult native-English speakers. The deaf students had an average age of 15;3; their mean hearing loss in the better ear across three pure-tone frequencies in the speech range was 95dB (range, 58dB to 120dB); their median reading comprehension score on the Stanford Achievement Test (normed for the hearing impaired) was 5th grade (range, second to twelfth grade). The normally-hearing third graders had an average age of 9;1 years, and a median reading comprehension level of 5th grade (range, third to eighth grade) on the Comprehensive Test of Basic Skills. The adults were 13 female and 7 male college students. Reference will also be made to the data from normally-hearing preschool children on the same structures (de Villiers et al., 1990; Roeper & de Villiers, 1991)

The Results

One of the first questions to be asked is whether the subjects show evidence of allowing long-distance movement of wh-questions in the structures a and b, where it is unambiguously allowed by preschoolers and adults. Table 2.9 shows the percentage of time the various groups (including the data from the previous research on preschoolers) understood the question word as having originated in either the upper or the lower clause.

There is a more marked asymmetry than expected between arguments and adjuncts, with arguments being interpreted as referring to the lower clause more frequently than adjuncts for the normally-hearing groups. Especially in their interpretations of adjuncts, the adults and third graders in this study are far more conservative about long-distance movement than the preschoolers tested orally in the previous work. This may reflect a difference between reading and hearing such stories and questions. In the case of the deaf students, long-distance interpretations for both arguments and adjuncts are particularly infrequent. The difference between the deaf children and the other two groups on these two structures without a medial question is highly significant ($F = 9.8$, $df = 89$; $p = .000$).

A second question to be asked is: Do the subjects show a constraint

TABLE 2.9
Long distance interpretations of Wh-Questions[a]

Argument	O medial	
a. Who did the boy _____ ask to call _____ ?		
Normally Hearing:		
Preschool	68%	32%
Third grade	42.5%	55%
Adult	25%	67.5%
Deaf:		
11 to 19	67%	18%
Adjunct	O medial	
b. When did the boy say _____ he hurt himself _____ ?		
Normally Hearing:		
Preschool	50%	44%
Third grade	82.5%	17.5%
Adult	75%	15%
Deaf:		
11 to 19	79%	10.5%

[a]The percentage do not add to 100% because we excluded cases where the subjects repeated back virtually the whole story by way of an "answer"—a prevalent tendency for the deaf subjects and some overcautious adults.

TABLE 2.10
Limitations on Long-Distance Interpretation

Adjunct	Adjunct medial	
c. When did the clown say _____ how he caught the ball _____ ?		
Normally Hearing:		
Preschool	48%	6%
Third grade	65%	35%
Adult	92.5%	5%
Deaf:		
11 to 19	67%	16%
Argument	Argument medial	
d. Who did the girl ask _____ what to feed _____ ?		
Normally Hearing:		
Preschool	70%	2%
Third grade	92.5%	5%
Adult	97.5%	0%
Deaf:		
11 to 19	75%	7.5%
Adjunct	Argument medial	
e. How did the girl ask _____ who to paint _____ ?		
Normally Hearing:		
Preschool	23%	8%
Third grade	92.5%	5%
Adult	90%	2.5%
Deaf:		
11 to 19	76.9%	7.5%
Argument	Adjunct medial	
f. Who did the boy ask _____ how to help _____ ?		
Normally Hearing:		
Preschool	63%	30%
Third grade	92.5%	2.5%
Adult	92.5%	5%
Deaf:		
11 to 19	77.5%	2.5%

against LD movement when the medial question is present? Table 2.10 shows the data from the groups on those structures (c through g) where it is clear that every group disallows LD movement under these circumstances.[3] However, with the almost complete absence of LD movement in the deaf children, it is not obvious that they show the contrast that young hearing children and adults do.[4]

A third question is: Do subjects incorrectly answer the medial question in

---

[3]The peculiar 35% of LD answers for the hearing third grade on structure c seems to reflect the operation of a bias in one particular story.

[4]Table 2.10 also reveals that structures like g) Who did John ask how to paint? were hardly ever given a LD interpretation by any group in this study, perhaps reflecting a difference between reading and hearing the questions, which we are exploring further.

TABLE 2.11
Incidence of Answering the Medial Question Word in COMP

Structures:	c Arg-Arg	d Arg-Adj	e Adj-Arg	f Adj-Adj
Normally Hearing:				
Preschoolers	28%	4%	68%	40%
Third grade	7.5%	0%	5%	5%
Adults	0%	0%	0%	0%
Deaf Students:	7.6%	0%	14.4%	13.5%

these structures? Preschool hearing subjects frequently answer questions such as:

(54) How did Big Bird ask who to paint?

by answering the argument medial question; for example, by saying "Kermit." This tendency could be argued to be due to the children considering that the medial is simply a copy of the initial question, a structure allowed in some dialects of German (see de Villiers, Roeper, & Vainikka, 1990; for a more complete rationale). Table 2.11 shows the prevalence of this type of answer for the groups tested on such structures. Although very prevalent for preschool children, it is vanishingly rare by third grade and also rather rare for the deaf children, who do not seem to consider the medial question to have real question status. No adult gives such an answer.

The deaf subjects' sometimes lengthy answers reveal a surprising command over the use of medial wh-embedded questions; 115 examples of medial wh-clauses are produced altogether. However, the majority of these answers — 68% — are directly borrowed from the structure of the preceding question, sometimes making for a rather tortuous response:[5]

(55) The boy ask his father how to help to her sister.
     The kitten learned how to swim by her mother teaching her.

Only five answers change the tense of the embedded clause, which is a significant change:

(56) Who did the boy ask how to help?
     The boy asked his father how he should help his sister.

---

[5]As mentioned earlier, deaf subjects were much more likely to give a full sentence answer than the other subjects, who mostly answered with a constituent. The deaf students may be masking the full extent of their problems by this strategy, but it should also be noted that their school emphasizes "complete answers," especially in written work.

Seventeen more change the embedded wh-word from "What" to "how," for example:

(57) How did the mother learn what to bake?
The mother learned how to bake a cake by watching TV.

which may be a way of allowing the initial "how" to take scope over the whole sentence, but at least it reveals the possibility of substitution across the CP nodes. Finally, it should be noted that there are some rare, but interesting, peculiarities in the spontaneous use of CP:

(58) He ask his father to how to help.
The girl decided to wear what by looking in a magazine.
Ask father that which of two decision is better.

Errors of that sort do not occur in our transcripts from hearing subjects of any age.

A fourth question is: How do the subjects treat structures with no CP? Table 2.12 provides a summary of the contrast between small clause and nominalizations.

Adults freely allow argument movement from small clauses, in fact, they prefer the LD reading here but nowhere else, as do preschoolers.[6] However, deaf children do not like that interpretation. Third-grade normal-hearing subjects fall between these two extremes. In fact, the adult preference becomes more likely as the third grader's reading level goes up ($F = 3.9$; $df = 17$, $p = .04$). However, a similar attempt to find variations in the deaf group by either their reading comprehension level (Stanford Achievement Test) or score on a test of English sentence syntax comprehension (The Rhode Island Test of Language Structure [RITLS]) was not successful, because practically no deaf students at any reading comprehension level or RITLS score gave LD interpretations for these sentences.

Why would deaf subjects not allow extraction of the wh-question from the small clause, because that is hypothesized not to involve CP, and we argued that it is one of the first forms of complementation that deaf children master? We cannot be sure at present. It is possible that the fragile cue differentiating the small clause from the nominalization (*him* vs. *his*) is not understood by the deaf subjects, given their known problems with

---

[6]It should be noted that all subject groups are again more conservative than adults in Roeper and de Villiers (1991), who received the stories and questions in the oral mode, and did allow argument LD movement from nominalizations, and adjunct LD movement from small clauses. Further research is needed to tell whether the differences are due to modality or to receiving such a large number of different questions in a booklet as in this task.

TABLE 2.12
Long-Distance Interpretation in Small Clauses and
Nominalizations

Argument	Small clause	
g. Who did the sister show _____ him copying _____ ?		?
Normally Hearing:		
Preschool	25%	62%
Third grade	62.5%	37.5%
Adult	17.5%	55.3%
Deaf:		
11 to 19	74.4%	4.5%
Argument	Nominalization	
h. Who did the sister show _____ is copying _____ ?		?
Normally Hearing:		
Preschool	53%	25%
Third grade	85%	2.5%
Adult	75.3%	7.5%
Deaf:		
11 to 19	75%	4.5%
Adjunct	Small clause	
i. How did the mother see _____ him riding_____ ?		?
Normally Hearing:		
Preschool	81%	18%
Third grade	90%	10%
Adult	65%	2.5%
Deaf:		
11 to 19	85.1%	4.5%
Adjunct	Nominalization	
j. How did the mother see _____ his riding_____ ?		?
Normally Hearing:		
Preschool	88%	12%
Third grade	85%	15%
Adult	75%	5%
Deaf:		
11 to 19	75.4%	10.5%

pronominalization (Wilbur, Montanelli, & Quigley, 1976). Notice in Table 2.12 that there is not a shred of evidence that deaf children differentiate the small clause from the nominalization, though the hearing groups clearly do for the argument questions. Deaf children's own productions of small clauses rarely have a pronoun in that role. If that is the case, they should err on the conservative side in interpreting these forms.

Alternatively, and speculatively, in the absence of any evidence that long-distance movement is possible in the language, children should err on the conservative side, or have no way to recover from their mistake (Baker, 1979). Given the impoverished nature of the speech addressed to deaf children and their lack of ability to read complex written material, it is likely that they have not recognized the possibility of long-distance movement in English.

Summary

In summary, our work in this area suggests serious shortcomings in the English grammars of oral deaf subjects with respect to subtle aspects of complex wh-questions and their interpretation. Our conclusions must be considered tentative because no data exist on the production of LD questions in deaf children. One can predict, however, that such structures will be very rare, as the production data from normally-hearing children is extremely sparse (de Villiers et al., 1990). In these cases, perhaps the only avenue of exploration is via comprehension studies, though Crain is developing techniques of elicited production that might prove valuable (Crain, 1989).

The comprehension studies reveal substantial group differences and a lack of similarity between the older deaf subjects and either normally-hearing third grade subjects (matched roughly to them by reading level) or much younger children tested in the oral mode. The data on the lack of LD readings suggests either: (a) an inflexibility of interpretation that represents a parsing conservatism, or (b) a failure to handle cyclic movement or any movement across more than a single clause. On the question of parsing conservatism, it should be noted that hearing adults and third grade subjects did show more conservative interpretations on the reading task than previous subjects tested orally. Nonetheless, they still showed a preference for LD readings on certain structures, which the deaf students never did.

The second proposal is compatible with the general notion of a delay in the acquisition of CP, and if it is combined with the aforementioned results on the severe delays and significant errors in acquiring relative clause structures, which also involve CP and movement within a clause, the case is strengthened. Yet the children's use of embedded questions in giving their answers reveals some use of medial CP, although almost 70% appear to be borrowed from the structure of the question asked immediately before. In the relative clause case, the task required completely spontaneous oral production, and performance was comparatively poor.

In conclusion, the lack of long-distance movement of questions provides the final piece of evidence in favor of the proposal that the deaf children's grammar is incomplete in the area of the C system.

DIRECTIONS FOR THE FUTURE

We have described evidence in support of the general hypothesis that most deaf children acquiring English develop an incompletely specified grammar. Furthermore, we have claimed that the character of their grammars is compatible with a more specific failure to develop an adequate I system or

C system. In current linguistic theory, it is argued that these functional categories may be subject to more variability across languages than the lexical categories, and hence require more information from the input. The kind of input that would allow the child to distinguish between language-specific versions of the C system or I system is dependent on functional elements, such as complementizers, auxiliaries, tense markings, and other elements that are frequent and readily available in the input of the hearing child. Unfortunately, access to these elements may be less readily available to the deaf child, because the triggering elements fall at the wrong extreme of the dimensions of phonological and semantic distinctiveness. As a consequence, the deaf child is in an especially disadvantaged position for building an appropriately articulated model of English syntax.

In Radford's (1988) account, the grammars of young hearing children are characterized as "lacking" functional categories at the beginning. Lebeaux (1988) argued that children may begin by expressing pure thematic structures — essentially the lexical categories. Those who seek a model of language acquisition in which children's grammar is continuous with the adult grammar, rather than radically different, have invoked the notion of maturation to explain the deviation exemplified by a small clause grammar (Radford, 1988; Wexler, 1990). On this view, it is important that the functional categories are absent only during a limited time of the child's life, perhaps when certain brain structures are still maturing. The implications of this for the present hypothesis are provocative. If the functional categories "mature," they should not be absent from the grammars of these older deaf children and adolescents. However, if they are dependent on input in the way we have proposed, maturation alone may not provide the evidence needed to fix the categories. Several lines of possibility open up. For example, second-language learners provide some sort of test, in that they have mature brains and access to the crucial input. Unfortunately, there are complications in assessing the hypothesis with respect to second-language learning. It has been postulated that the availability of Universal Grammar as a guide to language learning might itself have some kind of critical period and that second-language learners may be learning in a radically different way than first-language learners (e.g., Cook, 1988). Second, the very fact that functional categories vary across languages means that it is precisely in those areas of grammar that second-language learners may have most difficulty, even given appropriate access, because of the differences with their first language. There is no easy empirical test of the notion of maturation, but future work may illuminate the subtle differences and lead us to some important discoveries across these populations.

The functional elements have been regarded in some accounts as the less "essential" aspects of grammar, the additional niceties that provide only the nuances of meaning and expression. In contrast, the basic sentence structure and fundamental processes, such as recursion and embeddings, are regarded as the more central properties of language. But, on the contemporary account, the functional elements play a vital role in building the fundamental structures. For instance, consider the contrast above between small clause structures and nominalizations; a distinction cued only by the case — accusative versus genitive — of the pronoun in the lower clause. Yet that cue is used already by four-year-old normal-hearing children to discriminate the two structures.

What are the implications of this account? If a complete English syntax is to be acquired by deaf children, there are two possible avenues of access. One is to supplement the oral input by other means, such as early access to written English. In written form, the functional elements may be at less of a phonological disadvantage. However, it is not at all clear that children can acquire a complete grammar via the written mode if they do not have one in some first language beforehand. Obviously, it would be better to have a more complete grammar of spoken English first, but little is understood about how to achieve that. One thing is clear, though: Exposure to spoken language drills of simple English sentences will not expose the child to sufficient evidence for building the right kind of phrase structure.

The alternative is for the deaf child to acquire a complete system first in a modality to which the child could have unimpaired access, namely a formal sign language. Of course, access is not guaranteed to that for the majority of deaf children, those who are born into families that know no sign language and may not be able to learn one faster than their child. Very little is known yet about the linguistics of the I system and C system in American Sign Language, but it is highly probable that the systems are different in many ways from English. Nevertheless, advocates of signed input argue that it is vital to exploit the early readiness of children to acquire a full language, and that such a background will make more possible the acquisition of English as a complete second language. The debates about education of deaf students are too multifaceted to consider here, but proponents on all sides might consider the implications of the present evidence for their views.

REFERENCES

Abney, S. (1987). *The English noun phrase in its sentential aspects*. Unpublished doctoral dissertation, Massachusetts Institute of Technology, Cambridge, Ma.

Baker, C. L. (1979). Syntactic theory and the projection problem. *Linguistic Inquiry, 10,* 533–583.

Baumberger, T. (1986). *Acquisition of the past tense by oral deaf children*. Unpublished B. A. honors thesis, Smith College, Northampton, MA.

Baumberger, T., de Villiers, J. G., & de Villiers, P. A. (1986). *Phonological schemas for the past tense: Oral deaf and hearing children*. Paper presented at the 11th Annual Boston University Conference on language Development, Boston, MA.

Berko, J. (1958). The child's learning of English morphology. *Word, 14*, 150–177.

Bloom, L., Takeff, J. & Lahey, M. (1984). Learning *to* in complement constructions. *Journal of Child Language, 11*, 391–406.

Brown, R. W. (1973). *A first language: the early stages*. Cambridge, MA: Harvard University Press.

Bybee, J., & Slobin, D. (1982). Rules and schemas in the development and use of the English past tense. *Language, 58*, 265–289.

Chomsky, C. (1969). *The acquisition of syntax in children from 5 to 10*. Cambridge, MA: MIT Press.

Chomsky, N. (1981). *Lectures on government and binding*. Cambridge, MA: MIT Press.

Chomsky, N. (1986). *Barriers*. Cambridge, MA: MIT Press.

Cook, V. J. (1988). *Chomsky's universal grammar: An introduction*. Oxford Blackwell.

Crain, S. (1989, October). *Why production precedes comprehension*. Paper presented at the 14th annual Boston University Conference on language Development Boston, MA.

Crain, S. McKee, C., & Emiliani, M. (1990). Visiting relatives in Italy. In L. Frazier & J. de Villiers, (eds.), *Language processing and language acquisition*. Dordrecht: Kluwer.

de Villiers, J. G & de Villiers, P.A. (1973) A cross-sectional study of the acquisition of grammatical morphemes in child speech. *Journal of Psycholinguistic Research.* 2, 267-278.

de Villiers, J.G., & de Villiers, P.A. (1986). *Parallels and divergences in the acquisition of oral English by deaf and hearing children: Evidence for structural constraints*. Paper presented at the 11th Annual Boston University Conference on Language Development, Boston, MA.

de Villiers, P. A. (1988). Assessing English syntax in hearing-impaired children: Elicited production in pragmatically motivated situations. In R. R. Kretschmer, & L. W. Kretschmer, (Eds.), Communication assessment of hearing-impaired children: From conversation to classroom. *Journal of the Academy of Rehabilitative Audiology: Monograph Supplement, 21*, 41–71.

de Villiers, J. G., Roeper, T., & Vainikka, A (1990). The acquisition of long-distance movement. In L. Frazier & J. de Villiers (Eds.), *Language processing and language acquisition* . (pp. 257–297). Dordrecht: Kluwer.

Engen, E. & Engen, T. (1983). *Rhode Island Test of Language Structure*. Austin, TX: Pro-Ed.

Fukui, N. (1986). *A theory of category projection and its application*. Unpublished doctoral dissertation, MIT, Cambridge, MA.

Fukui, N., & Speas, M. (1985). *Specifier and projection*. MIT Working Papers in Linguistics (Vol 8).

Goldin-Meadow, S. (1982). The resilience of recursion. In E. Wanner & L. Gleitman (Eds.), *Language acquisition: The state of the art* (pp 51–77). New York: Cambridge University Press.

Hamburger, H., & Crain, S. (1982). Relative acquisition. In S. A. Kuczaj (Ed.), *Language development: Syntax and semantics* (pp. 245–274). Hillsdale, NJ: Lawrence Erlbaum Associates.

Koopman, H. (1984). *The syntax of verbs*. Dordrecht: Foris.

Kretschmer, R. R., & Kretschmer, L. W. (1978). *Language development and intervention with the hearing impaired*. Baltimore, MD: University Park Press.

Kuczaj, S. A. (1977). The acquisition of regular and irregular past tense form. *Journal of Verbal Learning and Verbal Behavior, 16*, 589–600.

Labelle, M. (1989, October). *Licensing of empty categories in child language*. Paper delivered at the 14th annual Boston University Conference on Language Development Boston, MA.

Labelle, M. (1990). Predication, wh-movement, and the development of relative clauses. *Language Acquisition*, 95–120.

Lebeaux, D. (1988) Language acquisition and the form of the grammar. Unpublished doctoral dissertation, University of Massachusetts, Amherst, MA.

Lebeaux, D. (1990). The grammatical nature of the acquisition sequence: Adjoin- A and the formation of relative clauses. In L. Frazier & J. de Villiers (Eds.), *Language processing and acquisition* (pp. 13–82). Dordrecht: Kluwer.

Limber, J. (1973). The genesis of complex sentences. In T. E. Moore (Ed.), *Cognitive development and the acquisition of language.* New York: Academic Press.

Magner, M., de Villiers, P. A., Hoban, E., & von Schlegel, J. (1988). *A multifaceted intervention program for improving deaf children's written English.* Paper presented at the Alexander Graham Bell Association Biennial Convention, Orlando, FL.

Maxfield, T., & Plunkett, B. (Eds.). (1991). Papers in the Acquisition of WH: Proceedings of the Umass Roundtable, May 1990. *University of Massachusetts Occasional Papers.*

Quigley, S. P. (1969). *The influence of fingerspelling on the development of language, communication, and educational achievement in deaf children.* Urbana, IL: Institute for Research on Exceptional Children.

Quigley, S. P., & King, C. M. (1980). Syntactic performance of hearing impaired and normal hearing individuals. *Applied Psycholinguistics, 1,* 329–356.

Quigley, S. P., Montanelli, D. S., & Wilbur, R. (1976). Some aspects of the verb system in the language of deaf students. *Journal of Speech and Hearing Research, 19,* 536–550.

Quigley, S. P., & Paul, P. (1984). *Language and deafness.* San Diego, CA: College-Hill Press.

Quigley, S. P., Smith, H.L., & Wilbur, R. (1974). Comprehension of relativized sentences by deaf students. *Journal of Speech and Hearing Research, 17,* 325–341.

Quigley, S. P., Wilbur, R., & Montanelli, D. S. (1974). Question formation in the language of deaf students. *Journal of Speech and Hearing Research, 17,* 699–713.

Quigley, S. P., Wilbur, R., & Montanelli, D.S. (1976). Complement structures in the language of deaf students. *Journal of Speech and Hearing Research, 19,* 448–457.

Quigley, S. P., Wilbur, R., Power, D. J., Montanelli, D. S., & Steinkamp, M. (1976). *Syntactic structures in the language of deaf children.* Urbana, IL: Institute for Child Behavior and Development.

Radford, A. (1988). Small children's small clauses. *Transactions of the Philological Society, 86,* 1–46.

Roeper, T., Akiyama, S., Mallis, L., & Rooth, M. (1985). Empty categories in acquisition. Unpublished manuscript, University of Massachusetts, Amherst, MA.

Roeper, T., & de Villiers, J. G. (1991). Ordered decisions in the acquisition of wh-questions. In H. Goodluck, J. Weissenborn, & T. Roeper (Eds.), *Theoretical issues in language development.* Hillsdale, NJ: Lawrence Erlbaum Associates.

Stowell, T. (1981). The origin of phrase structure. Unpublished doctoral dissertation, MIT, Cambridge, MA.

Tavakolian, S. (1981). The conjoined clause analysis of relative clauses. In S. Tavakolian (Eds.), *Language acquisition and linguistic theory* (pp. 167–187) Cambridge, MA: MIT Press.

Weinberg, A. (1990). Markedness versus maturation: The case of subject–auxiliary inversion. *Language Acquisition, 1,* 165–194.

Wexler, K. (1990). On unparsable input in language acquisition. In L. Frazier & J. de Villiers (Eds.), *Language processing and language Acquisition.* Dordrecht Kluwer

Wilbur, R., Montanelli, D. S., & Quigley, S. P. (1976). Pronominalization in the language of deaf students. *Journal of Speech and Hearing Research, 19,* 120–140.

Williamson, M. (1985). The assessment of question production in oral deaf children. Unpublished B. A. honors thesis, Smith College, Northampton, MA.

3 Morphology in a Child with a Congenital, Left-Hemisphere Brain Lesion: Implications for Normal Acquisition

Yonata Levy
The Hebrew University, Jerusalem

Naomi Amir
Ruth Shalev
Sharei Zedek Hospital, Jerusalem

INTRODUCTION

This chapter is concerned with the development of Hebrew morphology in a child with a congenital left hemisphere brain-lesion documented by CT, which is the result of cerebral infarction in the distribution of the left Middle Cerebral Artery (MCA). Such lesions destroy the traditional left hemisphere language areas. Elsewhere, we present a detailed description of the study and its findings (Levy, Amir, & Shalev, 1992). Here we describe the theoretical background for the study, give a brief summary of the findings, and consider the implications for language learning.

Two major issues are addressed in this chapter:

1. Does the development of Hebrew morphology in our subject follow the conventional course? That is, is it possible to demonstrate plasticity in the actual process of acquisition?
2. Does this data bear upon existing models of normal development like those outlined earlier?

In the context of neuropsychological theories, the significance of cases like these concerns the issues involved in brain plasticity. Those have traditionally been associated with claims concerning the equipotentiality of the brain hemispheres early in life. We include a short summary of the theoretical background of these issues.

The maturational theory of language lateralization, which argues for the equipotentiality of the brain hemispheres for language functions early in life, was proposed by Lennenberg (1967). Proponents of this theory claim that, although the left hemisphere is the site of language in most normal dexteral individuals, the right hemisphere is potentially capable of language in the event of damage to the left side language areas. This is so, provided that this damage is incurred early in life so that areas which have the potential for mediating language have not yet been committed to other functions (see Bishop, 1988b, for a discussion). The main empirical support for this claim derives from reports of the nonsevere, transitory nature of aphasic symptoms following trauma to the left hemisphere in young children (Basser, 1962).

However, recent studies that have looked at cerebral dominance in the young child suggest that the pattern of lateralization, which is responsible for the presence of language in the left hemisphere in most adults, may already be essentially complete soon after birth.

Woods (1984) reported on anatomical and behavioral studies which support the invariance hypothesis. Studies of diachotic ear preference in children (Hiscock, & Kinsbourne 1977; Woods, 1980), evoked responses in infants (Molfese, Freeman, & Palermo, 1975), and autopsy examination of neonatal brains (Wada, Clark, & Hamm, 1975), all suggest that there are both anatomical and behavioral asymmetries between the hemispheres early in life and that language and language-related functions are lateralized to the left side probably from birth, or very soon thereafter. A reanalysis of Basser's (1962) data, on which the maturational lateralization hypothesis was originally based, and data from a number of other studies since 1962 (Carter, Hoenegger, & Satz, 1982), controlled for age of patients and handedness, suggest that the hypothesis cannot, in fact, be supported. Woods and Teuber (1978) reported on the frequency of aphasia in children following unilateral brain trauma. Their data, as well as earlier work that they reviewed, showed a marked fall in the incidence of crossed aphasia in children in most studies following the year 1941. In the authors' view, this result was due to the availability of antibiotics for the treatment of systemic bacterial infections, which affected many of the cases of childhood aphasia and cases of hemiparesis reported in the literature. The important point here is that such infections result in diffuse brain changes, which may appear bilaterally. In other words, the incidence of crossed aphasia that was reported in the past was probably a result of methodological problems in the studies, such as sampling errors and inaccurate diagnosis.

In a rebuttal of the anti-equipotentiality view, Bishop (1988a) found serious methodological flows in all but one of the studies that purport to support it. She concluded that the claim that the right hemisphere has some inherent limitations on the degree of linguistic sophistication it can achieve remains an unproven possibility.

Note that the behavioral studies, of which ours is one, in fact address the question of brain plasticity which, although related, is not identical to the question of the equipotentiality of the hemispheres. The latter raises the question of the developmental nature of lateralization, whereas the former refers to the ability of the secondary hemisphere to develop language in cases of damage to the left hemisphere.

Researchers have not agreed on the interpretation of the plasticity thesis. Witelson (1977) and Woods (1980) argued that the plasticity of the brain hemispheres may not be without limits. They claimed that the evidence in favor of the plasticity hypothesis was not based on well-controlled populations. Robinson (1981) reviewed cases of brain trauma and concluded that when the site, nature, and severity of the injury are comparable, the child suffers equally with the adult. Dennis (1980), Dennis and Kohn (1975), and Dennis and Whitaker (1977) argued that in individuals in whom language is mediated through the right hemisphere following insults to the left side of the brain, certain sophisticated linguistic functions seem impaired. As already mentioned, Bishop (1988b) found methodological flows in these as well as in other studies (Aram, Ekelman, Rose, & Whitaker, 1985; Aram, Ekelman, & Whitaker, 1986; Kohn, 1980; Leleux & Lebrun, 1981; Rankin, Aram, & Horowitz, 1981) that, in her view, suffice to reject the whole model.

A different way of interpreting the plasticity issue is in relation to the developmental course that may be observed in such children. Studying the developmental sequence and the types of errors that these children make compared to the normal course may be important for an understanding of possible consequences of very early lateralization and the implications of brain plasticity for learning.

Can the study of language development in children with congenital LH infarcts contribute to theories of language acquisition in normals? Clearly, a demonstration of brain plasticity logically precedes all discussions of possible relevance of such data to the study of normal development. Assuming that such a demonstration is possible, we believe that the gain may be methodological as well as substantive.

In a healthy infant who is in full possession of all five senses and has an intact brain, language evolves in temporal conjunction with other competences, all of which unfold over a period of a few years in early childhood. Learning takes place in a condensed manner and everything is temporally interdependent. From the point of view of developmental research, this situation is unfortunate, for variables seem hopelessly confounded.

The slowing down of the process of acquisition is a hallmark of language development in pathology. Controlled studies, as well as clinical observations of children with focal brain-lesions such as our subject, report a marked delay in language development and rarely describe a child without problems in language, at least through the late preschool years (Aram & Whitaker, 1987). In other words, assuming that there is brain plasticity, the effect of left-hemisphere lesions incurred early in life may be a slowing down of the process of acquisition in the face of a relative preservation of the normal course of development. If this is indeed the case, as we show for certain aspects of morphology, uncovering an ordered continuum of linguistic systems as they slowly emerge in these children may contribute to a clarification of theoretical issues in language acquisition.

Consider the long-lasting debate concerning the *cognition hypothesis* the *functionalistic approach* and the *linguistic approach* to language acquisition:

In a review article, Cromer (1986) described the *cognition hypothesis* as the approach that stressed the dependency relations that exist between language and cognition. This position postulates the centrality of semantics and the underlying conceptual system to language development in its early phases. It stresses existing correspondences between cognitive and linguistic categories and expressions and suggests that those are exploited by the prelinguistic child as an entry point into the linguistic system.

Functionalistic approaches to language development consider the fact that language communicates thoughts, feelings, requests, and emotions as central in the acquisitional process. Despite apparent differences, functionalism and the semantic/cognitive approach share a basic theoretical tenet. Both positions involve a commitment to the following statement: Language subserves cognitive and/or social functions. Structures found in young children's speech may be described in cognitive/semantic/pragmatic terms. Language acquisition should be explained as a function of these underlying structures.

The *linguistic approach*, as argued by Curtiss (1989), for example, opposes this view. It assumes a modular view of language that presupposes the dissociation of various language aspects. The modules are said to have different properties, which may be selectively impaired or preserved. Inspired primarily by work in generative grammar, this model assumes that the structural aspects of language are guided by innate principles. Acquisition, although triggered by experience, is largely a matter of choosing between innately available options. For those who espouse the linguistic approach and do not subscribe to specific claims made by nativist theories, the assumption that formal linguistic categories and rules are available to the child from the inception of language development is still very central.

An empirical evaluation of either of these positions in young children who are still in the course of learning language presents difficult methodological problems. Of prime concern is the fact that the actual language that 2-year-olds speak lends itself to accounts that are consistent with all positions. The limited universe of little children, the emergent cognitive faculties, and the small size vocabularies do not allow for a full manifestation of grammatical abilities, even if they exist.

Theoretical debates have centered around the nature of early categories. However, when one looks at the data, restricted syntactic categories, semantic categories, or functional speech-acts seem to offer equally plausible accounts for first word combinations. In other words, a research strategy that attempts to look at structural aspects of language runs into serious problems when one attempts to separate form from function and meaning in the syntax of very young children, because of their limited linguistic repertoire. For example, in English, the familiar syntactic instances of structural constraints that are divorced from meaning involve long and grammatically complex utterances of the kind that young children do not typically use (e.g., Pinker, 1989). Yet, even in English, there are examples, such as the count-mass distinction in nouns, that involve both syntactic and morphological manipulations (Gathercole, 1985; Gordon, 1985) or the operation of concord that may be observed even in beginners.

New possibilities open up when one looks at the development of languages with complex morphologies because these systems are used even by very young children. As will become clear in the next section, Hebrew morphology, which is the language acquired by the subject of the present study, offers several opportunities for teasing apart strictly formal, linguistically constrained systems from meaning-dependent systems.

Indeed, such data cannot directly address the issue of the nature of early syntactic categories. Its importance concerns the notion of *ease of acquisition* as it affects order of emergence. Specifically, we argue that the theoretical positions outlined earlier make different predictions as to which linguistic subsystems will be more accessible to the young child and, therefore, earlier to emerge. Consequently, a demonstration of order of emergence of linguistic structures is one way in which the plausibility of one position may be strengthened, as compared to the others.

Because the *meaning first* view assumes the availability of prelinguistic, cognitive, or social structures to the child, it is reasonable to assume that systems will be more penetrable if their linguistic systematization may be achieved through their meanings or functions. Linguistic expressions that relate directly to cognitive notions and pragmatic functions, which form part of a young child's conceptual and social systems, should be learned earlier, whereas linguistic categories which do not have well-defined meanings for the child will pose particular difficulties in acquisition. Thus, in places in the grammar where there is a correspondence between semantic or pragmatic categories and classifications and grammatical ones, learning will occur earlier and more easily than for subsystems that are systematized solely on the basis of linguistic data.

The *linguistic approach* claims that the development of grammar will be essentially independent of other developmental milestones. From this viewpoint, ease of acquisition and, thereby, order of emergence are determined by considerations that are internal to the linguistic module. This can only be true of grammatical phenomena that are not a function of extragrammatical features. With regard to such grammatical phenomena, the prediction is that, for young children, formal linguistic categories will be as accessible as functionally or semantically determined categories.

FACTS ABOUT HEBREW MORPHOLOGY

The following exposition is restricted to details that are necessary to an understanding of the developmental data.

Hebrew is a Semitic language. Its vocabulary is composed of consonantal roots, cast in vocalic word patterns. The roots are usually triconsonantal, and the patterns are in the forms of vocalic infixes, prefixes, and suffixes. There are seven verb patterns (*binyanim*) and about three dozen noun patterns-(*mishkalim*). In general, for both nouns and verbs in Hebrew, the roots express the semantic core of the lexical item and the patterns determine class membership. The system is morphologically complex, yet quite systematic. It consists of sets of alternations conditioned by morpho-phonological environments. Thus, *binyanim* and *mishkalim* are essentially word-paradigms which may partially serve to convey meanings.

For example, the *binyanim* may serve to express a set of predicate relations, such as transitivity, reciprocity, reflexivity, passive, inchoative, causative, and so on. However, the system is definitely not regular. For example, the same function may be expressed by more than one pattern, and the same pattern may serve to express more than one meaning or may be "basic."

All verbs may be analyzed into root + pattern, but this is not the case for all nouns. Furthermore, there are many more noun patterns, *mishkalim*, than verb patterns, and the semantics of the patterns are reduced, although they are functional in important segments in the vocabulary.

The following are examples of verbs and nouns from the root *B-Š-L*: Verbs are in III per. mas. sg.

- *BiŠeL* "cooked" (trans.)
- *BuŠaL* "was cooked"
- *hiVŠiL*[1] "ripened"
- *huVŠaL* "was ripened
- *hitBaŠeL* "cooked" (intran.)

---

[1]In Hebrew, there are stop-spirant alternations such as b-v in derivatives of the root *B-Š-L*. Throughout this chapter, root consonants are in capitals.

- *BiŠuL* "cooking" (noun)
- *BŠeLut* "maturity"
- *haVŠaLa* "maturation"
- *miVŠaLa* "brewery"

Verbs in Hebrew are inflected for tense, number, person, and gender. Nouns are inflected for plurality and classified for gender. Other noun inflections, such as possession, are restricted in colloquial use.

What is the psychological status of this system? It is important to note that the notion of a root is formal and abstract; it may be inaccessible to speakers without explicit tutoring, mainly because of the existence of "defective" roots, which characteristically have less than three consonants in their surface structure. However, there is little doubt that the identification of the root consonants, when they are overtly expressed in words (i.e., the "consonantal skeleton" of Hebrew words), as well as their crucial role in the structure of words, are fully appreciated by speakers of the language. Recent studies of normal children demonstrated that this is true of children at various ages (Clark & Berman, 1984; Levy, 1988a; Walden, 1982). Even before age 3, Hebrew speakers seem particularly attentive to the consonantal skeleton of their words. Interestingly, similar findings have been reported for Arabic, another Semitic language (McCarthy, 1981).

Knowledge of Hebrew entails the ability to do word internal analyses, combine roots with word patterns and introduce inflections. Likewise, speakers seem to know the probabilistic nature of the semantics of the *binyanim* and *mishkalim*. Thus, processes that are peripheral to Indo-European languages are central to Semitic grammars and are part and parcel of normal speakers' knowledge from early on.

ACQUISITION OF HEBREW MORPHOLOGY BY NORMAL CHILDREN: A SUMMARY

Data from studies such as those by Berman (1985a, 1985b), Kaplan (1983), Levy (1983, 1988a, in press), and Walden (1982), present a detailed picture of the development of morphology in normal Hebrew-speaking children of ages 2–3 years. We summarize the major findings:

The earliest morphological distinctions to emerge in Hebrew speakers are the linguistic manifestations of plurality. This seems to be the first inflection that children master in other languages as well (Slobin, 1985). Person is another category that emerges rather early in all the languages where it is overtly marked (Slobin, 1985). Third person typically follows the development of the second person.

Berman (1985b) reported on the learning of the Hebrew tense system in children between the ages of 2 and 3. Early in the third year, children start varying tenses in some relation to the semantics of individual verbs. Children under 3 seem to possess a partial knowledge of the semantics of the tense system. In particular, they seem ignorant of the fact that it denotes an aspect of events that is not tied to the nature of the predicate or to its specific meaning. That is, they do not know that the notion of time applies to all predicates and is independent, for example, of whether the predicate is an activity verb. The morphological system per se presents no particular difficulties. In other words, children produce all tense forms even when they are not entirely clear on their uses. Similar findings were reported in a cross-linguistic study of temporality involving five different languages (Berman & Slobin, 1987).

Gender, as it affects the assignment of inflectional endings on nouns or verbs, is acquired by Hebrew-speaking children during their third year (Levy, 1983). Two-year-olds, although not in control of the whole system, know that the choice of plural suffixes is determined by the final syllable of the singular form of the noun and that plural formation triggers certain phonological changes in that syllable. They also know that verbs are marked in agreement with the classification of the head noun.

Two-year-olds' primary difficulty with the assignment of gender has to do with nouns that refer to animates — in other words, in cases in which linguistic gender is determined by the sex of the referent in the external world. As a consequence, confusion between masculine and feminine plural forms and verb agreement in reference to animates are found long after choice of plural affixes is done faultlessly in reference to inanimate objects. As in the case of the temporal system, the morphology involved in marking gender distinctions is not by itself the source of difficulties for the young.

Of particular importance to the present study is the development of the Hebrew verb system, *binyanim*. Recall that the typically Semitic word-formation process (i.e., that of casting consonantal roots in vocalic patterns to create new words) is most regular in the verb system. The *binyanim* present a complex, yet very regular, system of pattern manipulations that serve in part to convey meaning relations. In analogy to the gender studies, one may observe here the differential learning of aspects of form and meaning.

Data on very young children, in the early months of the third year, suggest that they differentiate between the root consonants and the vowel patterns. Root consonants are consistently preserved, whereas errors occur on the vowel patterns and the inflectional endings. As the example in Section 2 illustrates, verbs and nouns have common roots with patterns that are unique to each word class. Very young children seem sensitive to these facts and refrain completely from crossing word-class boundaries, often adopting a more strict criterion than the language, in fact, requires. This has been interpreted as an indication that, at some rudimentary level, even young 2-year-olds know about the combinatorial nature of Hebrew words and about word classes (Levy, 1988a).

Researchers agree that children under 3 do not yet appreciate the semantics of the system and the flexibility in introducing meaning that the language allows through the use of these pattern manipulations. However, research has repeatedly shown that, from very early on, children use all the *binyanim* in a variety of inflections and in keeping with the morpho-phonological constraints on word formation.

Berman (1985a) studied the *binyan* system extensively. She found that children 4 years old and above, unlike younger ones, typically move between *binyanim*, capitalizing on the meaning distinctions that may be thus achieved. Order of acquisition of the semantics of the *binyanim* at this time seems to be affected by conceptual development as well as by relaxation of overrestricted linguistic constraints. This period is character-ized by neologisms that attempt to carry the semantics of the *binyanim* further than linguistically permissible. Finally, children come to appreciate the partial correlations between meaning and form that are characteristic of the *binyanim* and do not overgeneralize.

In summary, data concerning the acquisition of Hebrew morphology suggest that, in normal development, inflectional morphology is generally not problematic. Rather, the reverse seems true: When the system is regular, even if complex, children acquire it early and with no noticeable difficulties. Furthermore, there is no necessary priority in learning to aspects of morphology that serve to introduce meaning distinctions. The system is learned qua system; the mapping of form to meaning is an additional factor which may or may not facilitate learning, according to the conceptual distinction that it serves to introduce. A similar trend seems true cross linguistically (for more details, see the cross-linguistic data in Slobin, 1985).

MORPHOLOGY IN A CHILD WITH A CONGENITAL LH INFARCT

Background

The present case report is part of a prospective study of language development in which children with congenital lesions in either the right or the left distribution of the Middle Cerebral Artery (March of Dimes Birth Defects, No. 12-175) have been studied. Children were selected to produce as homogeneous a group of subjects as allowed by modern diagnostic measures and as recommended by psychological practices, even at the cost of limiting their number. Although this seems like an elementary method-

developmental neuropsychology it has too often gone unnoticed, no doubt due to diagnostic difficulties.

Our intention in selecting the children for the present study was to assure, to the extent possible, that these children had no additional brain damage except the wedge-shaped lesion visible on the CT, which was the result of a congenital infarction in the area distribution of the MCA. The lesion was identified as affecting the left, posterior, frontal lobe and the posterior portion of the left temporal gyrus — in other words, the classical Broca's and Wernicke's areas. The children were all full-term babies, with normal weights appropriate for term infants. History of handedness in the family was noted. The children exhibited normal development, except for motor abnormalities such as hemiparesis, hypotonia, etc. Excluded from the study were children who had a focal injury with an etiology that gave reason to suspect that there might have been additional, unidentified, damage to the brain. Thus, those excluded were children with:

1. Birth asphyxia: This causes a global cerebral injury and may culminate in a focal injury. It would be difficult to quantify the health of the less injured hemisphere if asphyxia was the underlying provocation of the stroke.

2. CT evidence of more than one stroke outside the distribution of the MCA.

3. Meningitis, polycythenia, hydrocephalus, overt obstetrical trauma, somatic dysmorphism: All of these may result in a more widespread cerebral injury, despite the fact that the most obvious CT abnormality may be confined to one vascular territory.

4. Epilepsy: There is continuous controversy over the role of the epileptic process per se and the cognitive behavioral disturbances induced by anticonvulsants.

Despite stringent neurological criteria which were applied in the selection of subjects, clinical experience has given us reason to believe that the children will probably be functionally different. A discussion of this fact is beyond the scope of this chapter. Let us just say that this may be the result of current shortcomings of diagnostic procedures or, more interestingly, it may be a reflection of some principles which concern the relationship between neuroanatomical facts and behavioral patterns.

In a similar vain, recent discussions in the literature have questioned the appropriateness of group studies in adult neuropsychology (Badecker & Caramazza, 1985; Caramazza, 1988; McClosky & Caramazza, 1988; Shallice, 1979). The claim has been that criteria for the selection of subjects have yielded either trivially similar or nonhomogeneous groups. Case studies have been advocated instead. A similar conclusion seems unavoidable in developmental neuropsychology, where an additional factor, namely that of development, adds to the difficulties of prognosis.

Our aim is to produce a series of case studies of language development in children with congenital LH infarcts. Whether those will culminate in some generalizable statements in reference to the group as a whole remains to be seen.

Dan

Dan is a fourth child of nonconsanguineous, dexterous parents. Pregnancy and delivery were unremarkable. Birth weight was normal. Early milestones were considered normal. Dan was alert, made eye contact easily, demonstrated conjugate pursuit movements at 6–8 weeks, turned in both directions at 5 months. At that age he was first diagnosed as having a right spastic hemiplegia. CT scan disclosed a wedge-shaped hypodense area in the area of distribution of the left Middle Cerebral Artery which, in the case of this young child, covered all of what would be the classical language areas. Dan never had a seizure or a syncopal event and, therefore, received no medication.

Dan walked independently at 2 years. He spoke single words at 16 months and had a vocabulary of about 30 words at 24 months. Dan started to combine two words when he was 3. At the onset of the study, Dan was 3;6 and was attending a regular kindergarten. At that time, he was receiving regular physiotherapy. Speech therapy had not started until after our study was completed.

Controls

To study Dan's language development, a decision had to be made regarding the issue of controls. This is a point of major concern in studies of pathological populations and merits at least brief consideration.

When one compares naturalistic studies, particularly longitudinal ones, with extensive sampling, the issue of control for type of task does not arise. The problem in those cases becomes one of finding the appropriate points in time for different children. In studies of language acquisition in normal preschool children, chronological age and MLU (Brown, 1973) are common general estimates of linguistic development. Aram and Whitaker (1987) mentioned stage of development, grade-level performance, chronological age, IQ, and sibling controls as the practice found in recent experimental studies of language in pathological populations of children.

Recall that Dan did not start to combine two words until he was 3. Thus, no research was needed to rule out chronological age as a measure on which he could be equated with normal children. MLU (Mean Length of Utterance), or rather MPU (see following), was considered next.

Despite known weaknesses, MLU is still used as a rough, general estimate of a child's linguistic development. For synthetic languages like Hebrew, such a measure, which relies heavily on the word as the major unit of analysis, cannot be used. Instead we used MPU – a specially devised counting system for Hebrew (Dromi & Berman, 1982). The usefulness of both MLU and MPU depends upon the assumption that growth in mean utterance length reflects growth in grammatical knowledge, as evident in the occurrence of syntactically complex utterances. The possibility of the use of MPU as defining a point of reference for a comparison of the linguistic development of Dan with that of normal children, is examined here. Dan's MPU and percentages of complex utterances in his speech samples will be compared to the established norms for Hebrew (Dromi & Berman, 1982; Kaplan, 1983).

Reading through Dan's transcripts during the first month of data collection suggested that he was already past the one- and possibly the two-word stages of language development. In the first three sessions of the study, up to 16% of Dan's speech were utterances longer than four units. In other words, Dan had structured language that suggested he should be compared to children who show the beginnings of syntax. Dan's MPU at 3;6, when data collection started, was 1.9. It rose to 2.4 nine months later (see Fig. 3.1).

An examination of percentage of structured utterances, along with MPU values for 2-year-olds acquiring Hebrew (Dromi & Berman, 1982; Kaplan, 1984) reveal a developmental picture that is very different from Dan's. In normal children, at a mean age of 2;0, MPU is 2.02, with hardly any utterances longer than three units. MPU rises to 2.3 at the next developmental stage (age 2;2). At this time about 15% of the children's utterances are four, five, and six units long, about the percentage of complex speech that Dan showed, with an MPU of 1.9. In normal children, MPU continues to rise until it reaches 4.8 at age 3;6, when 40% of the children's utterances are longer than three units. Thus, at 3;6, Dan's MPU was four stages below the expected count for his age and the percentage of complex utterances in his speech was similar to that found in healthy 2-year-olds. Nine months later, he was still way below his healthy peers on both measures.

Could the differences in MPU be due to Dan's frequent use of one -word utterances, such as *Ok, good, yes, no, I want?*. To check for this possibility, MPU was calculated excluding one-unit utterances from the samples. Dan's MPU at 3;6 rose to 2.8 when one-word utterances were excluded – in other words, still well below what is expected for his age.

These figures point to some of the fundamental difficulties with quantitative measures such as MPU. Being a mean, MPU is sensitive to the

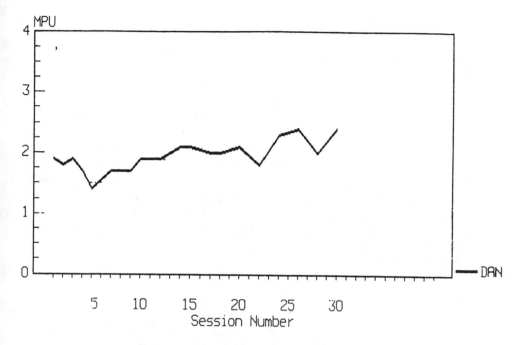

FIG. 3.1.   MPU for Dan.

quantity of long sentences in the samples and not simply to their presence. Dan's speech contained few long utterances. As a consequence, MPU values marked him far below his normal peers, as did percentages of complex utterances in his speech. A somewhat different analysis of findings from English has likewise demonstrated the inappropriateness of MLU for the purpose of comparing pathological populations of children (Aram & Whitaker, 1987).

In the present project, a decision was made to compare the course of Dan's development, from age 3;6 on, to the established course of language acquisition in children who are just past the two-word stage. Typically these will be "young 2s" showing the beginnings of complex syntax, followed up to the end of their third year.

Method

Dan was seen in his home for a period of 9 months, for which we have 30 recorded sessions. Our materials consist of naturalistic speech samples obtained in the course of play and daily routines, in the presence of members of the family, usually Dan's mother and sometimes his siblings. Testing Dan was out of the question: He refused to cooperate on even the most simple verbal tests. In view of this limitation, particular effort was exerted to vary the natural situations in which the data was collected. Excerpts from Dan's language in the beginning, middle, and end of the study are given in the Appendix.

Dan's articulation was quite good. Apart from a few words which he consistently distorted (e.g., *telezivia, *kaseka), his speech was clear and accurate. Each session was computer coded for syntactic, morphological, and meaning aspects. The latter included semantic and pragmatic features of the utterances. The coding system was specifically devised for Hebrew. It codes inflectional and derivational morphology in great detail. Special attention has been devoted to the coding of linguistic measures that may express either dissociations or interactions between various linguistic subsystems. Because quantitative measures reveal little change from one week to the next, the data was divided in half in a way that maintained regular intervals. Each half served as control for the other. The following data are from one half of the files.

Summary of Findings

In the summary presented here, we are especially concerned with demonstrations of dissociations between strictly formal, morphological subsystems and those which are dependent upon meaning selections (more detailed presentation and data concerning syntax can be found in Levy, Amir, & Shalev, 1992). As already stated, this is of crucial importance to the questions that this study addresses.

Variability of Verb Forms

Dan's corpus included 138 different roots. These appeared appropriately in a variety of verb patterns, binyanim. Only 7 roots (5%) occurred in more than one pattern, for example, RaXaC ("washed") and hitRaXeC ("washed himself"). Thus, binyan manipulations were few and involved mostly roots that served to create very common verbs (R-/ʕ/-H to form see and show; R-X-C to form wash and wash oneself). This fact characterizes early speech in normal children as well.

Consideration of the different inflectional forms in which these roots appeared reveals an impressive richness of forms. Dan used most inflected options, though not always in a contextually appropriate way. Some verbs appeared in up to 11 different inflectional forms.

The distribution of tense forms attests to the fact that Dan was using all four tense forms. Person and number were not as varied as tense, probably because during these sessions Dan typically interacted with one other individual.

The data suggest that Dan was using the inflectional system productively. Not enough variability was found in the transcripts to warrant such a conclusion with regard to the derivational paradigms.

Distribution of Errors

Table 3.1 gives the distribution of error types in three gross categories: (a) morphology, (b) meaning, and (c) syntax. Imitations, repetitions, and utterances of length 1 were excluded from the count. Errors of meaning, as they appear in Table 3.1, exceed errors of syntax and particularly errors of morphology.

In other words, generally speaking, problems of word choices, pragmatic inappropriateness, factual knowledge, discourse problems, logical contradictions, and lack of appropriate reference were more common than either syntactic or morphological difficulties. This possibility is further investigated in Table 3.2.

Tables 3.2 gives the distribution of Dan's morphological errors. Dan made remarkably few errors of gender in inanimates. Yet, errors of gender assignment to animate nouns, for which one has to know the sex of the referent in the real world, abound. There are almost no errors in person selection (p). This could be the result of the discourse situation, which did not typically call for the use of third person pronouns. Tense (t) and number (n) did not cause major difficulties either. Errors marked "F" concern

TABLE 3.1
Distribution of Error Types(%) in Utterances Longer than MPU 1

File	MOR	SY	MEANING
1	13	53	33
2	28	32	40
3	33	21	46
4	21	25	54
5	22	22	56
6	24	27	49
7	11	33	57
8	25	23	52
9	18	36	46
10	29	27	43
11	38	26	35
12	11	26	63
13	27	13	60
14	10	20	70
15	25	39	37
16	27	14	59

Note. Calculations are based on number of utterances in the file *excluding* imitations, repetitions, and units of MPU 1.

TABLE 3.2
Errors of Morphology(%)

File	g/an	g/in	t	n	p	F	in	rc	bn	nnc
1	11	—	5	—	—	22	47	16	—	—
2	64	—	—	—	—	29	7	—	—	—
3	45	—	—	—	—	27	—	9	9	9
4	—	—	—	13	—	25	25	25	—	12
5	14	—	7	—	—	10	29	34	—	7
6	19	10	—	19	—	34	9	9	—	—
7	11	2	2	2	2	13	29	36	2	2
8	13	—	4	—	1	11	27	38	1	4
9	11	—	—	—	—	6	49	26	3	5
10	13	—	2	2	2	7	46	23	—	5
11	15	—	2	—	—	2	40	34	5	3
12	20	—	—	—	—	—	—	80	—	—
13	11	—	11	—	—	11	33	22	11	—
14	—	—	—	—	—	50	50	—	—	—
15	24	—	2	—	—	2	44	27	—	—
16	7	—	—	—	—	—	53	20	20	—

Note. g/an = gender/animate F = 3 or more features wrong
g/in = gender/inanimate in = inflectional morphemes
t = tense   rc = root or stem morphemes
n = number   bn = *binyan*
p = person   nnc = nonce form

instances in which three or more inflectional categories were wrong. The assignment of such words to a special category, rather than decomposing them to the affected categories, reflects our conservatism in the coding process. Errors marked "in" refer to the word pattern. Those concern mostly wrong vowels. No systematicity was found in the errors affecting these patterns. Errors in root consonants (rc) involved 47 different roots. Of the 172 erroneous forms, 55% occurred in derivatives of three roots — the verbs *glue*, *want*, and *cut with scissors* — in which the same consonant was consistently dropped. In other words, the large percentages that appear in this column are the result of repeated difficulties with the same three roots. There were few instances in which the wrong *binyan* was chosen (bn). Instances of nonsense words (i.e., words that do not exist and are not legitimate innovations [nnc]) were rare in these corpora.

In summary one can say that formal morphological aspects were not particularly deficient in Dan's speech. Had it been otherwise, we would expect relatively more errors in gender in inanimate nouns, *binyan* alternations, and nonsense words. The fact that root consonants are generally preserved and inaccuracies are common in the vowel patterns is another indication that the child had a sense of the internal makeup of Hebrew vocabulary. F errors are, in our view, an indication of confusion that resulted in many things going wrong at the same time.

In Levy (in preparation) longitudinal, naturalistic data on two normal children between the ages of 1;10 and 2;11 was analyzed using the same coding system we used. Results were remarkably similar to Dan's: A prevalence of meaning errors over syntax and morphology was found for these children as well. The distribution of morphological errors was likewise very similar to that found for Dan although, overall, the healthy children made fewer mistakes. However, F errors were very rare. In our view, here lies one of the major differences between Dan and his normal controls: Whereas he had moments of confusion in which the system looked as if it was approaching a breakdown, normal children could rely on a smoother performance.

GENERAL DISCUSSION

Dan's knowledge of Hebrew morphology, particularly as it is reflected in types and amount of errors relative to other linguistic aspects, suggests that despite his massive, focal, LH lesion, as far as formal linguistic aspects are concerned, his language development followed the normal pattern. A marked difference between Dan and healthy children was apparent, however, in the overall delay, as reflected in the age at which language learning was taking place, his limited MPU relative to age-mates, and a higher error rate overall.

With regard to the plasticity thesis, these data imply the following general conclusion: In cases of early focal lesions in the LH, the course of acquisition of formal morphological aspects of language remains unaffected. Plasticity is not without cost in time and speed of acquisition.

These findings seem in accord with those found in other studies of language in pathology. Leonard Sabbadini, Leonard, and Volterra (1987) studied morphology in the speech of specifically language-impaired Italian and English children. The different status of morphology in the two languages allowed some interesting comparisons. Contrary to expectations, it was found that deficits were related to the opacity of the rules involved, to homonymity between morphemes, and to phonological difficulties, rather than to formal grammatical properties within the verb system or in any other place in the grammar. Cromer (1986), Curtiss (1989), and Yamada (1988) looked at later stages of linguistic development in retarded children with a variety of pathologies. Similarly to Dan, the children that they studied seemed less impaired on formal linguistic aspects, whereas their most severe difficulties were with functional and semantic aspects of language.

Cromer (1986) viewed the findings from retarded populations of children as contradicting the *cognition hypothesis*. Curtiss (1989) and Yamada's

(1990) case studies of retarded adolescents support this conclusion. In other words, these data, as well as ours, suggest that if order of acquisition is considered, formal linguistic systems that are totally unrelated to cognitive distinctions and may be totally unimportant functionally, are nevertheless "easy" to acquire. Yet, a rejection of the *cognition hypothesis* still does not explain what it is about these grammatical subsystems that accounts for their ease of acquisition. In this last section, we attempt such an explanation.

Fodor (1983) described input systems, including language comprehension, as "a family of modules: domain-specific, computational systems characterized by informational encapsulation, high-speed, restricted access, and neural specificity" (p. 101). Modules are "impenetrable" to types of information other than that to which they were specifically designed to react. The flow of information is bottom–up — that is, from the input data, through the processor, to the final output. Interestingly, informational encapsulation, which Fodor considered the most important feature of modules, characterizes the morphological systems which have been referred to as "formal." We consider such a property, when found in linguistic systems, as that of "autonomy." Our conjecture is that autonomy is one of the features determining ease of acquisition and, thereby, order of emergence of linguistic structures in the child.

A system is considered autonomous if its primitives and rules are defined within the paradigm, with no recourse to information that is external to it. In logic, such systems are viewed as "closed" and their definition as circular; the system is defined in terms of its rules and primitives, which are internally postulated by reference to that same system. An instatiation of a system is a statement that is expressed in terms of the primitives allowed and that abides by the rules of that same order.

In the case of morphology, an externally imposed categorization of words seems necessary prior to the formation of such paradigms. The distinction between verbs and nouns is of crucial importance. From that point on, the work will be done through morphophonological patterning defined over instances of each paradigm. Note that what is arrived at through such an analysis are paradigms that make use of information of a single type. Furthermore, systems which may be characterized in such a way are not unique to morphology. For example, there are structural configurations that condition syntactic operations, which may be construed as autonomous. This means that neither the whole of morphology, nor the whole of syntax are autonomous, in any strict sense of the term. Rather, where linguistic systems are concerned, autonomy seems to be a matter of degree.

As an example, consider again the case of linguistic gender. In many languages, among them Hebrew, the gender of inanimate nouns is determined by reference to the noun's phonological properties. Gender is often involved in the choice of plural suffixes. Of course, one need not refer to this classificatory system as gender and to the added suffixes as plurals. One may describe it in the following way: In Hebrew, the choice of the suffix -*im* or -*ot* as well as the allomorphic alternations that are required when those are added to the noun are fully determined by morphophonological properties of that noun. To use the terminology that has already been introduced, plural formation is an example of a closed and, therefore, autonomous system.

As for animate nouns, although the same morphophonological pattern-ings are generally preserved, precedence is given to the sex of the referent in the real world. In other words, if a morphologically "masculine" name is given to a girl, as is fashionable nowadays, inflections and agreement are done in the feminine. Therefore the, system is less autonomous than in the case of inanimate nouns, because it requires an *additional* type of informa-tion besides morphophonology.

Interactions among different types of information are likewise required in gender agreement. This is a syntactic phenomena involving thematic roles, internal components of the noun phrase, morphophonology, and, in the case of animate nouns, knowledge about the sex of the referent in the real world.

We propose that autonomy in the sense we have defined contributes to the simplicity of the learning task, whereas interactions increase its com-plexity. Therefore, it is predicted that linguistic systems that are autono-mous will emerge early in the developing child.

Let us point out that whereas Fodor's (1983) thesis concerns the structure of the mind, we are proposing that similar structural properties when found in the input data may affect the learning of language. The concerns are substantially different, yet the parallelism here may not be accidental.

Another analogy that comes to mind is between autonomy and what Schneider and Shiffrin (1977) called *Automatic Processes* and what Seuren (1978) termed *Routine Procedures* (RT). A system becomes automated following the use of controlled processes that are necessary for learning. An automated system is not easily open to introspection; it is quite specific in nature and executed with no control by the subject. There is affinity here with the notion of autonomy, for autonomous systems are the best candidates for quickly becoming automated or routinized.

Consider data from the acquisition of language by normal children. Investigations of the acquisition of Hebrew showed that, of the entire linguistic gender system, learning to select the correct gender suffix of inanimate nouns in the marking of plurality or case, including the intro-duction of the appropriate phonological changes in the final syllable, present the least difficulties, whereas the selection of animate pronouns and case endings continue to cause problems. In other words, the part of the gender system that is closed and autonomous emerges first, earlier than parts involving more than one type of information. A similar course characterizes the learning of gender in many languages (Levy, 1983, 1988b). Likewise, the development of the Hebrew verb system (*binyanim*) and the temporal system suggest that parts of these systems that can be considered autonomous are earlier in acquisition.

Data from Hebrew (Levy, 1988a) and other languages (Clark, 1982; Macnamara, 1982) suggest that young 2-year-olds know about classes of words that roughly correspond to nouns and verbs. This is crucial because our analysis suggests that such a distinction is a prerequisite for the formation of paradigms.

Investigations of the development of the count-mass distinction in English show that older children use both semantic and syntactic cues to countability, whereas young children predominantly use surface syntax [Gathercole, 1985; Gordon, 1985]. Tracy (1986) argued with reference to German-speaking children, that inflections are used productively at a very young age, and only later they are seen as cues for underlying semantic relations. Weist and Witkowska-Stadnik (1986) contrasted word order, inflectional information, and pragmatic information in young children learning Polish. They argued in favor of the existence of syntactic categories, which are distributionally defined from as early as 1:6. Weist and Witkowska-Stadnik agreed completely with Hyams (1984), who suggested a model of acquisition where semantics and syntax develop in a parallel fashion. Apart from a rejection of the primacy of any one of these components over the other, this model suggests that interaction between these separately developing systems will increase the complexity of the learning task.

Meisel (1986) studied German-French bilingual children. He rejected the contention that new formal devices are acquired to satisfy functional needs. His study demonstrated the emergence of formal morphological markings with no functional correlates. In his view, new forms are acquired because they are part of the linguistic system to which the child is exposed. In our terminology, this is yet another study suggesting that interactions increase complexity and, therefore, may delay acquisition.

If it is true that a system that is autonomous in the previously described sense is simpler and, therefore, earlier in acquisition, we may have an explanation for the pathological data. The fact that, in populations of children with various pathologies, formal linguistic structures develop with relative ease when compared to meanings and to functional properties could be a function of the simplicity of the former, that is, their degree of autonomy as defined earlier. This notion of simplicity rests upon the plausibility of viewing interactions as contributing to the complexity of a problem space. Notice that the analogy we propose between the learning of morphology by our subject Dan and the development of syntax by the English-speaking children of Cromer (1986), Curtiss (1989), and Yamada (1990) may mean that in cases in which plasticity may be assumed, the exact nature of the brain damage is of a lesser consequence than the fact that the children are learning language with less than an intact brain.

Clearly, the presence of interactions is not the only factor affecting simplicity. Another important point concerns the amount of opacity in a system, which seems to be strongly correlated with sequence of emergence. Opacity is affected by the presence of homonymity, fusion of forms, and number of exceptions. Order of emergence is likewise affected by semantic and pragmatic factors. When there is a pressing pragmatic reason for making a linguistic distinction, it may precipitate development. Likewise, when a conceptual distinction is cognitively available to children, it may have an effect on the development of the relevant linguistic expression. However, if these variables are not confounded and an estimate of the degree of autonomy of a linguistic system is possible, the latter is seen as a major determinant of order of emergence.

The data from the pathological cases further suggest that closed linguistic systems may be more robust than systems which are highly interactive—in other words, degree of autonomy may be inversely related to vulnerability. In cases of acquired aphasia in which recovery is observed, the prediction would be that the first to recover will be the more autonomous systems, for they require less of an effort to be put back in place.

In summary, we suggest that the interactive nature of linguistic subsystems contributes to their complexity. As a consequence, acquisition of a system is simpler if it is "informationally encapsulated" (Fodor, 1983) or, in our terminology, more autonomous, that is if it can be defined with reference to fewer types of rules and primitives. Our claim has been that the degree of autonomy of a linguistic system is a major predictor of its ease of acquisition and, consequently, its order of emergence. Furthermore, in circumstances that predict vulnerability, the interactive systems risk breakdown more often than the simple systems. The notion of autonomy, as we have defined it, may explain the early emergence of formal morphology in normal children, as well as the relative intactness of such morphological structures in our subject Dan and the exceptional syntactic abilities revealed in other cases of pathology.

ACKNOWLEDGMENT

This work was supported by the March of Dimes Birth Defects grant no. 12-175.

APPENDIX

EXCERPTS FROM CONVERSATIONS WITH DAN

We illustrate Dan's language in the beginning, middle, and end of data collection. Utterances marked with an * are grammatically deviant. In translating the texts, we tried to maintain comprehensibility and to indicate missing or wrong elements. It is a compromise between a literal and a free translation.

Dan, age 3; 8:1 — File 4.

Res: ma lehadbik? (What shall I glue?)
Dan: kan (Here.)
Dan: *lo ciyona naxon? (Not ciyona, right? = you are not ciyona, right? Pronoun omission not acceptable in Hebrew.)
Res: ma yes kan? (What do we have here?)
Dan: *roce tashir oto (Want you leave it. Unacceptable deletion of "that")
Res: ma? (What?)
Dan: *roce tashir titor shelax (Want you [mas.] leave your transistor. Wrong gender on the verb; unacceptable deletion of "that.")
Res: bo tistakel, ma yes kan? (Come look. What's here?)
Dan: lo shel ima? (Not Mommy's?)
Res: ma? (What?)
Dan: eyfo ima? (Where's Mommy?)
Res: ma? ma ima? (What? What Mommy?)
Dan: *roce gozer oto (Want cut it. Wrong choice of form for the verb cut.)
Res: ma ze? (What's this?)
Dan: ima (Mommy)
Res: ze ima? ze macxik ma sheata omer (This is Mommy? It is funny what you are saying.)
Dan: *kaseta axer (Another cassette. Wrong gender of qualifier.)
      hine kaseta (Here's a cassette.)
      lehaxzir od kaseta (Return another cassette.)
Res: ma ata roce? (What do you want?)
Dan: lirot et hakaseta (To see the cassette.)

Dan, age 3;11:2 — File 17

Dan: ze lo shelax (This is not yours)
      *ima kona lanu od axeret (Mommy buys for us more, another one. Wrong gender of qualifier.)
Res: ima kona ma? (Mommy buys what?)

Dan: *axeret (Another one. Unacceptable omission of head noun.)
Res: axeret? ma axeret? (Another one? What another one?
Dan: *kmo kaze (Like, like this. Duplication unnecessary.)
Res: kmo kaze? ma ze? (Like, like this? What's this?)
Dan: *kmo kadur kaze (Like, like this ball.)
Res: lama hi kona axer? (Why will she buy a different one?)
Dan: im praxim (With flowers.)
Res: ki ma? (Because of what?)
Dan: *ima kanu li im praxim (Mommy buy [pl. 3 per] with flowers.)
Res: ima kanta ma? (Mommy bought what?)
Dan: im hapraxim (With the flowers.)
Res: kadur im praxim? (A ball with flowers?)
Dan: shel me ze? (Whose is this?)
Res: ze sheli (This is mine.)
Dan: shel titor (Of the transistor.)
Res: naxon. bo nire ma nadbik (Right. Let's see what we can glue.)
Dan: naxon asinu? (Is it right that we did?)
Res: ze asinu paam,naxon. ma carix? (This we did once, right. What do
      we need?)
Dan: *lizor (To cut. Consonant missing.)
Res: ma carix (What do we need?)
Dan: misparaim (Scissors.)

Dan, age 4;3:2—File 29

Res: OK, Dan, bo necayer kcat (OK, Dan, let's draw some.)
Dan: ce kodem tabalon (Want first the balloon).
Res: kodem tabalon? (First the balloon?)
Dan: kodem (First.)
Res: ma naase ito? (What shall we do with it?)
Dan: *lenapeax (To blow. Wrong verb form.)
Res: ata yodea eix? (Do you know how?)
Dan: tenapxi li (Blow for me!)
Res: ma asita? eifo haita? (What did you do? Where were you?)
Dan: *beaba (In aba. Wrong preposition.)
Res: eifo? (Where?)
Dan: bavoda shall aba (At Daddy's work.)
Res: ma haya sham? (What was there?)
Dan: dvarim (Things.)
Res: ma ata mecayer? kavim? (What are you drawing? Lines?)
Dan: ken, ani ose bayad (Yes, I am doing with the hand.)
      ose yad. *ata roe? (Doing a hand. Do you [-mas.] see? [-mas] Wrong
      gender of pronoun and verb.)

Res: ani roa (I see. -[-fem.]
Dan: *rim yad (Lift hand. Wrong gender on the verb.)
Res: rega tigmor [-mas] (One moment, you finish.)
Dan: *axshav li, axshav li (Now to me. Wrong preposition.)
Res: rega, sim et hayad (One moment, put the hand.)
Dan: hine yad sheli, ze shelax? (Here's my hand. This yours?)
Dan: *bo se od yad (Let's do another hand. Wrong gender of verb.)
Res: od paam? (One more time?)
Dan: ken (Yes.)

REFERENCES

Aram, D. M., Ekelman, B. L., Rose, D. F., & Whitaker, H. A. (1985). Verbal and cognitive sequelae of unilateral lesions acquired in early childhood. *Journal of Clinical and Experimental Neuropsychology, 7*, 55–78.

Aram, D. M., Ekelman, B. L., & Whitaker, H. A. (1986). Spoken syntax in children with acquired unilateral hemisphere lesions. *Brain and Language, 27*, 75–100.

Aram, D. M., & Whitaker, H. A. (1987). Cognitive sequelae of unilateral lesions acquired in early childhood. In D.L. Molfese & S. J. Segalowitz (Eds.), *Developmental implications of brain lateralizations* (pp. 124–159). NY: Guilford.

Badecker, W. & Caramazza, A. (1985). On considerations of method and theory governing the use of clinical categories in neurolinguistics and cognitive neuropsychology: The case against agrammatism. *Cognition, 20*, 97–125.

Basser, L. S. (1962). Hemiplegia of early onset and the faculty of speech, with special reference to the effects of hemispherectomy. *Brain, 85*, 427–460.

Berman, R. A. (1985a). The acquisition of Hebrew. In Slobin, D. I. (Ed.), *The cross-linguistic study of language acquisition* (pp. 255–372). Hillsdale, NJ: Lawrence Erlbaum Associates.

Berman, R. A. (1985b). *Acquisition of tense-aspect by Hebrew-speaking children.* (Final Report). U.S.–Israel Binational Science Foundation, Jerusalem, Israel.

Berman, R. A. & Slobin, D. I. (1987). *Five ways of learning how to talk about events: A cross-linguistic study of children's narratives* (Report No. 46). Berkeley: University of California, Cognitive Science.

Bishop, D. V. M. (1988a). Can the right hemisphere mediate language as well as the left? A critical review of recent research. *Cognitive Neuropsychology, 5(3)*, 353–367.

Bishop, D. V. M. (1988b). Language development after focal brain damage. In Bishop, D. V. M., &, Mogford, K. (Eds.).*Language development in exceptional circumstances,* (pp. 203–219). London: Churchill Livingstone.

Brown, R. (1973). *A first language: The early stages.* Cambridge, MA: Cambridge University Press.

Caramazza, A. (1988). On drawing inferences about the structure of normal cognitive systems from the analysis of patterns of impaired performance: The case for single-patient studies. *Brain and Cognition, 5*, 41–66.

Carter, R. L., Hoenegger, M. K., & Satz, P. (1982). Aphasia and speech organization in children. *Science, 218*, 797–799.

Clark, E. V. (1982). The young word maker: A case study of innovation in the child's lexicon. In E. Wanner & L. R. Gleitman (Eds.), *Language acquisition — The state of the art.* New York: Cambridge University Press.

Clark, E. V. & Berman, R. A. (1984). Structure and use in the acquisition of word-formation. *Language, 60*, 542–590.

Cromer, R. F. (1986). Differentiating language and cognition. In L. L. Lloyd, & R. L. Schiefelbusch (Eds.) *Language perspectives* (Vol. 2, pp. 237-268). Baltimore: University Park Press.

Curtiss, S. (1989). The independence and task-specificity of language. In M. Bornstein, & Lawrence Erlbaum Associates. (Eds.), *Interaction in human development* (pp. 105-137). Hillsdale, NJ: Bornstein, M.

Dennis, M. (1980). Capacity and strategy for syntactic comprehension after left and right hemidecortication. *Brain and Language*, *7*, 153-169.

Dennis, M., & Kohn, B. (1975). Comprehension of syntax in infantile hemiplegics after cerebral hemidecortication: Left hemisphere superiority. *Brain and Language*, *2*, 472-482.

Dennis, M., & Whitaker, H.A. (1977). Hemispheric equipotentiality and language acquisition. In S. J. Segalowitz, & F. A. Gruber (Eds.), *Language development and neurological theory*. New York: Academic Press.

Dromi, E., & Berman, R. A. (1982). A morphemic measure of early language development: Data from Modern Hebrew. *Journal of Child Language*, *9*, 169-191.

Dromi, E., & Berman, R. A. (1986). Language-specific and language-general in developing syntax. *Journal of Child Language*, *13*, 371-387.

Fodor, J. A. (1983). *The modularity of mind*. Cambridge, MA: MIT Press.

Gathercole, V. C. (1985). "He has too much hard questions": The acquisition of the linguistic count-mass distinction in *much* and *many*. *Journal of Child Language*, *12*, 395-415.

Gordon, P. (1985). Evaluating the semantic category hypothesis: The case of the count-mass distinction. *Cognition*, *20*, 209-242.

Hiscock, M., & Kinsbourne, M. (1977). Selective listening asymmetry in preschool children. *Developmental Psychology*, *13*, 217-224.

Hyams, N. (1984). Semantically based child grammars: Some empirical inadequacies. *Papers and Reports on Child Language Development*, *23*, 58-65.

Kaplan, D. (1984). *Order of acquisition of morpho-syntactic categories among Hebrew speaking 2- to 3-year-olds*. Master's thesis, Tel-Aviv University, Tel-Aviv.

Kohn, B. (1980). Right hemisphere speech representation and comprehension of syntax after left cerebral injury. *Brain and Language*, *9*, 350-361.

Leleux, C., & Lebrun, Y. (1981). Language development in two cases of left hemispherectomy. In Y. Lebrun & O. Zangwill (Eds.), *Lateralization of language in the child*. Liss: Swets & Zeitlinger.

Lenneberg, E. (1967). *Biological foundation of language*. New York: Wiley.

Levy, Y. (1983). It's frogs all the way down. *Cognition*, *15*, 75-93.

Levy, Y. (1988a). The nature of early language knowledge: Evidence from the development of Hebrew morphology. In Y. Levy, I. M. Schlesinger, & M. D. S. Braine, (Eds.), *Strategies and processes in language acquisition* (pp. 73-98). Hillsdale, NJ: Lawrence Erlbaum Associates.

Levy, Y. (1988b). On the early learning of formal grammatical systems: Evidence from studies of the acquisition of gender and countability. *Journal of Child Language*, *15*, 179-187.

Levy, Y. (in prep.).*Formal grammatical structures in the language of 2-year-old Hebrew speakers*.

Levy, Y., Amir, N. & Shalev, R. (1992). Linguistic development of a child with a congenital, localised L.H. lesion. *Cognitive Neuropsychology 9* (1), 1-32.

Leonard, L. B., Sabbadini, L., Leonard, J. S., & Volterra, V. (1987). Specific language impairment in children: A cross-linguistic study. *Brain and Language*, *32*, 233-252.

Macnamara, J. (1982). *Names for things*. Cambridge, MA: MIT Press.

McCarthy, J. J. (1981). A prosodic theory of nonconcatinative morphology. *Linguistic Inquiry*, *12*, 373-418.

McClosky, M., & Caramazza, A. (1988). Theory and methodology in cognitive neuropsychology. *Cognitive Neuropsychology* , *5*, 583-623.

Meisel, J. M. (1986). Word order and case marking in early child language. Evidence from simultaneous acquisition of two first languages: French and German. *Linguistics, 24*, 123–186.

Molfese, D. L., Freeman, R. B., & Palermo,D. S. (1975). The ontology of brain lateralization for speech and nonspeech stimuli. *Brain and Language, 2*, 356–358.

Pinker, S. (1989). Language acquisition. In M. I. Posner (Ed.), *Foundations of cognitive science* (pp. 359–399). Cambridge, MA: MIT Press.

Rankin, J. M., Aram, D. M., & Horowitz, S. J. (1981). Language ability in right and left hemiplegic children. *Brain and Language, 14*, 292–306.

Robinson, R. O. (1981). Equal recovery in child and adult brain? *Developmental Medicine and Child Neurology, 23*, 379–382.

Schneider, W., & Shiffrin, R. M. (1977). Controlled and automatic human information processing. *Psychological Review, 84*, 1–66.

Seuren, P. (1978). Grammar as an underground process. In A. Sindair, R. J. Jaravella, & M. J. V. Levelt (Eds.), *The child's conception of language*. Berlin: Springer-Verlag.

Shallice, T. (1979). Case study approach in neuropsychological research. *Journal of Clinical Psychology, 1*, 183–211.

Slobin, D. I. (1985). *The cross-linguistic study of language acquisition* (Vol. 2). Hillsdale, NJ: Lawrence Erlbaum Associates.

Tracy, R. (1986). The acquisition of case morphology in German. *Linguistics, 24*, 47–78.

Wada, J., Clark, R., & Hamm, A. (1975). Cerebral hemispheric asymmetry in humans. *Archive Neurology, 32*, 239–246.

Walden, Z. (1982). *The root of roots*. Unpublished dissertation, Graduate School of Education, Harvard University, Cambridge.

Weist, R. M., & Wilkowska-Stadnik, K. (1986). Basic relations in child language and the word-order myth. *International Journal of Psychology, 21*, 1–19.

Witelson, S. F. (1977). Early hemisphere specialization and interhemisphere plasticity: An empirical and theoretical review. In S.J. Segalowitz & F. A. Gruber (Eds.), *Language development and neurological theory* (pp. 213–287). New York: Academic.

Woods, B. T. (1980). Observations on the neurological basis for initial language acquisition. In D. Caplan (Ed.), *Biological studies of mental processes* (pp. 149–158). Cambridge, MA: MIT Press.

Woods, B. T. (1984). Dicotic listening ear preference after childhood cerebral lesions. *Neuropsychologia, 22*, 303–310.

Woods, B. T., & Teuber, H. L. (1978). Changing patterns of childhood aphasia., *Annal Neurology, 3*, 273–280.

Yamada, J. (1990). *Laura—A case for the modularity of language*. Cambridge, MA: MIT Press.

4 Language Development After Early Unilateral Brain Injury: A Replication Study

Heidi M. Feldman
University of Pittsburgh

Two fundamental theoretical issues have motivated the study of language abilities after unilateral injury in childhood: the degree to which the left hemisphere is specialized for language functioning early in life, and the degree to which plasticity is possible after early brain injury (Aram, 1988). Studies of children with early unilateral brain injury over the last decade have undergone major methodological improvements that have forced a reevaluation of theoretical positions. Modern neural imaging techniques, such as computerized tomography scans (CT) and magnetic resonance imaging (MRI), have become the primary method for defining the location of brain injury (Aram, Ekelman, Rose, & Whitaker, 1985; Aram, Ekelman, & Whitaker, 1986, 1987; Feldman, Holland, Kemp, & Janosky, 1992; Marchman, Miller, & Bates, 1991; Rankin, Aram, & Horowitz, 1981; Thal et al., 1991; Vargha-Khadem, O'Gorman, & Watters, 1985). A decided improvement over the traditional method of inferring lesion location from the clinical evaluation of hemiplegia, neural imaging permits a description of the precise location and the extent of the lesion in addition to the identity of the affected hemisphere. Objective assessments, including formal testing and analysis of language samples, have become the accepted method of characterizing the language abilities of the subjects (Aram et al., 1985, 1986, 1987; Feldman et al., 1992; Kiessling, Denckla, & Carlton, 1983; Marchman et al., 1991; Rankin et al., 1981; Thal et al., 1991; Vargha-Khadem et al., 1985; Woods & Carey, 1979). Unlike traditional clinical evaluations of language abilities, these objective methods allow selective descriptions of the vocabulary, syntax, comprehension, and production.

Recent studies that have incorporated these methodological advances have challenged the view popularized by Lenneberg (1967) that the two hemispheres have comparable potential for learning language at birth. Evidence has been accumulating that the left hemisphere (LH) is specialized for language very early in life. Early LH injury has been associated with subtle deficits in sentence comprehension (Kiessling et al., 1983; Rankin et al., 1981; Vargha-Khadem et al., 1985; Woods & Carey, 1979) and sentence production (Aram et al., 1986; Kiessling et al., 1983). Deficits in lexical comprehension and production have been described after LH damage (Woods & Carey, 1979) but also have been documented after damage to the right hemisphere (RH) (Aram et al., 1987; Kiessling et al., 1983; Vargha-Khadem et al., 1985).

Most of the studies to date have been retrospective in design, basing their conclusions on single observations of the subjects at varying times after the brain injury. The issue of plasticity in the retrospective studies has been addressed by comparing language abilities in children with relatively early damage to language abilities in children with relatively late damage (Aram et al., 1987; Vargha-Khadem et al., 1985; Woods & Carey, 1979). The key variable is the age at which the injury was sustained and not the age of the child at the time of assessment. Woods and Carey (1979) found greater deficits in children who sustained LH damage after 1 year of age than in children who sustained injury before 1 year of age. Similarly, Vargha-Khadem et al. (1985) found a negative relationship between age at lesion and accuracy of naming, although this study divided subjects into three categories on the basis of age of injury. Both of these studies thus suggest that plasticity is greater the younger the child's age at the time of injury. However, using a similar strategy, Aram et al. (1987) found no differences within the group with LH damage on lexical tasks as a function of age at the time of injury.

An alternative approach to the issue of plasticity that has recently emerged is the prospective longitudinal study of children with early brain injuries (Feldman et al., 1992; Marchman et al., 1991; Thal et al., 1991). The effect of brain injury on subsequent functioning has been shown in animals (Goldman, 1974) and in humans (Levine, 1993) to depend in part on the developmental status of the subject at the time of assessment. Patterns of stability and change over time have been identified as important variables for understanding the nature of the neural mechanisms of plasticity and also of cerebral specialization (Goldman, 1974; Levine, 1993). The important variable is the age or developmental stage of the child at the time of the testing rather than age at the time of injury. Developmental delays may be detected early in the developmental course. This pattern of results suggests that the injured neural tissue is typically involved in the skill at that developmental time; the loss of relevant neural substrate causes the developmental delay. However, if the delay resolves over time, the results suggest that uncommitted neural substrate can be recruited to serve that function. By contrast, deficits may not be present initially but may emerge over time. This pattern suggests that injured tissue becomes involved with that skill in a later developmental period; because the relevant neural substrate is lost from the developing system, the injury causes a functional deficit late in the developmental course (Goldman, 1974; Levine, 1993).

The three longitudinal studies completed to date have, surprisingly, all found similar developmental patterns despite their use of different methods to assess different aspects of language. Early developmental delays have been documented following injury to either hemisphere. Some subjects show relatively rapid recovery in the early years. Marchman et al. (1991) studied the phonology of early communicative babbling and the development of word use in five children with pre-and perinatal unilateral injury. All subjects, the four with LH damage and the one with RH damage, showed delays in use of communicative gestures, babbling, and word use. However, three of the subjects showed improvement in standing relative to normal learners by 2 years of age. Thal et al. (1991) evaluated lexical comprehension and production from a parent report instrument in eight children longitudinally and an additional 19 children cross-sectionally. As a group, the children showed delays in both comprehension and production. The children with posterior LH damage showed more protracted delays in language production than the children with injuries to other brain regions. Feldman et al. (1992) described the development of the lexicon and syntax in nine children evaluated longitudinally. For this study, language samples were generated from parent–child interaction. Seven children showed initial delays in word use and five in onset of multiword sentences. However, by 24 months of age, four of five children with LH damage and two of four with RH damage had syntactic skills comparable to children developing typically.

The purpose of this chapter is to describe the development of word use and sentence production in a new group of six children, three with LH injury and three with RH injury, using the same methodological approach as Feldman et al. (1992). Because the number of children with unilateral brain injury is relatively small, the contribution of this study is to enlarge the sample of children who have been evaluated longitudinally. In general, the hypothesis is that this study will replicate previous findings of developmental delays and rapid recovery in some affected children.

As in a previous study (Feldman et al., 1992), the principles of growth modeling have been followed in describing the subjects. Growth modeling is a methodological approach in which multiple observations are made on individuals over time (Willett, 1988, 1989, 1990). In this approach, the first phase of data analysis describes longitudinal changes within each child, asking whether the individual's growth proceeds smoothly and along a stable and recognizable trajectory. Visual inspection of individual growth trajectories is used to select appropriate mathematical models to characterize the growth pattern. If stable growth patterns are found within individuals, then a second phase of analysis compares the growth trajectories across individuals in order to determine whether some attributes of the child, in this case side of unilateral injury, predicts the type of pattern.

In summary, several questions are asked in this descriptive replication study. Do children with early brain injury show stable patterns of change over the time frame of our observations? What mathematical function best describes the developmental course? How do the growth trajectories for children with LH injury compare to the growth trajectories for children with RH injury? How do the patterns in these children compare with the patterns that have been described previously (Feldman et al., 1992)?

METHODS

Subjects

Children have been referred to the study by local child neurologists or neonatologists on the basis of a nonprogressive destructive brain lesion documented by a modern neural imaging study, either ultrasonography, CT scan, or MRI. Sixty-six children have been referred to the project to date, 20 with unilateral damage and 46 with nonfocal injuries. Nine of the children with unilateral lesions have been described previously (Feldman et al., 1992). The six children selected for this report all had evidence of unilateral LH injury or RH injury on their imaging study and had been evaluated on at least three occasions.

Table 4.1 describes the children who are referred to using three letter code names. These are the names by which they are identified in the Child Language Data Exchange System data base (MacWhinney, 1991). The code names are retained to allow researchers to identify the files of these subjects when their data is made publicly available. The table includes their sex and socioeconomic status, calculated using the Hollingshead two-factor method and converted to a class score (Hollingshead, 1965). It also includes their clinical history. BEY was born prematurely, and ages of observation found on the tables and figures for this child have been corrected for the degree of prematurity. Four of the other children had serious complications soon after their term births. It is possible that these clinical conditions led to some additional or diffuse injury that was too small to be detected by the neural imaging technique employed. Though this is a potential confounder, it is a problem for all studies of children with focal brain injury. The neural imaging techniques used here are the most sensitive and specific techniques that were available at the time the children required scanning.

TABLE 4.1
Demographic, Clinical, and Neurological Characteristics of Subjects

Hemisphere	Name	Sex	SES	Clinical History	Lesion Type	Lesion Location	Neurological Examination
L	BEY	F	4	Premature Birth, IVH	POR PVL	Parietal	R hemiparesis
L	BEA	M	4	Meconium aspiration	Infarct	Parietal	Normal
L	SNO	M	3	Congenital Heart Disease	Infarct	Parietal	R hemiparesis
R	GIG	F	3	Term birth Neonatal sz	Infarct	Parietal	Normal
R	HAT	M	4	Term birth Neonatal sz	Infarct	Parietal-Occipital	Normal
R	ROM	M	3	Term birth Neonatal sz	Infarct	Fronto-Parietal	Normal

L = left, R = Right; M = male F = female; Infarct = Infarction; POR = porencephalic cyst; PVL = periventricular leukomalacia; Sz = seizure.

Neural imaging studies revealed two different types of brain injuries in these children. One child (BEY) sustained periventricular leukomalacia (PVL) and an adjacent porencephalic cyst. PVL was originally identified only at the time of autopsy (Banker & Larroche, 1962) but can now be identified *in vivo* because of the improvements in neural imaging. The lesion is most likely caused by ischemic injury to regions of brain that fall in the so-called watershed areas, zones whose blood supply comes from the small terminal branches of the blood vessels of two major vessels systems. In the premature infant, white matter adjacent to the ventricles is vulnerable to ischemic damage. In this child, an area of brain tissue adjacent to the white matter sustained damage, resulting in a porencephalic cyst. The other five children (BEA, SNO, GIG, HAT, and ROM) have evidence of a cerebral infarction. This lesion represents disruption of a major cerebral artery, resulting in destruction of cortical gray matter and adjacent white matter. Four of these children (BEA, GIG, HAT, and ROM) sustained the injury in the pre- or perinatal period. SNO had a congenital cardiac lesion. He sustained a cerebral infarction at the time of cardiac catheterization when he was 1 month of age.

Procedures

Initial Testing. At the initial visit and on subsequent visits near the child's birthday, a test of general development functioning was administered. The Bayley Scales of Infant Development (Bayley, 1969) was administered to children less than 30 months of age (and scored based on corrected age for BEY). The McCarthy Scales of Children's Abilities (McCarthy, 1972) was administered at 36 months of age. Table 4.2 provides standard scores for each subject.

Language Samples. Language samples from semi-structured parent–child interaction were obtained in the clinic of the Child Development Unit, Children's Hospital of Pittsburgh and analyzed to describe language skills. Interactional analysis was not taxing enough to reveal differences between school-age children with left and right hemidecortication (Dennis & Kohn, 1975; Dennis & Whitaker, 1976). We used the technique for two reasons: (a) It allows direct observation of multiple language subsystems simultaneously in toddlers and preschoolers who cannot cooperate with extensive testing; and (b) it generates the same measures over the entire age range of the study to permit longitudinal analyses.

In order to generate the language samples, the children and their parent(s) participated in five separate activities as follows:

1. Warm-up play with toy cars, a tea set, puppets, and small human figures.
2. Ball play.
3. Coloring with crayons and blank paper.
4. Reading using a Richard Scarry book with a large variety of pictures of common objects and animals.
5. Teaching from an activity book.

Sessions were videotaped and audiotaped simultaneously for transcription.

Transcription. Language samples were transcribed directly from both audiotape and videotape to an IBM computer by trained speech and language pathologists who served as research assistants. Transcription, coding, and analysis utilized the Child Language Data Exchange System

TABLE 4.2
Cognitive Scores From the Bayley Scales and the
McCarthy Scales

Name	*Bayley Scales* *MDI*	*McCarthy Scales* *GCI*
BEY	119	—
BEA	102	—
SNO	89	79
GIG	106	105
HAT	89	90
ROM	143	127

(ChiLDES) (MacWhinney, 1991). ChiLDES is a system of computer programs designed for automated analysis of language transcripts. It includes a detailed set of conventions for orthographic transcription and coding (CHAT), and programs for analysis of the transcripts (CLAN). The corpus is segmented into utterances based on terminal intonational contour. The speaker's name and an exact transcription of what is said is recorded on the "main tier." Additional coding or comments are placed on a "dependent tier." The automated analyses can operate from either the main tier or a dependent tier. Twenty minutes of interaction were analyzed for each child at each session.

One activity from each child at each visit was retranscribed by a second research assistant. Interobserver agreement was calculated as the number of utterances with perfect agreement divided by the number of utterances. Interobserver agreement for transcription was above 92% on all files.

Measures.   The primary measure of syntactic development was Mean Length of Utterance (MLU). This is a direct measure of sentence length, but it is highly correlated with sentence complexity in children without brain injury who are in the earliest stages of language development (Brown, 1973). We followed standard procedures for calculating MLU as described in Miller (1981), with the exception of using all of the utterances in the language sample (not requiring or limiting analysis to 50 utterances).

An additional measure of the development of syntax was the Index of Productive Syntax (IPSYN score) (Scarborough, 1990). This measure reflects the number of mastered and emerging syntactic devices. It credits the child for one or two exemplars of 50 different syntactic structures, such as placement of an article in front of a noun or creating the past tense of an irregular verb. The score has been found to be predictive of future functioning in young children at risk for reading disability; norms have been established for children from 24 to 42 months of age (Scarborough, 1990) based on 100 utterances. We followed the standard instructions for calculating IPSYN score with the only exception being that if fewer than 100 utterances were obtained we used the entire corpus without adjusting the score. IPSYN scores were recalculated by a second research assistant. Intercoder agreement was greater than 94% for all files. Disagreements were discussed until consensus was reached.

The primary measure of vocabulary was the number of different words (lexical types) used by the child in the session. An alternative measure, the total number of words used in the session (tokens), yielded similar results.

Data Analysis.   Following the growth modeling perspective (Willett, 1988, 1989, 1990), individual growth trajectories were prepared for each language measure, MLU, IPSYN score, and the number of different words.

Each dependent variable (y-axis) was plotted as a function of the child's age rounded to the nearest quarter year (x-axis). Visual inspection of the resulting growth trajectories for each function of each child suggested the appropriate models for each measure and each child. For purposes of presentation, the growth trajectories for children with LH and RH injury were graphed together on separate figures.

Normative data from the literature were used as a comparison for the performance of these children to avoid costly data collection and analysis of large cohort of children developing normally. For MLU, we used means and standard deviations reported by Miller (1981) for children aged 18 to 60 months at 3-month intervals. To validate the use of these normative data for children in this protocol, we collected and analyzed language samples from 36 healthy children without brain lesions interacting with a parent on the same protocol in the same laboratory. Children for this validation study were siblings of subjects and children enrolled in the local day-care center. The MLU for all the normal children fell within $+/-$ 2 standard deviations from the mean on the Miller (1981) normative data, suggesting the appropriateness of these norms for the purposes of comparison. Figures 4.1 and 4.2 were prepared to record the growth trajectories of MLU for children with LH injury and RH injury, respectively. On the figure, the white background area denotes MLU values within $+/-$ 1 standard

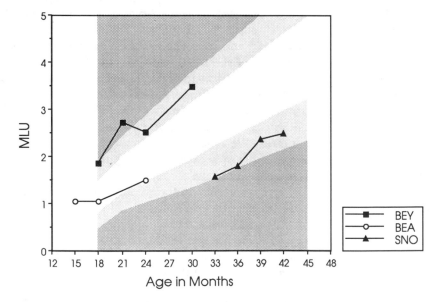

FIG. 4.1.   Mean length of Utterance (MLU) as a function of age in children with left hemisphere damage.

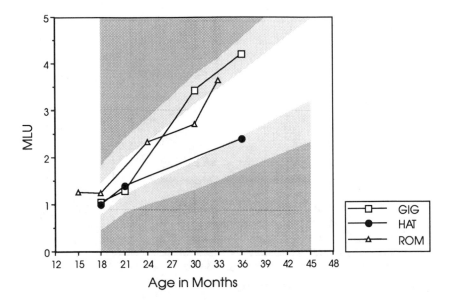

FIG. 4.2.   Mean length of Utterance (MLU) as a function of age in children with right hemisphere damage.

deviation from the mean of the normative data (Miller, 1981); light gray area represents $+/-$ 1 to 2 standard deviations from the mean; dark gray represents values greater than $+/-$ 2 standard deviations from the mean.

The language samples of these normal children were analyzed for IPSYN score. The same validation procedure was used. IPSYN scoring for all normal children fell within the range of $+/-$ 2 standard deviations of normative data (Scarborough, 1990) at 24, 30, and 36 months of age; two normal children fell slightly below this range at 42 months of age. Figures 4.3 and 4.4 were prepared to record growth trajectories for IPSYN scores for children with LH injury and RH injury, respectively. The white background area denotes MLU values within $+/-$ 1 standard deviation from the mean of the normative data (Miller, 1981); light gray area represents $+/-$ 1 to 2 standard deviations from the mean; dark gray represents values greater than $+/-$ 2 standard deviations from the mean.

Expectations for the number of different words that a child uses in a particular protocol is highly dependent on the materials and methods of the protocol. In order to generate an expected range for vocabulary size in this protocol, we determined the minimum and maximum vocabulary size for each age at 3-month intervals in the sample of 36 children without brain injuries. In some cases, a younger child used more words than all of the children at the next age interval. In these cases, we used the vocabulary size

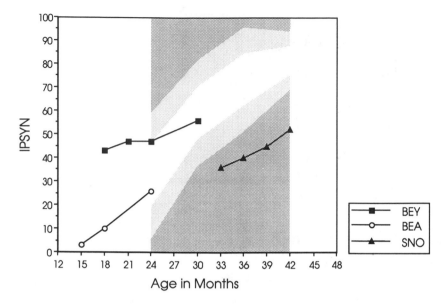

FIG. 4.3. IPSyn scores as a function of age in children with left hemisphere damage.

of the younger child as the upper limit at the older age. All of the normal 15- and 18-month-old children used words in the protocol. Figures 4.5 and 4.6 were prepared to show the number of different words used during each session for children with LH injury and RH injury, respectively. The white area in the background indicates the observed range of vocabulary size for children without brain injuries, and the shaded area represents values outside the observed range.

RESULTS

Figures 4.1 and 4.2 display the growth trajectories for MLU in children with LH and RH injury, respectively. Visual inspection of the data revealed improvements over time in MLU for all children. The growth trajectories were best summarized by simple straight line models. The estimated slope of the fitted growth curves for children with LH damage ranged from .11 to .12; the estimated slope of the fitted growth curves for the children with RH injury ranged from .11 to .19. The estimated slope for the linear growth curve fitted to the means of the normative data is .10. All of the children fell within the normal range of MLU at all of the visits (although HAT had only one utterance at the 18-month visit).

Figures 4.3 and 4.4 display the growth trajectories for IPSYN scores in

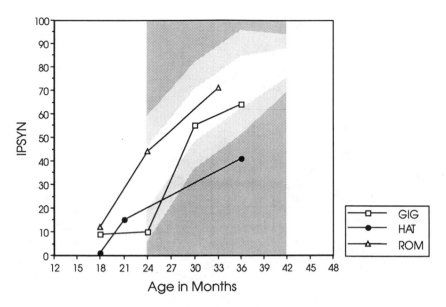

FIG. 4.4.   IPSyn scores as a function of age in children with right hemisphere damage.

children with LH and RH injury, respectively. Visual inspection of the data revealed steady improvements over time in IPSYN scores for all children. The growth trajectories were best summarized by simple straight-line models. The estimated slope of the fitted growth curves from children with LH damage ranged from 1.04 to 2.57; the estimated slope of the fitted growth curves for the children with RH injury ranged from 2.06 to 3.86. The estimated slope for the linear growth curve fitted to the means of the normative data is 2.73. One child with LH damage, SNO, and one child with RH damage, HAT fell more than 2 standard deviations below the mean on IPSYN sore.

Figures 4.5 and 4.6 display the growth trajectories for number of lexical types in children with LH and RH injury, respectively. Visual inspection of the data revealed overall improvements over time in number of lexical types for all children. The growth trajectories were best summarized by simple straight-line models. One child with LH damage, SNO, and one child with RH damage, HAT, fell outside the expected range on this measure.

DISCUSSION

In summary, the six children described here with early unilateral brain injuries sustained prior to 1 month of age showed stable patterns of change

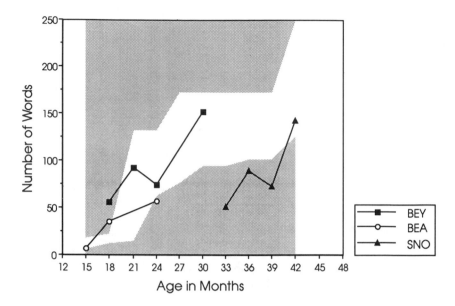

FIG. 4.5.   Number of different words used as a function of age for children with left
hemisphere damage.

during the early period of language development. Despite variations in their
levels of language skill, they all demonstrated steady improvements over
time in MLU, IPSYN score, and vocabulary size. Given steady developmental progress, the growth trajectories for each child on each measure
were best described by straight lines. The rate of progress on MLU and
IPSYN scores — that is, the slopes of the linear models that were fitted to the
growth trajectories — were similar for the children with brain injuries and
children developing typically. In addition, the slopes were comparable for
children with LH and RH injury. One exception was BEY's slope on the
IPSYN score; the slope of the growth curve for this child was less steep than
the slope for the children with RH damage. However, BEY, a child with LH
injury, was relatively advanced in syntactic capabilities at the first observation, so her rate of progress was slower than the other subjects from that
point.

This study replicates several findings from our previous research
(Feldman et al., 1992). LH injury was not invariably associated with
persistent language delays in the toddler-preschool era. In this population,
BEY, a child with LH injury, was the most accomplished speaker of the
sample before age 2. Similarly, RH damage was sometimes associated with
delays in language acquisition. HAT, a child with RH injury, had persistent
delays in language abilities during the time frame of the study.

Both vocabulary and syntactic development were delayed throughout the

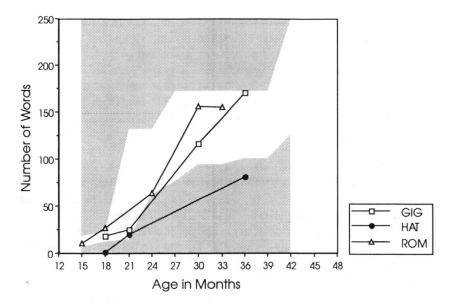

FIG. 4.6.   Number of different words used as a function of age for children with right hemisphere damage.

study in two of the children described, SNO with LH injury and HAT with RH injury. Neither of these boys caught up to normal learners. Their rate of development was close to average, so that their performance paralleled the performance of the normative sample. In our previous study, we observed children with delayed onset and rapid improvements by 24 months of age. We also observed one child with protracted delays in language development who acquired vocabulary and syntactic skills at a normal rate once she began to develop. Thus, although she progressed, she remained below the normal curve through age 4. The two children in this cohort followed a similar course.

The data from this study seem to conflict with the recent reports of selective language impairment, particularly in syntactic development, following unilateral left hemisphere brain injury (Aram, 1988; Aram et al., 1985, 1986; Kiessling et al., 1983; Rankin et al., 1981; Thal et al., 1991; Woods & Carey, 1979). Several variables may explain differences in results. First, the children with LH injury in our study population may have sustained different or less severe injuries than children in the other studies. In this cohort, as well as in our previous study (Feldman et al., 1992), children with LH porencephalic cysts and PVL generally performed well within the normal range on language measures. It is possible that these injuries spare the language areas of the brain. The two children we have followed with infarction of left middle cerebral artery, SNO in this series and MAG in previous studies (Feldman et al., 1992; Feldman, Holland, & Brown, 1992) have performed below the normal range in both syntactic and vocabulary measures. It is possible that this injury destroys tissue that is highly specialized for language function. A second possible reason for the differences between ours and other studies is that developmental measures from analysis of parent–child interaction may not be sufficiently sensitive to detect subtle weaknesses in sophisticated syntactic processing. In studies of older children who have undergone hemidecortication, analysis of conversational language did not reveal subtle language difficulties (Dennis & Kohn, 1975; Dennis & Whitaker, 1976). Unfortunately, the assessment battery available for use with young children is quite limited. Until children reach an older age, analysis of language samples remains an excellent method for language assessment. In further studies, we will look in more detail at specific linguistic structures and at error rates to try to describe language difficulties not well captured by the traditional developmental measures.

Finally, evidence of language deficits may not emerge until children are beyond the early stages of language acquisition. Heralding back to the logic of the longitudinal research design (Goldman, 1974; Levine, 1993), if we were to detect differences between children with LH and RH injuries at school age that were not detected at preschool age, the data might suggest that regions of the LH do not mediate language exclusively in the early stages of language acquisition, but are typically recruited for higher level language functions in later development.

Another difference between the results reported here and some of the other studies of children with unilateral brain injuries is that some children with RH lesions have shown developmental delays in language abilities. In this study, HAT was similar to SNO in the rate and pattern of language development. One possibility is that HAT had other reasons for delays in language acquisition, based on his genetic endowment or environmental circumstances. On the other hand, because we have identified other children with a similar developmental delay after RH injury, this explanation is not sufficient. We have found that children with infarction of the RH are more likely to suffer developmental delays than children with PVL. One possible explanation for developmental delays after RH cortical injury is that the RH is involved with naming and vocabulary development (Aram et al., 1987; Kiessling et al., 1983; Vargha-Khadem et al., 1985). Given the close relationship between the lexical and syntactic development in the earliest phases of language acquisition, RH injury might impact both word and sentence development.

It is important to note that all of the children studied prospectively thus far have proceeded to develop language during the toddler-preschool era. Moreover, the pattern of development is strikingly similar to the pattern of development in children with no neurological injuries. These findings demonstrate that the acquisition of early language, particularly early grammar, is a robust phenomenon. It can proceed in a relatively normal manner and at a normal rate, at least in the earliest stages, in the face of brain injury. This finding suggests that the neural substrate underlying language development may be highly redundant such that unilateral injuries do not severely distort the course of language learning nor delay its developmental time table.

ACKNOWLEDGEMENTS

This project was supported by National Institute of Child Health and Human Development Grant No. PO1-HD23388-01A1 and March of Dimes Social and Behavioral Science Grant No. 12-210. The author gratefully acknowledges the important contributions of Rosalyn Brown, Nancy Wareham, Carol Hallberg, Brian MacWhinney, John Willet, and Audrey Holland; and the gracious cooperation of these children and their families throughout the project.

REFERENCES

Aram, D. M. (1988). Language sequelae of unilateral brain lesions in children. In Plum F, *Language, Communication, and the Brain*. New York: Raven Press.

Aram D. M., Ekelman, B. L., Rose, D. F., Whitaker, H. A. (1985). Verbal and cognitive sequelae following unilateral lesions acquired in early childhood. *Journal of Clinical and Experimental Neuropsychology*, 7, 55–78.

Aram, D. M., Ekelman, B. L., & Whitaker, H. A. (1986). Spoken syntax in children with acquired unilateral hemisphere lesions. *Brain and Language*, 27, 75–100.

Aram, D. M., Ekelman, B. L., & Whitaker, H. A. (1987). Lexical retrieval in left and right brain lesioned children. *Brain and Language*, 31, 61–87.

Banker, B. Q., & Larroche, J. C. (1962). Periventricular leukomalacia of infancy. *Archive of Neurology*, 7, 32–57.

Bayley, N. (1969). *Bayley Scales of Infant Development*. New York: Psychological Corporation.

Brown, R. (1973). *A first language: The early stages*. Cambridge, MA: Harvard University Press.

Dennis, M., & Khon, B. (1975). Comprehension of syntax in infantile hemiplegics after cerebral hemidecortication: Left-hemisphere superiority. *Brain and Language*, 2, 472–482.

Dennis, M., & Whitaker, H. A. (1976). Language acquisition following hemidecortication: Linguistic superiority of the left over the right hemisphere. *Brain and Language*, 3, 404–433.

Feldman, H. M., Holland, A. L., & Brown, R. E. (1992). A fluent language disorder following antepartum left hemisphere brain injury. *Journal of Communication Disorders, 25*, 125–142.

Feldman, H. M., Holland, A. L., Kemp, S. S., & Janosky, J. (1992). Language development after unilateral brain injury. *Brain and Language*, 42, 89–102.

Goldman, P. S. (1974). An alternative to developmental plasticity: Heterology of CNS structures in infants and adults. In D. G. Stein, J. J. Rosen, & N. Butters (Eds.), *Plasticity and recovery of function in the central nervous system* (pp. 149–174). New York: Academic Press.

Hollingshead, A. B. (1965). *Two-factor index of social position*. Unpublished manuscript, Yale Station, New Haven, CT.

Kiessling, L. S., Denckla, M. B., & Carlton, M. (1983). Evidence for differential hemispheric function in children with hemiplegic cerebral palsy. *Developmental Medicine and Child Neurology, 25*, 7, 27–734.

Lenneberg, E. H. (1967). *Biological foundations of language*. New York: Wiley.

Levine, S. C. (1993). Effects of early unilateral lesions: Changes over the course of development. In G. Turkowitz & D. A. Devenny (Eds.), *Developmental Time and Timing* (pp. 143–166). Hillsdale, NJ: Lawrence Erlbaum Associates.

MacWhinney, B. (1991). *Manual for use of the CHAT transcription coding system of the Child Language Data Exchange System*. Pittsburgh: Carnegie Mellon University.

Marchman, V. A., Miller, R., & Bates, E. A. (1991). Babble and first words in children with focal brain injury. *Applied Psycholinguistics, 12*, 1–22.

McCarthy, D. (1972). *MaCarthy Scales of Children's Abilities*. San Antonio, TX: Psychological Corporation.

Miller, J. F. (1981). *Assessing language production in children*. Baltimore: University Park Press.

Rankin, J. M., Aram, D. M., & Horowitz, S. J. (1981). Language ability in right and left hemiplegic children. *Brain and Language, 14*, 292–306.

Scarborough, H. S. (1990). Index of productive syntax. *Applied Psycholinguistics, 11*, 1–22.

Thal, D. J., Marchman, V., Stiles, J., Trauner, D., Nass, R., & Bates, E. (1991). Early lexical development in children with focal brain injury. *Brain and Language, 40*, . 491–527.

Vargha-Khadem, F., O'Gorman, A. M., & Watters, G. V. (1985). Aphasia and handedness in relation to hemispheric side, age at injury, and severity of cerebral lesions during childhood. *Brain, 108*, 677–696.

Willett, J. B. (1988). Questions and answers in the measurement of change. In E. Z. Rothkopf (Eds.), *Review of research in education (Vol 15*, pp. 345–422). Washington, DC: American Education Research Association.

Willett, J. B. (1989). Some results on reliability for the longitudinal measurement of change: Implications for the design of studies of individual growth. *Educational and Psychological Measurement, 49*, 587–602.

Willett, J. B. (1990). Measuring change: The difference score and beyond. In H. F. Walberg & G. D. Haertel (Eds.), *The international encyclopedia of educational evaluation*. Oxford, England: Pergamon Press.

Woods, B. T., & Carey, S. (1979). Language deficits after apparent clinical recovery from childhood aphasia. *Annuals in Neurology, 6*, 405–409.

5 The Course of Language Learning in Children with Down Syndrome

Anne E. Fowler
Bryn Mawr College
Haskins Laboratories

Rochel Gelman
University of California at Los Angeles

Lila R. Gleitman
University of Pennsylvania

A large body of research on first language acquisition has led to the general consensus that young children bring to the language-learning task certain predispositions for how to organize a grammar:

1. Numerous studies have demonstrated that young children typically progress through an early language stage, with common thematic relations, consistent word order, and an absence of closed class functors (e.g., Bloom, 1970; Brown, 1973; Gleitman & Wanner, 1982).
2. Well-studied cases of overgeneralizations within derivational and inflectional morphology suggest that children are driven to extract regularities from the input provided (e.g., Bowerman, 1982; Brown, 1973).
3. Examination of the syntactic structures that characterize the speech of young children suggests a well-ordered and rapidly completed sequence of development without obvious violations of general syntactic constraints (e.g., Bellugi, 1967; Hamburger & Crain, 1982).

As exemplified by the chapters in this volume, compelling evidence for internally driven linguistic constraints derives further support from the study of language acquisition under the most adverse learning conditions. Children who are blind from birth, deaf-isolate children who are born deaf and denied access to signed language, and children exposed only to impoverished "pidgin" languages all construct grammars similar in crucial respects to those developed under normal learning conditions (Feldman, Goldin-Meadow, & Gleitman, 1978; Landau & Gleitman, 1985; Newport, 1981; Sankoff & Laberge, 1973; see Gleitman, 1984, for a review and discussion). Because the children in each of these cases produce grammars that go well beyond the input provided, it can be argued that the "learning process itself may contribute certain types of organizational characteristics to languages" (Newport, 1981, p. 120). The linguistic commonalities observed derive not so much from a carefully arranged highly structured input, but should be crucially dependent on the child's intact cognitive/linguistic system, which governs the learning process.

But what if the cognitive/linguistic system is itself disrupted in some way? Will these same constraints and organizational characteristics continue to apply? In this chapter, we consider the applicability of general features of language learning to individual cases where general cognitive impairment is associated with limited syntactic function. Specifically, we focus on the language of several mentally retarded children with Down syndrome, trisomy 21, who apparently lack sufficient cognitive or linguistic function to formulate a fully specified grammar. The children under study, like most individuals with Down syndrome, have achieved only limited success in language learning; their general cognitive deficit is evident as well in such areas as conceptual development, number knowledge, memory, and visual spatial function. Given that language learning is not complete, we can ask several questions bearing on the role of general cognitive factors on the character of language:

1. How far does learning progress and what seems to prevent further development?

2. Are certain facets of the developing grammar relatively more disrupted than others by general cognitive impairment?

3. How do these children get as far as they do? Do they induce rules, impose word order, and follow the canonical developmental sequence observed when intelligence is fully intact? Is there evidence that the cognitively impaired child, like the normally intelligent child, actively constructs a coherent and internally consistent grammar that goes beyond the individual instances presented? Or, are different learning strategies present?

It is recognized, of course, that the search for the effects of cognitive impairment on language learning begs many questions. For instance, if a child with Down syndrome obtains an IQ score of 50 and also acquires very little syntactic function, this cannot necessarily be attributed to general intellectual function. After all, language may be disrupted even in cases of normal to superior intelligence, as can be readily attested to by the much studied case of specific language delay, where extremely delayed language proceeds alongside otherwise normal intellectual function (e.g., Bishop & Edmundson, 1987; Johnston, 1988; Rescorla, 1989; Rescorla & Schwartz,

1990). Similarly, if a child with an IQ of 50 develops full syntactic competence, this does not necessarily imply that no "general" cognitive processes were brought to bear. Rather, both findings may suggest only that not all cognitive abilities proceed in lock-step. One area (e.g., spatial organization) may be so disrupted as to yield an extremely low score on an omnibus IQ test; relatively normal language function in such a case tells only that syntax is represented independently of spatial cognition. Just this situation appears to be the case in the child with William syndrome (Thal, Bates, & Bellugi, 1989). For these reasons, it is important to avoid thinking of cognition as a unitary construct and to resist the temptation to generalize from one case of impaired language associated with "general" cognitive impairment to all others. The goals of this enterprise are considerably more modest. Here, I can only note that language learning can become disrupted and look closely to determine how the nature of such disruptions may bear revealingly on the normal learning process.

The study of retarded children with Down syndrome to explore the effects (or noneffects) of cognitive impairment on the language learning process is hardly new. Indeed, the endeavor, which began with the pioneering work of Lenneberg, Nichols, and Rosenberger (1964), has been studied so often and has yielded such consistent findings that it is often dismissed with a single phrase, as being a remarkably uninteresting case of "delay, without deviance." This characterization rests on several observations:

1. No study of children with Down syndrome, or of any other mentally retarded group to date, has provided conclusive evidence for outright deviancies that would contradict constraints on learning postulated by linguistic theorists; no linguistic structures have been observed that have not also been found in normally intelligent children.[1]

2. Language complexity increases in a similar fashion across both mentally retarded and normally intelligent populations, whether thematic relations, grammatical functors, or complex syntactic structures are under study (Graham & Gulliford, 1968; Lackner, 1968). Retarded children, like young normally intelligent children, appear to produce and comprehend speech in what appears to be a coherent rule-governed fashion.

These conclusions have led to a developmental account of language delay in which retarded children proceed through the same stages as the normally

---

[1]Although some researchers claimed to observe deviant imitation or comprehension patterns (Cromer; 1972, 1974; Haber & Maloney, 1979), it is not clear that the controls were appropriately selected. Similar responses would be observed if younger children, at a language level more akin to the retarded children, had been selected.

intelligent child, but at a slower rate of acquisition and with an ultimately lower level of attainment commensurate with the degree of retardation. To return to our initial concern with constraints on language learning, these data might be interpreted as suggesting that even children whose cognitive/linguistic system is clearly not intact, as evidenced by failure across cognitive domains, are nonetheless bound to construct the same grammar from the input; as far as they do progress, it seems they must follow the same path as the brightest of children. On the face of it, all constraints are met and linguistic theory is intact.

However, without challenging the general finding of delay without deviance, we maintain that a close examination of language impairment in individuals with Down syndrome provides an interesting perspective on language learning. In particular, there are two features of language learning in individuals with Down syndrome that bear specific attention and explanation:

1. Although not often remarked upon, the absolute levels of linguistic attainment in individuals with Down syndrome are strikingly low, even taking the general retardation into account. A celebrated few notwithstanding (e.g., Seagoe, 1965), children and adults with Down syndrome tend to cluster at quite limited syntactic levels, lagging far behind both chronological and mental age expectations (Fowler, 1990; Miller, 1988; Wisniewski, Miezejeski, & Hill, 1988). Both clinical observation and a careful reading of the literature suggest that few individuals with Down syndrome move beyond the simple phrase-structure grammars that characterize the normally intelligent 2-year-old; this is true even for those individuals studied by Lenneberg et al. (1964).[2] Given the severity of the limitation, it is of great interest to examine the linguistic features of the stopping point and consider what prevents further development.

---

[2]The fact that consistently limited language levels associated with Down syndrome have received little attention presumably stems from the uninterpretability of this fact—after all, a small number of children with Down syndrome in any sample (including our own) do acquire full competence. Furthermore, early demographic studies pointing to a specific deficit in language associated with Down syndrome failed to take into account factors such as institutionalization; more recent research, including our own, have not controlled for such potentially contributing factors as low parental and teacher expectations, and the high prevalence of hearing loss resulting from chronic otitis media. Whether children who have been raised in supportive and optimistic home environments, who have not suffered a hearing loss because of appropriate medical intervention, and who have participated in early childhood intervention programs yield a different language outcome remains to be determined. Although such a survey of ultimate language achievement informed by such variables is highly desirable to understand how Down syndrome affects language learning, our present goal is somewhat different. Here, to better understand the basic processes of and constraints on language learning, we are primarily interested in the form that slow language learning can take, irrespective of the factors contributing to the delay.

2. The limitations on structural language development are even greater than deficits in other areas of language, more broadly defined. Carefully designed studies indicate that children with Down syndrome are relatively more advanced in both receptive vocabulary (Miller, 1988) and communicative skills (Beeghly, Weiss-Perry, & Cicchetti, 1990) than they are in language structure. Suspending the assumption that language, or even syntax, is one bounded and homogeneous system, it becomes possible to investigate differential delays, with different structures developing at different rates. Further investigation of this developmental disparity may provide insight regarding both the coherence of syntax and its dependence on general cognitive versus specifically linguistic factors.

It might be noted that these two features of atypical language development are not exclusive to individuals with Down syndrome. For example, children with left hemispherectomies and autistic children also fail to acquire full language mastery (e.g., Dennis & Whitaker, 1977; Scarborough, Rescorla, Tager-Flusberg, Fowler, & Sudhalter, 1991). Still more common is a discrepancy between structural aspects of language (syntax and phonology) compared to growth in vocabulary and/or communication skill. Such a discrepancy is, for example, a hallmark of specific language delay (Gathercole & Baddeley, 1989; Rescorla, 1989). Nonetheless, as a window on partial language failure, Down syndrome offers many advantages:

1. Children with Down syndrome are easily and objectively identifiable. The syndrome is comparatively well studied and is uniformly associated with general cognitive deficits, which may vary from mild to severe (for overall reviews see Beeghly, Weiss-Perry, & Cicchetti, 1990; Gibson, 1978; Nadel, 1988; Pueschel, 1988).
2. Full trisomy 21 has consistently been associated with impairments in language structure (Fowler, 1990; Miller, 1987; Wisniewski et al., 1988).
3. Large numbers of children with Down syndrome are currently being raised at home in supportive and hopeful environments.

Given what is known about cognitive development in children with Down syndrome, we entertained several hypotheses about how language development might be affected. First of all, because it has often been noted that individuals with Down syndrome are characterized by severe limitations on both memory and articulation (e.g., Bleile & Schwartz, 1984; Crosley & Dowling, 1989; Marcell & Weeks, 1988; Varnhagen, Das, & Varnhagen, 1987), we hypothesized that we might find some disparity between syntactic competence and performance. That is, we expected that memory and production factors might impose an apparent ceiling on some indices of language development, especially utterance length, while masking more advanced syntactic abilities. Thus, we hypothesized that children with Down syndrome, carefully studied, would show evidence of syntactic structures not yet mastered by a comparison group of normally developing children matched on mean utterance length.

As noted, the mean length of an utterance is a good indicator of the kind of morphological and syntactic structures a normal-IQ child has acquired and is apt to use. However, beyond the very earliest stages, length does not logically have to mirror complexity. Although *Whose book did you read?* is complex by virtue of wh-movement and subject–auxiliary inversion, it includes the same number of morphemes (five) as the more straightforward construction *They walk to the store.* If children with Down syndrome are held back in utterance length only by a memory and/or production limit, then one might plausibly find evidence for constructions that are short enough to fit within the production limit, but more complex than those ordinary found at that MLU stage in normally intelligent children.

The second hypothesis was that some aspects of language are more affected than others by general intellectual factors. Because it is well documented that language structure lags behind MA expectations (Fowler, 1990; Miller, 1987), one might expect that those facets of language most closely tied to general intelligence (as captured in the MA level) proceed in a different fashion from the more purely structural aspects. Of particular interest in this regard was the acquisition of closed-class vocabulary, that area of language which is at once least semantic and most vulnerable to environmental factors. The class of "little" words that glue sentences together includes grammatical inflections, articles, prepositions, and pronouns. These "functors" have been characterized as carrying no content, which distinguishes them from the content words that include nouns, verbs, adjectives, and adverbs. They also constitute a class in the historical development of languages by virtue of their finite nature: The language acquires new closed-class elements at an extremely protracted rate (over hundreds of years) as distinct from the open-class system which acquires hundreds of words per year. Furthermore, closed-class terms fall together as a phonological class in that they, as opposed to open-class words (nouns, verbs, adverbs, adjectives) lose stress within the total intonation of the sentence, resulting in *he's* for *he is*, *can't* for *cannot*, and the like (Kean, 1977; see Gleitman & Wanner, 1982, for an in-depth overview of the open-class/closed-class distinction). The closed-class system is fragile in many respects, hence, the expectation that it might be more impaired in retarded populations. It develops relatively late in child language (e.g., Bloom, 1970; Brown, 1973) and is missing in pidgin languages (Newport, 1982; Sankoff & Laberge, 1973) and in the invented language (homesign) of deaf isolates (Feldman et al., 1978). It is selectively impaired in Broca's aphasia (Kean, 1977) and is more dependent on input characteristics than other language components (Gleitman, Newport, & Gleitman, 1984). Despite the well-attested fragility of closed-class grammar and its distinctive developmental course, it has not been adequately determined whether this specific aspect of language is differentially affected in individuals with Down syndrome.

A third hypothesis concerned the possibility of different language-learning strategies. Whereas prior research has provided little support for such a hypothesis by way of deviant language structures, we felt that longitudinal research might provide some revealing information regarding how it might be that the very same generalizations might be mastered at greatly protracted rates. Furthermore, because mental age measures have consistently proven to greatly overestimate language skill in individuals with Down syndrome (Fowler, 1990; Miller, 1987), it is possible that interesting differences may yet show up when a more sensitive matching procedure is employed. To this end, in both studies presented in this chapter, children with Down syndrome were matched to normally developing preschoolers, not on mental age, but on an anchor measure of language-development MLU (mean length of utterance in morphemes; Brown, 1973). As a measure of internal syntactic complexity, MLU surpasses any other single measure of linguistic competence in the early stages of language development, in both its predictive powers and its breadth of application across child language studies (Bloom, 1970, 1973; Brown, 1973; Nelson, 1973; Newport, Gleitman, & Gleitman, 1977; Shipley, Smith, & Gleitman, 1969). In particular, descriptive studies of early language development found MLU to be a useful independent variable against which to predict (a) the expression of semantic relations (Bloom, Lightbown, & Hood, 1975), (b) the productive use of certain grammatical inflections and functors (Brown, 1973; deVilliers & deVilliers, 1978; Klima & Bellugi, 1966), and (c) the emerging structure of negative and interrogative constructions.

In the first of the two studies, we (Fowler, Gelman, & Gleitman, 1980) focused on the linguistic stopping point of four adolescents with Down syndrome who naturally fell together as a group in terms of MLU. To place their achievement within a developmental context, their language was compared in detail to the language of normally developing preschoolers functioning at the same MLU level. By matching the two groups on a global language measure and juxtaposing performance on several internal measures of syntactic development, the intention was to identify differential delays to distinguish those areas of language most and least affected by Down syndrome retardation. Specifically, it was hypothesized (a) that length would be more compromised than syntactic complexity, and (b) that the closed-class system would be more affected than either open-class vocabulary or sentence length. We predicted that the grammar of adolescents with Down syndrome would be relatively more advanced in terms of syntactic complexity (as in embedding) and vocabulary measures and less well developed on measures of morphological development. Although we were quite interested in observing evidence for linguistic strategies or generalizations that do not occur in the normal developmental sequence, we did not anticipate finding such evidence in this cross-sectional comparison.

STUDY I
LANGUAGE STRUCTURE OF ADOLESCENTS WITH DOWN SYNDROME COMPARED TO NORMALLY INTELLIGENT CHILDREN MATCHED ON MLU

Method

Subjects

The subjects included four moderately retarded adolescents with Down syndrome in a stimulating parochial day school. The four were selected for homogeneity of age (CA 10;9 to 13;0 years; mean = 12;7), intelligence level (Stanford-Binet IQ 46 to 56; mean = 51; MA 6 to 7 years; mean = 6;3), and language level (all were in Stage III, using the criteria of Brown, 1973). This language level (MLU 2.75 to 3.25; mean = 2.98) was representative of adolescent children with Down syndrome at that school and appears to be in keeping with other studies of adolescents with Down syndrome (Mein, 1961; Ryan, 1975; Semmel & Dolley, 1971). As a comparison group, non-MR youngsters were sought who had MLUs as close to 3.0 as possible. This was not easy; by 36 months of age, children have moved well beyond that language level and one has to "catch" younger children as they move through the level of interest. The controls in this study were 30 to 32 months of age, consistent with established norms (Bloom, 1970; Brown, 1973; Miller, 1980). The young age was surprising because the adolescents appeared, at least impressionistically, to be communicating well beyond a 3-year-old level. The resulting disparity in age (CA 12 vs. $2\frac{1}{2}$ years; MA 6 vs. 3 years) made dissociation all the more likely in the various analyses employed (refer to Table 5.1 for subject statistics).

Procedure

All analyses were based on spontaneous speech samples collected under naturalistic conditions. Children interacted with the experimenter at school in a half-hour of free play/conversation in a quiet room away from the classroom. The children had met and talked with the experimenter on

TABLE 5.1
Subject Characteristics

	Children with Down Syndrome (n=4)	MLU-Matched Controls (n=4)	T
Chronological age (years; months)			
Mean	12;3	2;7	18.25*
Range	10;9–13;0	2;6–2;8	
Mental age (years; months)			
Mean	6;3		
Range	6;0–6;9		
IQ			
Mean	51		
Range	48–50		
Utterance length statistics			
(based on spontaneous utterances)			
Number utterances produced	166.5	195.0	−0.86
MLU: mean length in morphemes	2.98	3.32	−1.32
Upper bound in morphemes	7.50	8.75	−1.56
Longest 10%: MLU in words	5.35	5.50	−0.29
Proportion one-word utterances	0.15	0.12	0.68
Word: morpheme ratio	0.95	0.92	1.63

Note. Groups were compared using independent sample two-tailed *t* tests.
*$p < .001$.

previous occasions. The conversation centered about a large three-dimensional house with miniature furniture and people. The children were encouraged to talk about the objects, to talk about own homes and families, and even to make up conversations using the objects as props (i.e., to play house). The sessions were videotaped and recorded on a hi-fidelity stereo tape recorder. The recordings were transcribed as soon as possible after the task by the experimenter. The utterance length measures were obtained as described below. In addition to these, internal analyses were performed to tap three different aspects of linguistic skill: (a) syntactic complexity, (b) grammatical morphology (closed-class knowledge), and (c) vocabulary (open-class knowledge).

Utterance Length Measures

MLU. The guidelines outlined in Brown (1973) served as the basis for the calculation of MLU, with some variations applied to both Down syndrome and control subjects. The primary deviation from his procedure was to incorporate in this analysis only those utterances initiated by the child; responses, imitations, and long lists without internal structure (e.g., counting or recitation of family names) were excluded. Additionally, only five tokens of any exact phrasing were included in the MLU analysis in order to relieve any possible bias introduced by repeated use of stock phrases such as *What's that?* Finally, analyses in this study were based on all utterances produced rather than on only the first 100 utterances of a transcript (see Fowler, 1984, for justification of these variations).

Two additional utterance length measures served as an index of optimal, as opposed to mean, performance. These included the *upper bound* (the length of the single longest utterance produced in the session, measured in morphemes, after Brown, 1973) and *MLU for the longest 10% of the utterances*. The fourth and final utterance length measure concerned the *distribution of utterance lengths*. Given an average length of utterance, the goal was to determine whether, perhaps as a function of usage factors, children with Down syndrome rely to a greater extent on very short utterances than other children with comparable syntactic skill.

Syntactic Measures

Newport Measures of Internal Complexity. As a first look at the internal structure of the utterances produced, counts were made of the number of major constituents (noun phrases and verbs) per utterance, and, in turn, of the number of words and morphemes entering into each constituent category. Length may derive from a greater number of sentential constituents (e.g., *see you help boy*) and from the internal length of few constituents (e.g., *going to the store*). These measures were developed by Newport et al. (1977), who found them to correlate highly with MLU in very young normally developing children.

This analysis was based upon a sample of 50 consecutive utterances from each child. Candidate utterances required a main verb other than *be* (explicit or not). A new MLU based on this sample was also computed. For this analysis, nouns were defined as nouns or pronouns, whether in subject or object position; they could also occur as objects of prepositions. Morphemes per noun phrase also included articles and inflectional markers; words per noun phrase excluded inflections. Verbs were defined to include only immediate verbal constituents: semimodals, auxiliaries, *not*, and the verb. Sentential elements not included in this count include optional elements such as adverbs, as well as particles and prepositions.

Expression of Thematic Relations. As a context-dependent measure of syntactic development, productions were analyzed for presence or absence of arguments made obligatory by certain verbs (or implied verbs). Does a child with Down syndrome choose to encode and delete the same thematic arguments as the non-MR child, when both are equally limited in productive language skill? Attention was focused on locative expressions for two reasons:

1. First, they were elicited in quantity by the task at hand—placing objects in a model house.

2. Normative developmental data on locatives are available (Bloom, Miller, & Hood, 1975); their analysis was the basis of the coding and scoring scheme relied upon here. Bloom et al. investigated three locative sentence frames: *Agent-Locative Action* utterances were defined as expressing the movement of an object (Patient) by an independent Agent, as in *I'm trying to put this back in here*. This sentence type requires an Agent (syntactic subject), Patient (object), Place and Verb. The *Mover-Locative Action* sentence type (e.g., *You can come my house*), includes those utterances specifying a movement in which the Agent was also the Patient moved, hence the Mover. This argument structure requires a Mover (subject), Verb, and Place. Bloom et al.'s third locative category, *Locative State*, specifies a state rather than a movement (e.g., *sleep, sit, be, belong*, and *go*, as in *This goes here*). This category also requires a Patient (subject), Verb, and Place.

Indices of Complex Syntax.   The two previous syntactic measures are useful in analyzing early language production, from the onset of two-word combinations in Stage I through Stage III. However, at the level of interest here, children are also on the verge of mastering aspects of complex syntax. Most notably, they must acquire the intricacies of the verbal auxiliary system (both movement rules and grammatical terminology) in order to produce correct negative and interrogative structures. Children just beyond this stage acquire many means of coordinating and embedding sentence clauses, such as conjunctions, relative clause structure, or preposing; here, too, they must master movement rules and grammatical markers. To measure progress made in this direction, in this study, a count was made of some of the earliest appearing aspects of complex syntax, such as those noted by researchers like Menyuk (1969) or Bellugi (1967). Constructions of interest included subordination and coordination, subject/auxiliary version in yes/no and wh-questions, passive voice constructions with *got* or *be*, and choice of negative markers.

Confirmation of syntactic development was sought via a quantitative measure of syntactic complexity devised by Scarborough (1990). The Index of Productive Syntax (IPSyn), based upon a 100-utterance sample, awards points for the occurrence of 56 kinds of morphological and syntactic forms. Baseline data for normal children are available, based on 48 transcripts from children aged 24 to 48 months; the scale is of potential value for children below and beyond this age range. Because full credit is awarded if a construction occurs twice in a 100-utterance transcript, this analysis serves as a measure of optimal rather than mean performance.

The Closed-Class System

It was suggested earlier that the acquisition of closed-class vocabulary might be more affected in individuals with Down syndrome than would the acquisition of open-class vocabulary. In particular, it was hypothesized that grammatical morphology might lag behind other aspects of syntactic development. This question was addressed first by the *word/morpheme ratio* calculated among the utterance length measures. This measure of use of bound inflections is calculated as the ratio of the number of "words" (defined phonologically) to the number of morphemes. The difference is made up by nominal and verbal markers, such as the plural or past tense markers.

Closed-Class Vocabulary. To assess the development of closed-class vocabulary, a count was made of all tokens of the five major closed-class categories: (a) pronouns, (b) prepositions, (c) modals, (d) wh-forms, and (e) demonstratives. This figure was compared to the total number of words in each speech sample. To supplement this measure of dependence on closed-class vocabulary, we also made a measure of lexical sophistication within these categories by looking at the diversity of vocabulary types falling into these and other categories of closed-class markers.

Use of Grammatical Morphemes in Obligatory Context. For a more fine-tuned measure of morphological development, an assessment was made of use in obligatory context of the first 14 grammatical morphemes to occur regularly in early child language. These include prepositions, verbal auxiliaries, and nominal and verbal inflections. Brown (1973) identified the contexts where these morphemes should appear, calculated the proportion of cases where they did appear, and tracked the development of each over the language-learning period. His methods were adapted for cross-sectional study by deVilliers and deVilliers (1978); their procedures were adopted here.

Open-Class Vocabulary

At the language level under study, it is difficult to make a fair assessment of productive vocabulary, especially in a single spontaneous speech sample. Nonetheless, a gross measure of vocabulary usage, the *type/token ratio*, was derived by calculating the ratio of different vocabulary types produced to the total number of words in the corpus (following Nelson, 1973).

Although this measure clearly does not explore the depth of the child's lexical knowledge for open-class items, it probably does provide a fair index of the closed-class lexicon, which is, after all, both finite and frequently used. The ratio also serves as a measure of information value independent of the syntactic structure employed.

Results

Utterance-Length Measures

By design, all subjects had MLUs falling within Brown's Stage III or IV. As seen in Table 5.1, MLU measures did not differ significantly across the groups. The average MLU of the group with Down syndrome was 3.0 (range 2.6 to 3.3); in the preschoolers, mean MLU was 3.3 (2.8 to 3.8). There was a generally low usage of inflectional morphology; in both groups, MLU in words was slightly, though comparably, lower than MLU in morphemes (2.8 and 3.0 for the children with Down syndrome and the comparison preschoolers, respectively). Similarly, word:morpheme ratios were high and not significantly different across the groups. The children with Down syndrome also did not stand out on optimal measures of utterance length. Their upper bound ranged from 7 to 9 morphemes; this was not significantly different from the upper bound found for the normally developing children (7 to 10). Both scores were in keeping with Brown's (1973) report of an upper bound of 9 at Stage III. Similarly, when only the longest 10% of the utterances were taken into account, the MLUs (in words) of the two groups were nearly identical (children with Down syndrome: 5.35; non-MR children: 5.50).

Although it might have been expected that the children with Down syndrome would be more variable in sentence length, alternating perhaps between long and very short utterances, this was not the case. The shape of the distribution of utterance lengths was similar across both groups. In each group, two-and three-word utterances made up more than 50% of the total and there was no utterance longer than 9 words. One-word utterances made up 15% of the utterances produced by the children with Down syndrome and 12% of the utterances produced by the non-MR children; this difference was nonsignificant.

Syntactic Measures

Newport Measures of Internal Complexity.   Measures of internal complexity are presented in Table 5.2. As can be seen, the mean length of the utterances fitting these criteria was identical across populations and there was virtually the same number of major constituents (noun phrases and

TABLE 5.2
Measures of Internal Complexity (Following Newport, Gleitman, & Gleitman,
1977) (Based on 50 Consecutive Nonequational Utterances)

	Children with Down Syndrome (n=4)	MLU-Matched Controls (n=4)	T
Mean words per utterance	3.68	3.73	−0.18
Major constituents per utterance			
Noun phrases/utterance	1.37	1.37	0.10
Verbs/utterance	1.07	1.01	1.81
Other (particles, adverbs)	0.36	0.55	−1.43
Internal structure of major constituents			
Words/nounphrase	1.62	1.72	−1.63
Morphemes/nounphrase	1.71	1.85	−2.44*
Morphemes/verbphrase	1.45	1.50	−0.40

Note. Groups were compared using independent sample two-tailed t tests.
*$p < .05$.

verbs) per utterance. There was, however, one internal difference: The group with Down syndrome relied upon significantly fewer morphemes per noun phrase. As will be supported by other measures, this is due, in part, to the fact the children with Down syndrome relied heavily on pronouns rather than on expanded noun phrases.

Expression of Thematic Relations. At the language level under study, children in both groups were explicit in expressing most of the obligatory thematic relations studied by Bloom, Miller, and Hood (1975). As shown in Table 5.3, of the 10 relations under study, 85.1% were expressed by the group with Down syndrome and 83.7% by the non-MR group. When scores were compared across individual and averaged categories, there were no significant differences across the two groups.

Although small numbers and potential differences in scoring procedures preclude statistical comparison with Bloom, Miller, and Hood's findings, the subjects in this study seemed to be performing as well as, if not better than, the children at the close of the normative study (MLU=3.0). In both studies, nonstative verbs were expressed virtually 100% of the time. In addition, the children in this study consistently included the place term across the three locative sentence types (Down syndrome: 95%; non-MR: 92% expressed); this was well beyond the 55% average quoted by Bloom, Miller, and Hood. In that normative study, stative locative verbs (*sits, belongs*, etc.) were consistently expressed (near 100%), just as were the nonstative verbs. In this study, however, nonstative verbs were often only implicit in both groups; subjects frequently produced utterances such as *the doll ___ upstairs* while placing a doll in a dollhouse, implying a verb such

TABLE 5.3
Obligatory Thematic Relations Expressed in Locative Utterances
(Proportion of Times an Argument or Verb is Expressed Where Obligatory)
(Following Bloom, Miller, & Hood, 1975)

	Children with Down Syndrome (n=4)	MLU-Matched Controls (n=4)	T
Locative Utterance Category			
Agent Locative (e.g., *I'm trying to put this in here*)			
Mean # in category	6.75	11.75	− 1.27
Agent	0.39	0.51	− 1.67
Verb	1.00	0.99	0.67
Patient	0.76	0.96	− 1.07
Place	0.87	0.99	− 1.25
Mover Locative (e.g., *Daddy going trolley*)			
Mean # in category	12.25	12.25	0.00
Mover (Agent *and* Patient)	0.65	0.69	− 0.23
Verb	0.65	1.00	0.00
Place	0.97	0.83	1.31
Locative State (e.g, *She sleep in bed*)			
Mean # in category	12.25	23.75	− 1.01
Patient	0.93	0.84	0.80
Verb/copula	0.79	0.62	0.80
Place	0.94	0.96	− 0.31
Average score for 10 thematic categories	0.85	0.84	0.38
Proportion Syntactic Categories Expressed[a]			
Nouns	0.72	0.75	− 0.45
Subject	0.70	0.68	0.30
Object	0.76	0.96	− 1.07
Verbs	0.93	0.92	0.22
Stative	0.79	0.62	0.93
Nonstative	1.00	0.99	0.00
Place terms	0.95	0.92	0.47

Note. Groups were compared using independent sample two-tailed *t* tests.

[a]Syntactic scores were obtained by averaging across thematic categories, according each sentence type equal weight.

as *goes* or *belongs*. In this regard, the difference between groups was not significant (children with Down syndrome: 79% expressed; nonMR children: 62%). In part, of course, this may arise from a failure to produce the contractible copula (*the doll's upstairs*).

When attention is restricted to obligatory nominal arguments, more variability is apparent. Overall, nominal arguments entering into locative relations were supplied 72% of the time by children with Down syndrome and 75% of the time by the non-MR group. The largest tendency to omit an obligatory nominal involved the Agent (subject) of Agent locative utterances, as in *put this right here*. Although the tendency not to express this form was somewhat greater among the Down syndrome group (39% supplied) than among the non-MR group (51% supplied), not one of the eight subjects supplied it more than 75% of the time. (Bloom, Miller, and Hood report an average score of 54%.)

The children were more apt to express the Mover in the Mover locative category. Although this category is similar to the Agent category in serving as sentence subject, thematically it also serves as Patient. The two groups performed comparably (64.8% Down syndrome; 68.8% non-MR), with two children in each group supplying this argument less than 75% of the time, and only one child (non-MR) supplying it more than 90% of the time.

Sentence subjects were most consistently supplied when functioning as the Patient in the locative state utterances (e.g., ___ *belongs in the kitchen*). Each child supplied this argument a minimum of 75% of the time, which was the mean performance reported by Bloom, Miller, and Hood. The high scores observed (92.8% Down syndrome; 83.5% non-MR) may be artificially inflated by coding procedures requiring that a minimum of two arguments be supplied in order to be included in the analysis. Thus *here*, meaning *this goes here*, would not be included in the analysis because it lacks both the noun and the verb.

Young children consistently supply the Patient in object position, as in Agent locative utterances (e.g., *I'll put ___ right here*), with 70% supplied from MLU 1.2 on (Bloom, Miller, & Hood, 1975). Consistent with these results, in the present study, each child in the non-MR group provided the locative Patient at least 90% of the time (group average 96%). Although the average score obtained by the group with Down syndrome (75.5%) did not differ significantly from the non-MR score, there was variability in the group with Down syndrome. Two of the children with Down syndrome, like the non-MR children, provided the Patient consistently; a third supplied it only 80% of the time and the fourth consistently failed to express it (22% supplied).

The focus in Bloom, Miller, and Hood (1975) was on the earliest stages of language; their observations were concluded at just the level of interest here. Although the children in the present study, like those at the close of Bloom, Miller, and Hood were more apt to express a nominal argument that incorporates both Agent and Patient than one which is Agent alone, the more obvious facts seem to concern grammatical categories. In the present study, although both groups tended to express sentence subject (children with Down syndrome 70%; non-MR children 68%) and grammatical object (children with Down syndrome 76%; non-MR children 96%), with differences failing to reach significance, there was a significant group by grammatical category interaction, indicating a greater split between these two categories in the non-MR group than in the group with Down syndrome.

Indices of Complex Syntax.   There was very little evidence for use of complex constructions in either group; what small differences existed between groups failed to reach significance (see Table 5.4a). Little use was noted in either group of the passive construction, subject/auxiliary inversions, the possessive form, or conjoined clauses. In both groups, the primary means of expressing negation was through negative modals, fitting with descriptions in the literature of negation at this stage (e.g., Klima & Bellugi, 1966). Primitive forms like *He have no chin* or *This not fit* were observed primarily in the non-MR group, whereas the children with Down syndrome tended to produce very few negatives overall.

Multiverb utterances were also rare, comprising less than 5% of the utterances in either group and consisting primarily of conjunctions and concatenations. Similar multiverb utterances were produced in both samples: A Down syndrome subject produced *put it on get more*, but *do that fix this* came from a non-MR child; *I want it shut* was produced by a child with

TABLE 5.4a
Indices of Grammatical Complexity
(Presented as Average Number of Occurrences per 100 Utterances)

	Children with Down Syndrome (n = 4)	MLU-Matched Controls (n = 4)	T
Utterances with 2 or more sentence nodes	3.83	2.38	1.39
Conjunction:			
Noun + noun	1.15	0.17	1.42
Verb + verb	0.40	0.00	1.00
Sentence + sentence	0.42	0.60	0.27
Prenominal adjectives	1.13	2.13	−1.62
Negative forms:			
No + verb	0.00	0.98	−1.31
Not + verb	0.20	1.18	−1.70
Negative modals	3.40	2.58	0.44
Passive forms:			
Got + verb	0.50	0.00	0.73
Be + verb	0.00	0.00	0.00
Use of possessive form:			
Noun's noun	0.85	0.60	0.37
Auxiliary inversion in yes/no questions	0.25	0.20	0.18

Note. Groups were compared using independent sample two-tailed *t* tests. There were no significant differences between groups.

Down syndrome and *and keep a door closed* by a non-MR child. Preverbal adjectives occurred rarely and in both samples consisted of such common constructions as *big truck* or *little boy*.

Index of Productive Syntax (IPSyn). The two groups also performed comparably in overall performance on Scarborough's (1990) IPSyn measure (children with Down syndrome 60.5; non-MR children 54.25). The scores of the group with Down syndrome were consistent with those reported by Scarborough for her 30-month-old group of nonhandicapped children; the non-MR group here was somewhat behind this average. Although the two groups in this study were highly comparable on the three subscales of this test tapping complexity of noun phrases, verbal auxiliary development, and devices for constructing negative and interrogative sentences, there was a notable difference regarding sentence complexity. This last subscale looks at means of embedding and coordinating sentence clauses; however, following Miller (1980), it is more concerned with movement rules and word order than it is with whether the particular grammatical markers are expressed. Thus, the child who produces *want my mommy come here* is credited with being able to produce infinitival sentences with a subject distinct form the matrix subject, despite the fact that the infinitival marker *to* was unexpressed. Although both groups, and Scarborough's as well, had this advantage (as shown in Table 5.4b), the group with Down syndrome were relatively more advanced on such constructions than were the non-MR children (though, see Scarborough, Rescorla, Tager-Flusberg, Fowler, & Sudhalter, 1991).

The Closed-Class System and Open-Class Vocabulary

The *word/morpheme ratio*, presented in Table 5.1, indicates that neither group made much use of inflectional morphology (Down syndrome .95;

TABLE 5.4b
Performance on Index of Productive Syntax (Based on Scarborough, 1990)

	Children with Down Syndrome (n = 4)	MLU-Matched Controls (n = 4)	T
Subscale:			
Noun phrase	16.25	15.75	0.29
Verb phrase	17.50	16.75	0.70
Questions and negatives	11.50	9.75	0.63
Sentences	15.50	12.00	2.18*
Total	60.50	54.25	1.89

Note. Groups were compared using independent sample two-tailed *t* tests.
*$p < .10$.

non-MR .92). The nonsignificant advantage that does occur for the non-MR group is a function of one child with Down syndrome who used very few inflections at all and one non-MR child who was more advanced on this measure.

Closed-Class Vocabulary. Pronouns, prepositions, modals, wh-forms and demonstratives made up a similar proportion, overall, of the lexical items produced by children with Down syndrome (31%) and by non-MR children (30%). Differences between groups within individual categories were not remarkable, although there was a marginally significant tendency for the non-MR children to use more demonstrative terms (*this*, *that*); this was complemented by a nonsignificant tendency on the part of the children with Down syndrome to use a greater number of pronouns (see Table 5.5). In terms of diversity of the closed-class items employed, children with Down syndrome had a slight, but nonsignificant, advantage over the non-MR children. This difference was particularly evident with modals and wh-forms, where it neared or attained significance (see Table 5.6).

Use of Grammatical Morphemes in Obligatory Context. Sufficient information was available for comparison across groups for 8 of the 14 morphemes (i.e., there were at least four identifiable obligatory contexts per subject); averaging across these morphemes the overall percentage supplied for each group was virtually identical: 68% for the group with Down syndrome, 66% for the non-MR group (Table 5.6). There appear, however, to be some differences regarding the pattern of acquisition for individual morphemes. This is evident in the scores for the progressive form (*-ing*), the first morpheme usually acquired. Although the non-MR children provided

TABLE 5.5
Usage of Closed-Class Vocabulary Tokens
(Mean Proportion of Words Falling into Each of Five Closed-Class Categories)

	Children with Down Syndrome (n=4)	MLU-Matched Controls (n=4)	T
Mean # words per corpus	468.25	474.75	−1.18
Closed-class categories			
Pronouns	16.56	13.81	1.57
Prepositions	3.66	4.52	−0.59
Modals/semimodals	3.23	1.97	1.21
Wh-terms	3.54	2.78	1.17
Demonstratives	4.01	6.68	−2.02*
Total	31.00	29.75	0.51

Note. Groups were compared using independent sample two-tailed t tests.
*$p < .10$.

TABLE 5.6
Proportion Usage of 14 Grammatical Morphemes in Obligatory Contexts
(following Brown, 1973, and deVilliers & deVilliers, 1978)
(# Subjects Reaching 90% Criterion Presented in Parentheses)

	Children with Down Syndrome (n=4)	MLU-Matched Controls (n=4)	T
Grammatical morphemes:			
Progressive marker - *ing*	0.61(0)	0.86(2)	−2.16*
Preposition *on*	0.84(1)	−(1)[a]	−
Plural *-s*	0.84(2)	0.92(2)	−0.59
Preposition *in*	0.73(1)	0.75(3)	−0.07
Past tense irregular	0.82(0)	0.63(0)	1.20
Articles *a* & *the*	0.43(0)	0.49(0)	−0.46
Possessive *'s*	−(0)	−(0)	−
3rd person irregular	−(0)	−(0)	−
Contractible copula	0.82(2)	0.62(0)	1.31
3rd person regular *-s*	0.25(0)	0.36(0)	−0.71
Past tense regular	−	−	−
Contractible auxiliary *be*	−(1)	0.39(0)	−
Uncontractible auxiliary *be*	(0)	−(0)	−
Overall proportion supplied[b]	0.68	0.66	0.16
Mean number morphemes acquired per child	2.25	2.25	0.00

Note. Groups were compared using independent sample two-tailed tests *t* tests.

[a]Averages were only calculated when there were more than four obligatory contexts for three out of four subjects.

[b]Overall proportion based upon just those 8 morphemes for which there was sufficient data for both groups.

*p < .10.

this form quite consistently (86% supplied), the children with Down syndrome were much more variable (61% supplied, $p < .10$). When performance is looked at case by case, there are eight cases of full mastery (90% usage in obligatory context) of the first 4 morphemes among the four non-MR children in this study. In contrast, there are only four such cases among the non-MR group. Interestingly, when a count is made of the number of cases of full mastery across the whole range of the 14 morphemes, the overall score is nine in each group. In some sense, the comparison preschoolers are "more normal," mastering the earlier morphemes first and only later going on to acquire the more difficult morphemes. Although one cannot infer the developmental sequence from this single point data, it appears that the Down syndrome group may have moved on to more difficult morphemes (notably, the copula) without having full mastered the simplest ones. It may well be that what the non-MR child learns he learns fully, hence rapidly reaching near 100% on the earliest morphemes. The child with Down syndrome, in contrast, may work on more constructions simultaneously but never acquire fully—or use consistently—even the earliest rules acquired.

Open-Class Vocabulary. On the open-class type-token ratio, the comparison preschoolers, with an average of 19.13 different open-class vocabulary types per 100 words produced, appeared to rely on a wider range of open-class vocabulary than did the children with Down syndrome, with a mean of 15.41 ($t = -2.10$; $p < .10$). This nearly significant difference derives almost entirely from the significantly greater tendency of the non-MR group to use different noun types (see Table 5.7). Thus, although PPVT scores indicate the children with Down syndrome should have access to a higher vocabulary, they tended not to rely upon a large (especially nominal) vocabulary in this spontaneous speech sample. As was observed in the analysis of closed-class vocabulary, the children with Down syndrome tended to rely on pronouns where possible.

Discussion

In summary, the adolescents with Down syndrome in this study appear to be at a linguistically stable, if extremely restricted, point of development,

TABLE 5.7
Measure of Lexical Diversity
(Presented as Number of Different Vocabulary Types per 100 Words)

	Children with Down Syndrome (n=4)	MLU-Matched Controls (n=4)	T
Number of words in corpus	468.25	474.75	-0.18
Open-class categories:			
Nouns	5.94	9.48	-3.69*
Verbs	5.52	5.79	-0.27
Adjectives	0.90	1.33	-0.70
Adverbs	3.05	2.54	1.08
Total	15.41	19.13	-2.10**
Closed-class categories:			
Pronouns	3.09	2.56	1.20
Prepositions	1.33	1.48	-0.66
Modals & semimodals	1.36	0.69	2.46*
Wh-forms	1.08	0.68	2.31**
Demonstratives	0.48	0.48	0.00
Quantifiers	0.93	0.87	0.22
Logical forms	0.25	0.42	-1.47
Total	8.50	7.18	1.82
Overall Total	23.90	26.47	-1.03

Note. Groups were compared using independent sample two-tailed t tests.
*$p < .05$. **$p < .10$.

with no syntactic or grammatical measure deviating from that stage. Overall, the combination of the syntactic measures employed reveal Down syndrome subjects to be at a level of simple phrase structure grammar — one that cannot be reduced, perhaps, to semantic generalizations (see Slobin, 1980, for a discussion of the normal course), but one that precedes, across the board, the dramatic changes required to build the complex syntax with its associated verbal auxiliary system, sentential embedding, and movement rules. Furthermore, despite the fact that this set of measures was chosen specifically with the aim of uncovering plausible differences between retarded adolescents and normally intelligent preschoolers, similarities across groups of children at the same language stage were more striking than were any small differences. Performance on each measure was within the expectations derived from the normal literature relevant to that stage and was confirmed on the basis of measures made on our own comparison group.

In contrast to our initial expectations, where differences did occur, it was usually the adolescent with Down syndrome who lagged behind the normally developing preschooler despite attested higher verbal MA. The adolescents supplied early grammatical morphemes and grammatical objects less consistently and produced less complex noun phrases. Despite relatively advanced receptive vocabulary scores, they relied more heavily on pronouns and produced only a limited set of nouns.

Even where the adolescents with Down syndrome maintained an advantage, there are important disclaimers. For instance, although they were somewhat more advanced in the acquisition of different closed-class terminology than non-MR children at this language level, other analyses make it apparent that they failed to use these forms appropriately and consistently to serve syntactic/grammatical functions. Similarly, although they produced complex sentences of appropriate length and word order, our results suggest that this level of syntactic complexity is not at all supported by appropriate grammatical markers. It is interesting that even within the closed-class system, then, one sees a relative advantage for vocabulary and relative deficit in structure (see Fowler, 1990, for further discussion).

There are, by now, many studies replicating the main finding of this study: When appropriate matching procedures are employed, internal analyses fail to distinguish the language structures employed by children with Down syndrome from those produced by normally developing children at the same language stage. This is true not only at the language level under study here, but at earlier levels of language as well (for reviews, see Fowler, 1990; Miller, 1988). Other studies are also in agreement with our findings concerning absolute level of language skill, consistently finding that individuals with Down syndrome tend to cluster at quite limited syntactic levels, lagging far behind both chronological age and mental age expectations (Fowler, 1990; Miller, 1988; Wisniewski et al., 1988).

From one perspective, then, the findings from this study and several related studies serve to strengthen the notion of retarded language as a monolithic indissociable "normal" system proceeding at a slower pace. On the other hand, this entire body of research, so consistent in its findings, fails to shed light on how they manage to acquire exactly the same system at dramatically slower rates, or why children with Down syndrome progress only as far as they do. Rather, this research serves only to highlight the dilemma with which we introduced the chapter: How is it that the child can be learning "normally" over a period of 12 years what is otherwise acquired in 30 months; what accounts for the failure to ever achieve the complex syntax that normal preschoolers appear to acquire rapidly and effortlessly? Where do individual differences in language learning show themselves, and what facets of language learning remain constant despite differences in cognitive skill? In an effort to understand how language learning can be slowed, without violating apparent constraints on the system, the next obvious step was to look at language learning over time. In terms of both overall language growth and the mastery of individual language structures, will longitudinal investigation reveal specific properties of the course and process of language acquisition that bear back revealingly on the normal case?

STUDY II

A LONGITUDINAL INVESTIGATION OF LANGUAGE ACQUISITION IN A YOUNG CHILD WITH DOWN SYNDROME

To account for extreme delays in language learning with no apparent deviancies, we undertook a detailed longitudinal study, examining the effects of Down syndrome retardation on the rate and character of language learning. By closely monitoring language growth in a young child with Down syndrome from the onset of two-word combinations (Brown's Stage I) to the achievement of the language levels examined previously (Brown's Stage III), we sought to develop a body of data directly comparable to the data available on normally developing children (e.g., Bellugi, 1967; Brown, 1973). We used this method to explore three different ways in which markedly delayed learning might differ interestingly from the normal case, with an eye toward understanding why language learning ceases where it does:

1. We first considered the rate and character of the overall learning curve for MLU. We considered two different possibilities. On the one hand, it is possible that language learning proceeds as a single accretion of information over time and practice conditions. If so, this accretion should be commensurately and uniformly slower in the retarded child, leading to an altogether flatter, stretched-out, language-learning curve. We contrasted this with the possibility that periods of learning at an apparently normal rate might be interspersed with periods of no learning at all. On this conceptualization, language acquisition is better characterized as a series of stages in which available information is reorganized and resystematized by learners (e.g., Bowerman, 1982; Karmiloff-Smith, 1979). Once having reached a stage, the retarded child should form generalizations in much the same way and at much the same rate as a normal child at the same language stage. The retarded child should, however, arrive at such stages late and show extreme difficulties in moving from one stage to another, ceasing altogether at a linguistically coherent ceiling.

2. The second area of investigation concerned the scope of linguistic generalizations, again looking at the character of language-learning curves, but in this case with respect to well-studied individual linguistic regularities, such as the plural morpheme or auxiliary inversion in questions. Here again, learning curves which are simply flatter in slow language learning suggest an inability to make generalizations of the same scope as normally observed. Again, it is possible that children with Down syndrome acquire rules of the normal scope but take longer between acquisition of these regularities, leading to a series of growth spurts and plateaus compared to the normal case.

3. Longitudinal investigation provides another window on the issue of differential delay addressed in Study I. Although, in that study, dissociation among language-production measures was not evident among adolescents with Down syndrome, it is possible that different facets of the developing systems follow distinct courses, with all reaching maximum potential at adolescence. In particular, we were interested in whether acquisition of different language structures varied, depending on how "semantic" or "syntactic" they were.

Because language learning in individuals with Down syndrome is widely assumed to occupy the first two decades of life, it is not surprising that longitudinal studies have rarely been undertaken. Longitudinal studies that do exist have not focused on language structure independently of vocabulary growth (Carr, 1988; Share, Koch, Webb, & Graliker, 1964). Even the most relevant and best known study of language delay in the retarded (Lenneberg et al., 1964) preceded the in-depth longitudinal research of normal children that so fundamentally shaped our ideas about language acquisition (e.g., Bloom, 1970; Brown, 1973). The measures taken by Lenneberg et al. (1964) were cursory and taken only at 6-month intervals. In the assessment of syntax, for example, subjects' speech was described as fitting into one of four categories: (a) one-word, (b) phrases, (c) sentences with errors, or (d) complete sentences. (Note, with regard to our earlier point about absolute levels of achievement, that only 2 out of 35 subjects ever moved beyond the phrase level during the entire period of study). The study is valuable in that it covers the entire period from 3 to 22 years of age; unfortunately, the learning curve presented was averaged over individual curves, each covering a 3-year period of observation.

What does seem apparent from Lenneberg et al. (1964) and other cross-sectional studies did not bode well for longitudinal research, leading one to expect that the language learning associated with Down syndrome is a painstakingly slow process, lasting from when the children were 3 or 4 years of age until puberty. However, pilot research and simple observations encouraged us to pursue a longitudinal investigation nonetheless. Consistent with Lenneberg et al. (1964), follow-up of the four adolescents studied in Experiment I revealed no further linguistic progress for the $2\frac{1}{2}$ to 4 years following the initial investigation; MLU remained within the range of 3.0 to 3.5, suggesting they had reached their final linguistic attainment. Cursory observation of younger children with Down syndrome (aged 8 or 9 years) attending the same school as our adolescents revealed that they too were functioning at a similar language level. In the one longitudinal study of children with Down syndrome that had mimicked the procedures of normal language acquisition, there seemed to be evidence for an extended period of "no growth," speaking to our "stage" hypothesis. In that study, Dooley (1977) conducted a year-long observational study of two moderately retarded children with Down syndrome (IQ 51 and 44; starting CA 3;10 and 5;2), examining individual growth curves using the language analysis procedures of Brown (1973). Throughout the study, both children remained in Brown's Stage I. Over the year, one child made approximately one month's progress (MLU 1.48 to 1.75) relative to non-MR children studied in Brown (1973); the other child actually declined somewhat in MLU (1.84 to 1.73). With the exception of the fact that they failed to change significantly over the period, the children were similar to Stage I non-MR children on internal measures (semantic relations, grammatical morphemes, utterance diversity, and size of lexicon). The only difference of note was a greater tendency on the part of the children with Down syndrome to rely heavily on routinized expressions and pro-forms (*it, they, here, there, do*), in keeping with our findings above. Dooley (1977), however, noted that this tendency also varies within the normal population. On the basis of these three observations, we hypothesized that perhaps most language learning takes place in a restricted age range, between 4 and 9 years of age, making a longitudinal project more feasible.

Method

Subject

The subject of our longitudinal study was Rebecca, a mild-to-moderately retarded child diagnosed at birth as having Down syndrome, trisomy 21. Her tested IQ on the Stanford-Binet was 57 at age 61 months. She and her nonretarded twin brother were the last-born of a large, supportive, middle-class family. Her family received public assistance in "infant stimulation" programs from a few months of age, and she was first enrolled in preschool at 2 years of age. She first came to our attention when she was 46 months old; at that time she had begun to speak in one-word utterances. Intensive longitudinal investigation began 5 months later, when she was 51 months old and attending a local parochial day school for handicapped youngsters; she remained at this school throughout the study. At that time, as noted by both the school speech therapist and ourselves, Rebecca was beginning to produce two-word combinations, making her comparable to the children at the outset of the Brown and Bloom studies.

Rebecca was an ideal subject for our observations for several reasons:

1. We caught her at the onset of syntax and were able to observe her in the very act of making progress.
2. From the beginning, her speech was relatively articulate for a child with Down syndrome, making transcription and interpretation straightforward for numerous undergraduate assistants.
3. She clearly enjoyed the attention and the interactions during which we collected language data, and was happy to play anything from "store" to "McDonalds" to "tea" for extended periods, providing us with volumes of data.

Procedure

Because we wished to compare her development to that of normally developing children, we tried to mimic as closely as possible both the methods and descriptive categories of Brown's (1973) and Bloom's (1970, 1973) classic investigations of speech development in the normal child. Thus, we visited Rebecca in her home once a month for an hour-long session from the age of 51 months to 89 months. At each visit, two experimenters would arrive with a bag of toys (toy town, dolls, drawing materials) and a high-fidelity tape recorder. Rebecca would play and chat with one of the experimenters; the other would take detailed notes on both speech and context. The audiotaped sessions were transcribed, either in full or until 250 useable utterances (i.e., intelligible, nonimitative, nonrepetitive, and nonelicited) from the subject had been recorded. Each transcript was fully checked by at least two listeners and discrepancies in the transcription were either resolved or removed from the analysis, leading to virtually complete interrater agreement. All further internal analyses were also submitted to double coding and scoring until full agreement was achieved among the experimenters. These analyses, much the same as those employed in the earlier experiment, are reviewed briefly.

Utterance-Length Measures

Following the classic language development studies, growth in utterance length served as our overall measure of language development and allowed for comparison with normally developing children on internal analyses. Three utterance-length measures were calculated. First, procedures outlined by Brown (1973) were duplicated exactly to yield the *Brown MLU*, allowing for direct comparison to his subjects. As a more optimal measure of language competence, we also calculated a spontaneous mean utterance length, *SMU*, following the procedures presented in Study I, in which responses, etc., were omitted. Our third index of utterance length was the *upper bound*, the length of the single longest utterance produced in the session, measured in morphemes (Brown, 1973).

On the basis of these three measures, transcripts were assigned to one of Brown's (1973) five language stages. This assignment allowed us to compare Rebecca's development on internal measures to growth in normally developing children. Although originally defined by Brown in quantitative terms (the upper bound for each midpoint increasing by 2 from 5 to 13), the stages have come to represent qualitatively distinct periods in development, each with a somewhat different focus of interest.

Internal Measures of Linguistic Complexity

Thematic Relations. Bloom's coding system for semantic/syntactic relations encoded in the earliest multiword utterances of young children serves as a measure of content and thematic complexity in Rebecca's language from Stages I to III (Bloom, Lightbown, & Hood, 1975). Our coding system followed hers closely. For purposes of comparison, we calculated a standard deviation for Bloom's subjects, and then determined by how many standard deviations Rebecca's performance deviated from that norm.

Grammatical Morphology.   To assess Rebecca's development of closed class morphology, we relied upon Brown's (1973) measure of use in obligatory context of the first 14 grammatical morphemes to appear reliably in child language. Individual learning curves and point of full acquisition (90% use in obligatory context across three sessions) were plotted for each of these morphemes.

Syntactic Measures.   As one measure of syntactic knowledge, we traced the development across stages of constructions with negative or interrogative intent. Here, we relied upon Bellugi (1967) for normative longitudinal data. As a clue to understanding the learning and generalizing procedures which characterize Rebecca's development, we were particularly interested in observing overgeneralizations in her attempts to acquire question and negative-formation.

Results

Stages of Language Development

Because the language stages laid out by Brown (1973) serve as major guideposts for the purpose of discussion and comparison, they are described briefly here, complete with MLU criteria from Brown (1973), normative chronological age data from Miller and Chapman (Miller, 1980), and discussion of how Rebecca's growth in MLU fits in (refer to Table 5.8).

Brown's (1973) Stage I covers MLU 1.0 to 2.0, with an upper bound of 5 words at the mean MLU of 1.75. This is the period in which children, typically between 18 and 24 months of age, begin to combine words into utterances; the focus in most studies at this stage has been on what meaning relations the child encodes with the minimal combinatorial power available; such analyses are available in Nelson (1973), Brown (1973), Bowerman (1973), and Bloom, Lightbown, and Hood (1975). For comparison with studies of normally developing children in Stage I, we have analyzed Rebecca's samples from 50 to 58 months of age. During this period, her MLU ranged from 1.2 to 1.8, her SMU from 1.3 to 2.0, and her upper bound was 5 morphemes.

Stage II covers MLU 2.0 to 2.5, with an upper bound of 7 morphemes at the mean MLU of 2.25 (Brown, 1973). Children, on average, traverse this stage between 24 and 30 months of age. Studies of normally developing children at this stage continue to focus on meaning relations. In addition, note is taken of the emergence of a few early functors and inflections; that endeavor continues up to and beyond Stage V. For comparison with Stage II children, we relied upon Rebecca's samples from 61 to 63 months. Her

TABLE 5.8
Utterance Length Statistics as a Function of Age in a Young Child with
Down Syndrome

Stage	Age in Months; Weeks	Brown MLU	UpperBound[a]	Spontaneous Mean Number of Morphemes per Utterance	Number of Spontaneous Utterances
I	50;1		3	1.57	35
	51;1	1.22	4	1.33	40
	53;0	1.21	4	1.43	102
	54;0	1.30	3	1.42	43
	55;0	1.36	4	1.49	286
	55;1	1.40	4	1.60	208
	56;2		5	1.88	123
	57;0	1.77	5	2.11	126
	57;2	1.60	5	1.93	194
	58;0	1.79	4	2.06	177
II	59;2	1.82	7	2.21	138
	61;0	2.03	8	2.31	192
	62;0	2.03	7	2.22	119
	63;0			2.61	
	64;0	2.30	8	2.85	222
III	65;0	2.42	9	3.04	128
	66;1	2.70	7	3.39	171
	67;0	2.70	9	3.37	350
	68;0	2.85	8	3.10	338
	69;0	2.39	8	3.16	585
	70;0	2.88	9	3.43	314
III/IV	71;0	2.52	13	3.51	304
	72;0	2.97	11	3.39	365
	73;0	2.64	10	3.48	151
	74;1	2.89	10	3.51	234
	75;1	2.73	13	3.52	293
IV	77;0	3.19	11	3.73	190
IV/V	78;0	3.55	14	4.34	166
	79;0	3.66	11	4.25	328
	80;0	3.02	18	3.98	369
	81;2			3.50	381
	82;2	2.86	10	3.52	525
	84;0	3.28	11	3.77	504
	86;1	4.45	16	4.45	502
	87;0	3.49	13	4.30	466
	89;0	3.21	16	4.19	479

[a]presented in morphemes; excludes lists.

MLU at this time was 2.0, her SMU ranged from 2.2 to 2.8, and her upper bound was 7 or 8 morphemes.

Stage III includes MLU 2.5 to 3.25, with an upper bound of 9 words at the mean MLU of 2.75. At this stage, most basic meaning relations have appeared and are used in conjunction with one another. Half a dozen grammatical morphemes are being used with 90% regularity; several others are being used erratically. It is at this point, when the child is between 30 and 36 months of age, that one can begin to track the development of such complex syntactic structures as negatives, wh-questions, and yes/no questions. The lack of verbal auxiliaries is a notable feature in these sentence types at this stage. This period is also notable for overgeneralizations such as *feets* or *goes*; it is a time when the child seems to be able to express whatever he or she wants, but in a "cute" childish fashion. For Stage III comparisons, we relied upon Rebecca's samples from 65 to 70 months, with an MLU ranging from 2.4 to 2.9, an SMU of 3.0 to 3.5, and an upper bound from 7 to 9 morphemes.

Stage IV covers MLU 3.25 to 3.75, with an upper bound of 11 words at the target value of 3.50. The 3-year-old child is typically at this stage and can form most negative and yes/no questions accurately, but has a way to go before full mastery of the intricacies of wh-questions. By the end of this stage, he or she has mastered 8 or 9 grammatical morphemes; most grammatical morphemes are supplied where required. The new feature at Stage IV is the embedding of one simple sentence within another, as in *I said you draw it*.

At this point, it becomes difficult to make direct comparisons between Rebecca and other children on the basis of utterance length alone. Between 71 and 75 months of age, Rebecca's MLU fluctuated between 2.5 and 2.9 (Stage III), her SMU varied between 3.5 and 3.7 (more like Stage IV), and her upper bound varied between 10 and 13 morphemes (also Stage IV). We refer to this period as Stage III/IV to indicate its intermediary status. In a later sample (77 months), all three measures converge on Stage IV assignment (SMU 3.7; MLU 3.2; upper bound 11); we use that sample for Stage IV comparisons.

Stage V covers MLU 3.75 to 4.25, with an upper bound of 13 at MLU 4.0. Once into this stage, the child (typically $3\frac{1}{2}$ years of age) can generally express what he or she needs to. MLU becomes more a measure of situational factors than of grammatical ability. Although the mastery of English grammar is not complete at this point, children at this level have strong mastery of most grammatical morphemes, supplying the first 14 90% of the time and producing auxiliaries appropriately in negative and interrogative constructions. There has been little longitudinal work beyond this level; at Stage V and beyond the child is considered to have mastered the basics of language (e.g., Crain & Fodor, in press). It is highly questionable whether Rebecca truly attained Stage V competence in the course of this study. Beyond the 77 month session, her utterance-length measures fluctuated erratically from MLU 2.9 to 5.6, SMU 3.5 to 4.5, and upper bound 10 to 16. For comparison purposes with studies in Stages IV and V, we have selected the last three sessions of the study: 86 to 89 months. In these samples MLU varied between 3.2 and 4.5, but SMU was consistently above 4.0 and upper bound was at least 13. These sessions are referred to as Stage IV/V.

Discussion of internal analyses divide naturally into two periods of development: (a) Stage I–III, and (b) Stages III and beyond.

Internal Analyses: Stages I–III

MLU.   After a slow start in early Stage I, Rebecca proceeded from Stage I to Stage III (55 to 66 months) in a strikingly normal fashion. On all measures taken, her growth was unremarkable both in rate and character. MLU progressed rapidly and consistently upward until attaining Stage III (refer to Fig. 5.1 for a comparison of Rebecca's MLU growth curves with those of normally developing children).

Thematic Relations.   Encoding of thematic relations progressed in an orderly fashion, although slightly in advance of other measures, including MLU. Usage of categories was consistent with that seen in Bloom's subjects; the only difference was a consistently greater reliance on Rebecca's part on nondevelopmental categories including stereotyped phrases, adverbs, and vocatives (see Fig. 5.2).

Rebecca's relative advantage in this area is particularly evident when one looks at the proportion of her multiword utterances expressing more than one thematic relation. By Stage II, Rebecca had attained or surpassed the level achieved by normally developing youngsters at the close of the study by Bloom, Lightbown, and Hood (1975). Rebecca continued to progress in this area, and by Stage III, had twice as many thematically complex utterances as her younger stage-matched peers (see Fig. 5.3).

Grammatical Morphology.   During Stages I–III, the first 4 of Brown's 14 grammatical morphemes were mastered to 90% criterion usage. These same 4 were the first acquired by each of Brown's three subjects, within comparable stages (refer to Fig. 5.4 to see growth on 14 grammatical morphemes). Growth curves for these same 4 individual morphemes were also calculated and are presented here. As can be seen in Fig. 5.5, Rebecca showed rapid mastery and consistent usage of *in* and *on* much like Eve, studied by Brown (1973). Her acquisition of the progressive *-ing* was more variable; again, this was also consistent with Brown's observations (see Fig. 5.6 for a comparison).

Syntactic Measures.   Rebecca's early negative and interrogative constructions paralleled normal acquisition, with a heavy reliance on intonation

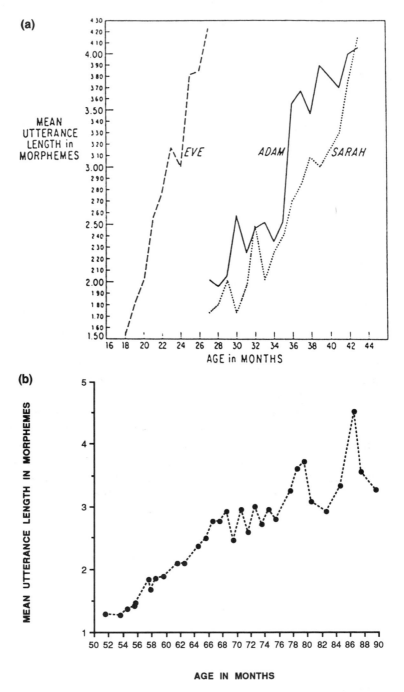

FIG. 5.1. Growth in mean utterance length in (a) three normally developing children studied by Brown, 1973, and in (b) Rebecca, a young child with Down syndrome. (Fig. 5.1a copied from *A First Language* by Roger Brown, 1973, Cambridge, MA: Harvard University Press. Copyright © 1973 by the President and Fellows of Harvard College. Reprinted by permission).

122

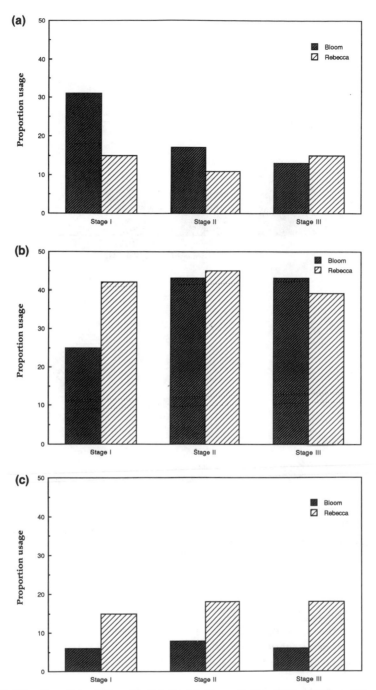

FIG. 5.2. Encoding of Thematic Relations in Normally Developing Children (Bloom, Lightbown, & Hood, 1975) and in Rebecca, a child with Down syndrome. (a) Functional categories (e.g., existence, recurrence, negation). (b) Verbal categories (e.g., actions, states). (c) Nondevelopmental categories (e.g., sterotype, routine, vocative).

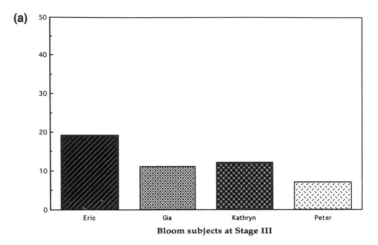

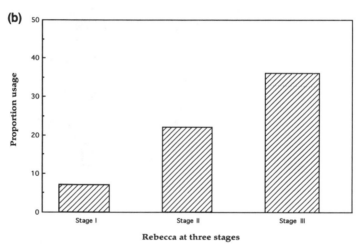

FIG. 5.3. Proportion of mulltiword utterances expressing more than one thematic relation in (a) four normally developing children studied by Bloom, Lightbown, and Hood (1975) and in (b) Rebecca, a young child with Down Syndrome.

(e.g., *I play this? This is yours?*), negative modals and the unadorned NOT (e.g., *I can't shut it, Her not go*), and a repertoire of unanalyzed wh-questions (e.g., *Where's NP? What's this?*). Examples of constructions at each stage are provided in Tables 5.9 through 5.11, together with comparison constructions collected by Bellugi (1967). During this period, there were no unusual or persistent overgeneralizations.

Internal Analyses: Stage III and Beyond

MLU.   Having achieved Stage III (MLU 3.5; 67 months), Rebecca's progress slowed sharply and began to differ in interesting respects. Growth

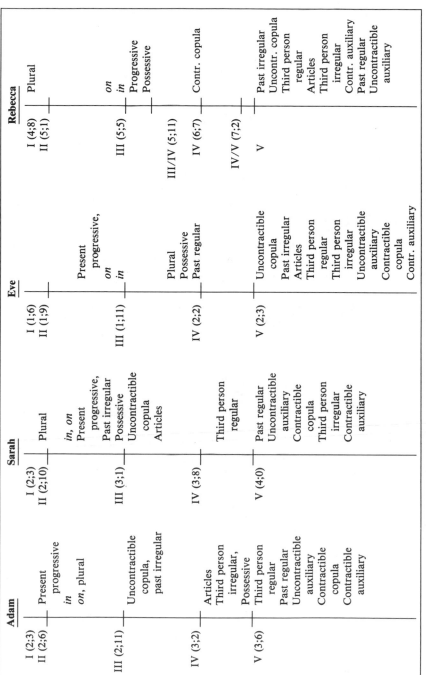

FIG. 5.4. The order of acquisition of 14 grammatical morphemes in three normally developing children studied by Brown, 1973, and in Rebecca, a young child with Down syndrome. Note: For all children, morphemes included below Stage V had not attained the 90% criterion at that point. (Adapted from *A First Language* by Roger Brown, 1973, Cambridge, MA: Harvard University Press. Copyright © 1973 by the President and Fellows of Harvard College. Reprinted by permission.)

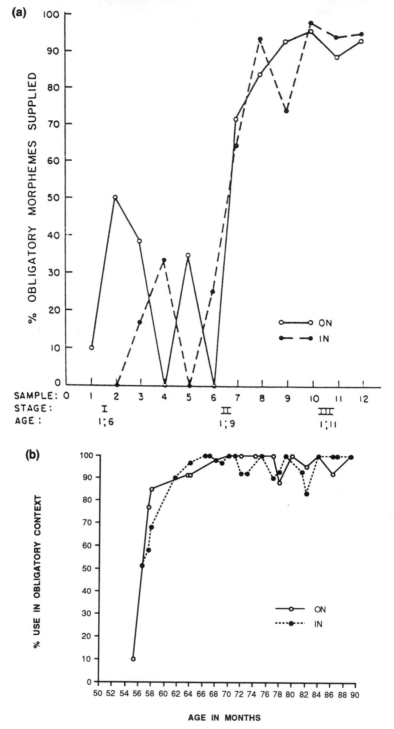

FIG. 5.5. Development of the prepositions *in* and *on* in (a) Eve, a normally developing child studied by Brown, 1973, and (b) Rebecca, a young child with Down syndrome. (Fig. 5.6a copied from *A First Language* by Roger Brown, 1973, Cambridge, MA: Harvard University Press. Copyright © 1973 by the President and Fellows of Harvard College. Reprinted by permission.)

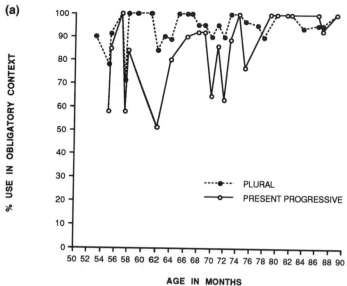

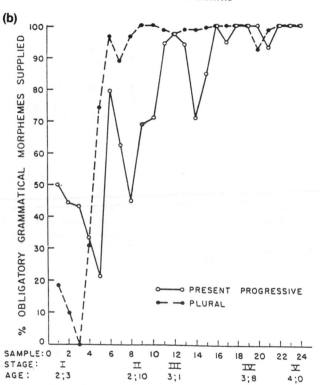

FIG. 5.6. Development of progressive and plural inflections in (a) Sarah, a normally developing child studied by Brown, 1973, and (b) Rebecca, a young child with Down syndrome. (Fig. 5.6a copied from *A First Language* by Roger Brown, 1973, Cambridge, MA: Harvard University Press. Copyright © 1973 by the President and Fellows of Harvard College. Reprinted by permission.

TABLE 5.9
Examples of Yes-No Questions Produced by Normally Developing Children, Studied by Bellugi (1967), and by Rebecca, a Child with Down Syndrome

Bellugi Subjects	Rebecca

Late Stage I

Bellugi Subjects	Rebecca
Fraser water?/	ə draw babies?/
Mommy eggnog?/	Play with it?/
See hole?/	Put your face?/
I ride train?/	My do it?/
Have some?/	Maxie going?/
Sit chair?/	Mommy cooking?/
No eat?/	Rebecca sit mommy's lap?/
Ball go?/	Eric watch t.v.?/

Stage III

Bellugi Subjects	Rebecca
See my doggie?/	Things in here?/
That black too?/	This is for you?/
Mom pinch finger?/	I play this?/
You want eat?/	You have a sister?/
I have it?/	I take?/
This can't write a flower?/	Is your name Raggedy Ann?/

Stage III/IV

Bellugi Subjects	Rebecca
Does the kitty stand up?/	You make it?/
Does lions walk?/	Binky, you talk?/
Is mommy talking to Robin's . . ./	I have phone now?/
Did I see that book?/	Mommy, I pour milk in here?/
Are going to make it with me?/	It's at your house?/
Will you help me?/	This is yours?/
Can I have a piece of paper?/	Do you?/
Can't it be a bigger truck?/	Can you leave that?/
Can't you work this thing?/	Will you carry me over snow?/

Stage IV/V

Bellugi Subjects	Rebecca
	Could I sit down next to Esther?/
	'n can I have some food?/
	These be good right here?/
	You feeling all right?/
	Now play dolls?/
	You want something to eat?/
	It's done?/

TABLE 5.10
Examples of wh-Questions Produced by Normally Developing Children, Studied by Bellugi (1967), and by Rebecca, a Child with Down Syndrome

Bellugi Subjects	*Rebecca*

Late Stage I

Who that?/	(What)'s that?/
Why?/	What a book name?/
What(s) that?/	How many in there?/
What cowboy doing?/	How 'bout this one?/
Where Ann pencil?/	Where are you?/
Where Momma boot?/	Where is it?/
Where kitty?/	Where taperecorder?/
Where milk go?/	Where the people?/
Where horse go?/	Mommy where they are where are scissors?/

Stage III

Where my mitten?/	Where's Mommy?/
Where me sleep?/	Where's people?/
What book name?/	Where her sit?/
What me think?/	What that?/
What soldier marching?/	What happened?/
Why you smiling?/	Where is it?/
Why you waking me up?/	What's Chris on here?/
Why not he eat?/	
Why not me sleeping?/	
Why not me drink it?/	

Stage III/IV

Where small trailer he should pull?/	Where's parking lot?/
Where I should put it . . ./	Now what's he go?/
Where the other toe will drive?/	Where's this little one sit/
Where's his other eye?/	Where was he?/
Where my spoon goed?/	Where is mailbox?/
What I did yesterday?/	What's Pat's phone number?/
What did you does?/	What's you want for your ice cream?/
What you have in your mouth?/	What's her want?/

(continued)

TABLE 5.10 *(Continued)*

Bellugi Subjects	Rebecca

Stage III/IV

Why the Christmas tree going?/   What's this called?/
Why kitty can't stand up?/   What's that kid you got on
Why Paul caught it?/   your hand?/
Which way they should go?/   What you writing for?/
How he can be a doctor?/   Who wants pizza?/
How that opened?/   What large?/

Stage IV/V

How much in?/
Where it goes?/
Where's purple in here?/
Who's eighteen?/
Where's food play with this?/
Where this go?/
What this be?/
'bout some more/
What's you gonna bring it Mom?
  20 minutes?/
When it's done yet?/
What's you want for some to eat?/
Which color for her shoes?/

in MLU ceased altogether for 10 months; further gains were offset by large and erratic shifts downward, varying as much as .85 morphemes/utterance between two sessions (see Fig. 5.1). Although by the end of the study (89 months) she had achieved an MLU as high as 4.45, it was not at all clear whether she would maintain this level.

Grammatical Morphology. Despite the promising start in Stages I through III, Rebecca made little further progress during the rest of the observation period. Over the 22 months from the onset of Stage III to the end of the study (at 89 months), Rebecca had mastered only one additional grammatical marker: the contractible copula (e.g., *it's gone*) and even that morpheme was not used altogether accurately. Despite its consistent appearance in appropriate contexts, leading to a high score on Fig. 5.4, the copula was also used in a wide variety of inappropriate contexts. (Note, for example: *she's eat; what's you want; mommy's go water*). This overgeneralization persisted throughout the entire period from 67 to 89 months. A further point of potential interest concerns the fact that other, earlier

TABLE 5.11
Examples of Negative Constructions Produced by Normally
Developing Children, Studied by Bellugi (1967), and by Rebecca, a
Child with Down Syndrome.

Bellugi Subjects	*Rebecca*

Late Stage I

Bellugi Subjects	Rebecca
More . . . no/	No read it/
No singing song/	No Easter/
No the sun shining/	No top/
No money/	No feet/
No sit there/	No • Carol's/
No play that/	No • me this one/
No fall/	Not Anne Mowrer picture/
No heavy/	Not me • Eric/
No want stand head/	No sit on table/
No Mom sharpen it/	Can't open it/
No Fraser drink all tea/	

Stage III

Bellugi Subjects	Rebecca
I can't catch you/	I can't shut it/
I can't see you/	I can't put it on her/
We can't talk/	Don't color/
I don't sit on Cromer coffee	Don't want it book/
I don't want it/	Don't put your hand in/
I don't like him/	No . . . that is trunk/
No . . . Rusty hat/	No color/
Book say no/	No hug/
Touch the snow no/	These not staying/
Don't leave me/	I not ready/
Don't wait for me . . . come in/	You got no curly hair/
That not "O," that blue/	She's no shoes/
That no fish school/	No monsters ride/
That no Mommy/	No holes/
There no squirrels/	Anne, this thing won't work/
He no bite you/	Nobody in there/
I no want envelope/	Not anyone's room/
I no taste them/	

(continued)

TABLE 5.11 (Continued)

Bellugi Subjects	*Rebecca*

Stage III/IV

Paul can't have one/	We can't play/
This can't stick/	I don't have broccoli/
I didn't did it/	Not you eyes closed • I like
I don't want cover on it/	your eyes open/
You didn't caught me/	I not cheat, AF/
I didn't see something/	I not get Pat yet/
Cause he won't let go/	Her not fall or anything/
No, it isn't/	No, I can't make it • AF does/
That was not me/	It's not funny • it's not/
I am not a doctor/	Miss Piggy's don't have cold/
This not ice cream/	We didn't have popsicle, we
This is no good/	have ice cream cone/
Paul not tired/	Ellen's not being good/
I not crying/	Her not talk, her clap/
He not taking the walls down/	Her not fit in there/
Don't put the two wings on/	Her's not sit too well/
I not hurt him/	Not for you/
I not see you anymore/	I not get these at store/
Ask me if I not made mistake/	Not start with that point . . ./
	Don't need anymore/
	Pat's not call me/

Stage IV/V

	'cause we can't open them/
	I don't need brown/
	Look - this doesn't work/
	'n tree . . . not no witch can't
	have any cookies/
	The count say she can't
	have any cookies/
	I not brought anything/
	Esther did not bring anything/
	Dog didn't ate it/
	Don't open it/
	It's not a message/
	I'm not/
	I not [i.e., won't] get it/

acquired, grammatical morphemes were now being used inconsistently. Whereas Brown (1973) reported that "once a curve has passed above the 90% line for several consecutive sessions, it levels off within a range of 90 and 100 percent" (p. 258), this failed to hold for Rebecca. For all but one of the six morphemes meeting this criterion, percentage correct dropped below 80% at some later point.

Syntactic Measures.   Beyond 67 months of age, Rebecca also failed to make further progress in mastering negative and interrogative constructions. Between 67 and 89 months of age, the auxiliary system underlying mature constructions, involving subject–auxiliary inversion and do-support, was almost totally lacking in Rebecca's grammar. Only in the final session were there clear signs of further progress in this domain. Once again, a persistent overgeneralization was apparent. In this case, the term *what* served to introduce most wh-questions, largely replacing other wh-terms *when, where, how*. For example, *what's you go?* was used to ask about location, and in *what's you gonna bring it, Mom? 20 minutes?* the omnibus wh-form is used to replace *when*.

Discussion

In this study, we examined language learning under conditions of cognitive impairment, seeking to determine what aspects are subject to variability (causing a slowdown) and what remain constant (causing "no deviance"). To this end, we examined growth in language in a young child with Down syndrome with a focus on the character of the language-learning curves and the appearance of overgeneralizations. We juxtaposed two hypotheses:

1. On the one hand, we considered whether language learning might proceed from a single accretion of information over time; this would be supported if learning curves are simply flatter than those of normally developing children.

2. In contrast to this possibility, we considered whether language learning might be better characterized as a series of stages in which the available information is reorganized and resystematized by learners over the course of cognitive-linguistic growth; we suggested this might be evident if periods of relative growth were interspersed with periods of no growth. By examining individual learning curves, and taking note of unusual overgeneralizations, we were specifically interested in the modifiability of rule learning. Finally, following up on Study I, we asked whether learning curves for different facets of development (e.g., MLU) would develop with the same synchronicity as in the normal case.

In the case of Rebecca, a child with Down syndrome, the fundamental differences between Stages I through III and beyond III provide suggestive evidence in support of a *stage reorganizational* account of language development. Once she began to provide two words in a productive fashion, Rebecca's growth progressed upward at a nearly normal rate, despite the fact that she was 3 years late at the outset. Interestingly, her progress was unaffected up until the point where simple phrase structure grammar could no longer suffice to describe her linguistic system. She, like the adolescents discussed in Study I, stopped short of the point where she had to analyze and represent a complex auxiliary system in order to master the intricacies of interrogative and negative formation. That Rebecca stalled at a language level characteristic of many adolescents with Down syndrome suggests to us that their stopping point is not due to the arbitrary imposition of a critical period at adolescence, but is concomitant with some fundamental change in the grammar. We are following up this observation with further experimental work comparing children, with and without Down syndrome, at either side of this threshold. On both comprehension of syntactic structures and, particularly, imitation of auxiliary structures, both normal children and those few children with Down syndrome who do break the barrier display dramatic increases in performance level once beyond Stage III (Fowler, 1990).

The case of Rebecca also bears importantly on the shallow generalization hypothesis, which suggests that the delay of children with Down syndrome might result from the acquisition of the same facts as are normally acquired, but in smaller pieces. Rebecca's development cannot be simply characterized as a flatter, slowed-down version of the normal case, with smaller generalizations taking the place of the rules observed in the normal case. Rather, a drive to extract regularities in the input is evident in the nature of her errors, in her far-reaching overgeneralizations that cut across the grammar, in her growth curves for individual grammatical morphemes, and in the synchrony of her development (or lack of development) across grammatical categories. In short, the tendency to regularize remains strong even where cognition is impaired.

OVERALL DISCUSSION

The two studies presented focus on partial language learning in children with Down syndrome, a well-documented case of extreme language delay associated with a more general cognitive impairment. Whereas the data obtained are consistent with the prevailing view of retarded language as "delayed, without deviance," they provide an interesting perspective on how constraints on language learning may continue to exert an effect, even in the case of language failure.

An initial concern, much neglected in prior research on language impairment, was to characterize just how far language learning progresses and to consider what might preclude further development. Although it remains to be determined whether other children with language impairment, or even with Down syndrome, will stop at the same point as the children studied here, the slowdown at Stage III observed in both adolescents and a much younger child raises the possibility that linguistic factors are one important determinant in explaining a child's failure to progress. It is difficult to ignore the fact that the stopping point in this group of children precedes the dramatic growth in syntactic development that has captured the imagination of linguists. Although this break is implicitly adhered to in child language research (syntacticians study children from age 3 and up; early child language folks study children up to age 3), in the present research it gains some empirical validity as a possible and important difference in language representation.

Unfortunately, the present studies contribute little to the question concerning exactly what factors might preclude further development, and why it is that these children fail to surmount this particular linguistic obstacle. For, although it might be quite simple to implicate "retardation," this account was deemed most unsatisfying early on in the discussion. Although it was noted that children with Down syndrome suffer particular problems with memory and articulation, the role of these factors in explaining language impairment could not be fairly addressed in the present studies. Here, only language production was assessed; further research is required examining whether the obstacle is evident even when memory and production factors are minimized (see, for example, Miller, 1988). We can at least report that a simple-minded view of the role these factors play will probably not account for the delay. For one thing, children with Down syndrome also display problems with comprehension of syntax (see Fowler, 1990, for review). A more complicated view of how memory and articulation may play into language acquisition could, however, prove very interesting, both for individuals with Down syndrome and for the normal case. With regard to yet other explanations for failure to progress, we refer you to a discussion in Fowler (1988); there, it was clear that age, IQ, and language level all played a role in determining rate of language growth.

A second concern addressed in the present research was whether certain facets of language acquisition are relatively more disrupted than others by a general cognitive impairment. Despite the large disparity between MLU and both chronological age and mental age, and despite intensive efforts to find disparities within the linguistic system, the language levels were very coherent, with very little deviation one way or the other. Where there was failure to progress, the failure appeared to be across-the-board. For example, where Bellugi had observed broad application of the use of a new auxiliary form, we observed broad nonapplication. This internal coherence of syntactic development was supported in the longitudinal study as well. Rebecca, at any point in the study, was comparable to preschoolers going through the same process. Whereas both experiments provide suggestive evidence that there is a difference between semantic and syntactic domains consistent with the MA/MLU disparity, this bears further study with more clearly delineated semantic measures.

Where we had anticipated – and found – a distinction between open- and closed-class items, this split was not inconsistent with the normal developmental course. Adolescents with Down syndrome, like very young children, are lacking in closed-class items. However, perhaps because complex syntactic structures crucially depend on these closed-class items, it was not the case that the adolescents made progress in one without the other.

The third area of interest concerned the possibility of different strategies of acquisition to yield the same effect, but at a slower pace. As discussed previously, we did not find evidence in the present research to support such a hypothesis. Indeed, the extreme normalcy of Rebecca's growth from Stage I through III, combined with Dooley's (1977) analyses of two other children with Down syndrome in Stage I, provides compelling evidence for constraints on language acquisition. These longitudinal studies suggest that a child either moves forward normally or fails to move at all. It would appear that language does not readily lend itself to piecemeal acquisition. Despite her lack of success, the case of Rebecca, once within Stage III, suggests that even the most language-impaired child will try to extract broad regularities from the input. The kinds of mistakes Rebecca displayed in overgeneralizing *what* to cover all wh-terms and in applying the copula *'s* in situations where it clearly does not apply are, we suspect, not wholly aberrant. Indeed, we have since observed both of these overgeneralizations, for brief periods, in the first author's own children. Rather, what separates Rebecca from the normally developing 3-year-old may be the inability to recover from the error, to learn anew.

Though not a strategy per se, one characteristic of language in children with Down syndrome does bear further mention. In both Study I and Study II, it was noted that once a structure was acquired, it was inconsistently applied. This particular observation is consistent with clinical report, but has not been addressed formally. Although we currently have no clear account for either this behavior or what effect it might have in making further progress toward linguistic mastery, it is clearly a replicable phenomenon that demands an explanation.

In summary, the story of language learning in children with Down syndrome is wholly consistent with the view that the language-learning process exerts a well-defined influence on the grammars a child will construct. Whereas a fully specified grammar clearly depends on an intact cognitive-linguistic system in order to move forward, it does appear that, in this group anyway, whatever forward progress is made or even attempted is governed by constraints on the learning process; the cases presented here do not permit alternate learning strategies. Finally, and most interestingly, the story of language learning in children with Down syndrome raises the possibility that cognitive factors may play an important role in advancing, or even reorganizing, the grammatical system. A slowdown at Stage III adds credence to the sense that there is a major stumbling block in language acquisition that needs to be addressed in syntactic theory and in theories of normal language development. We suspect that a focus on this stumbling block — this failure to progress — will force attention on the mechanisms of language growth and may yield important insight into the relation between language and cognition.

ACKNOWLEDGMENTS

The data presented here were presented by the first author in a doctoral thesis submitted to the University of Pennsylvania. Portions of these data have been presented at the Boston University Conference on Child Language Development (Fowler, Gelman, & Gleitman, 1980) and at the Society for Research in Child Development (Fowler, 1985; Fowler, Gleitman, & Gelman, 1981). We are grateful to the administrators, teachers, children, and parents of St. Katherine's Day School, whose cooperation made this work possible, to the many undergraduates who helped with data collection, transcription, and analysis, and to members of the research groups who discussed this work so intensively. Beneficial comments on earlier versions of this chapter were provided by Leslie Rescorla, Renee Baillargeon, and Marjorie Beeghly; Brain Doherty provided much appreciated assistance with the tables and references. The research was supported by a Program Project Grant (NICHHD 1 PO-HD-10965) to D. Premack, R. Gelman, and D. Kemler and by a grant (12-113) from the March of Dimes Birth Defects Foundation to R. Gelman, L. Gleitman, and A. Fowler. The chapter was written during the first author's tenure as a Science Scholar for the National Down Syndrome Society.

REFERENCES

Beeghly, M., Weiss-Perry, B., & Cicchetti, D. (1990). Beyond sensorimotor functioning: Early communicative and play development of children with Down syndrome. In D. Cicchetti & M. Beeghly (Eds.), *Children with Down syndrome: A developmental perspective* (pp. 329–368). Cambridge, MA: Cambridge University Press.

Bellugi, U. (1967). *The acquisition of negation.* Unpublished doctoral dissertation, Harvard University, Cambridge.

Bishop, D. V. M., & Edmundson, A. (1987). Language impaired 4-year-olds: Distinguishing transient from persistent impairment. *Journal of Speech and Hearing Disorders, 52,* 156–173.

Bleile, K., & Schwartz, I. (1984). Three perspectives on the speech of children with Down syndrome. *Journal of Communication Disorders, 17,* 87–94.

Bloom, L. (1970). *Language development: Form and function in emerging grammars.* Cambridge, MA: M.I.T. Press.

Bloom, L. (1973). *One word at a time.* The Hague: Mouton.

Bloom, L., Lightbown, P., & Hood, L. (1975). Structure and variation in child language. *Monograph of the Society for Research in Child Development, 40*(2).

Bloom, L., Miller, P., & Hood, L. (1975). Variation and reduction as aspects of competence in language development. In A. Pick (Ed.), *Minnesota symposium on child language* (pp. 3–55). Minneapolis: University of Minnesota Press.

Bowerman, M. (1973). *Early syntactic development.* Cambridge: Cambridge University Press.

Bowerman, M. (1982). Reorganizational processes in lexical and syntactic development. In E. Wanner & L. Gleitman (Eds.), *Language acquisition: The state of the art.* Cambridge, MA: Cambridge University Press.

Brown, R. (1973). *A first language.* Cambridge, MA: Harvard University Press.

Carr, J. (1988). Six weeks to twenty-one years old: A longitudinal study of children with Down's syndrome and their families. *Journal of Child Psychology and Psychiatry, 29*(4), 407–431.

Crain, S., & Fodor, J. (in press). Competence and performance in child language. In E. Dromi (Ed.), *Language and cognition: A developmental perspective.* Norwood, NJ: Ablex.

Cromer, R. F. (1972). Learning of linguistic surface structure cues to deep structure by educationally subnormal children. *American Journal of Mental Deficiency, 77,* 346–353.

Cromer, R. F. (1974). Receptive language in the mentally retarded. In R. L. Schiefelbusch & L. L. Lloyd (Eds.) Language perspectives: acquisition, retardation and intervention. Baltimore: University Park Press.

Crosley, P., & Dowling, S. (1989). The relationship between cluster and liquid simplification and sentence length, age, and IQ in Down's syndrome children. *Journal of Communication Disorders, 22,* 151–168.

Dennis, M., & Whitaker, H. A. (1977). Hemispheric equipotentiality and language acquisition. In S. J. Segalowitz, & F. A. Gruber (Eds.), *Language development and neurological theory.* New York: Academic Press.

deVilliers, J., & deVilliers, P. (1978). A cross-sectional study of the acquisition of grammatical morphemes in child speech. In L. Bloom (Ed.), *Readings in language development.* New York: Wiley.

Dooley, J. (1977). *Language acquisition and Down's Syndrome: A Study of Early Semantics and Syntax.* Unpublished doctoral dissertation, Harvard University, Cambridge.

Feldman, H., Goldin-Meadow, S., & Gleitman, L. (1978). Beyond Herodotus: The creation of language by linguistically deprived deaf children. In A. Lock (Ed.), *Action, symbol, and gesture: The emergence of language.* New York: Academic Press.

Fowler, A. (1984). *Language acquisition in Down's syndrome children: Production and comprehension.* Unpublished doctoral dissertation, University of Pennsylvania, Philadelphia.

Fowler, A. (1985, April). *The acquisition of syntax by a Down syndrome child: A longitudinal case study.* Poster presented at the Biennial Meeting of the Society for Research in Child Development, Toronto.

Fowler, A. (1988). Determinants of rate of language growth in children with Down Syndrome: A longitudinal investigation. In L. Nadel (Ed.), *The psychobiology of Down syndrome.* Cambridge, MA: Bradford/MIT Press.

Fowler, A. (1990). Language abilities in children with Down syndrome: Evidence for a specific syntactic delay. In D. Cicchetti & M. Beeghly (Eds.), *Down syndrome: The developmental perspective.* New York: Cambridge University Press.

Fowler, A., Gelman, R., & Gleitman, R. (1980, October). *A comparison of normal and retarded language as a function of MLU.* Paper presented at the 5th Annual Boston Child Language Conference., Boston MA.

Fowler, A., Gleitman, L., & Gelman, R. (1981, April). *Towards a characterization of delay without deviance in retarded language acquisition.* Paper presented at the Symposium on Individual Differences at the Biennial Meeting of the Society for Research in Child Development, Boston.

Gathercole, S., & Baddeley, A. (1989). The role of phonological memory in normal and disordered language development. In C. v. Euler, I. Lundberg, & G. Lennerstrand (Eds.), *Brain and Reading*. New York: MacMillan Press.

Gibson, D. (1978). *Down's syndrome: The psychology of mongolism*. London: Cambridge University Press.

Gleitman, L. (1984). Biological predispositions to learn language. In P. Marler & H. Terrace (Eds.), *Dahlem konferenzem*. New York: Springer-Verlag.

Gleitman, L., Newport, E., & Gleitman, H. (1984). The current status of the Motherese hypothesis. *Journal of child Language, 11*, 43–79.

Gleitman, L. R., & Wanner, E. (1982). Language acquisition: The state of the art. In E. Wanner & L. R. Gleitman (Eds.), *Language acquisition: The state of the art* (pp. 3–48). New York: Cambridge University Press.

Graham, N. C., & Gulliford, R. A. (1968). A psychological approach to the language deficiencies of educationally subnormal children. *Educational Review, 20*, 136–145.

Haber, L., & Maloney, C. (1978). Linguistic development in mentally retarded children. In D. Farkas et al. (Eds.), *Papers from the 14th regional meeting of the Chicago Linguistics Society*. Chicago: University of Chicago Press.

Hamburger, H., & Crain, S. (1982). Relative acquisition. In S. Kucjaz (Ed.), *Language development: Vol. 1. Syntax and semantics*. Hillsdale, NJ: Lawrence Erlbaum Associates.

Johnston, J. (1988). Specific language disorders in the child. In N. Lass, L. McReynolds, J. Northern, & D. Yoder (Eds.), *Handbook of speech-language pathology and audiology* (pp. 685–715). Philadelphia: B. Decker.

Karmiloff-Smith, A. (1979). *Language as a formal problem space for children*. Nijmegen: Max. Planck Gesellschaft.

Kean, M. L. (1977). The linguistic interpretation of aphasic syndromes: Agramatism in Broca's aphasia, an example. *Cognition, 5*, 9–46.

Klima, E., & Bellugi, U. (1966). Syntactic regularities in the speech of children. In A. Reibel & S. A. Schane (Eds.), *Modern studies in English* (pp. 448–466). Englewood Cliffs, NJ: Prentice-Hall.

Lackner, J. (1968). A developmental study of language behavior in retarded children. In D. M. Morehead & A. E. Morehead (Eds.), *Normal and deficient child language*. Baltimore: University Park Press.

Landau, B., & Gleitman, L. (1985). *Language and experience: Evidence from the blind child*. Cambridge, MA: Harvard University Press.

Lenneberg, E. H., Nichols, I. A., & Rosenberger, E. F. (1964). Primitive stages of language development in mongolism. *Research Publications, Association for Research in Nervous and Mental Disease, 42*, 119–147.

Marcell, M. M., & Weeks, S. L. (1988). Short-term memory difficulties and Down's syndrome. *Journal of Mental Deficiency Research, 32*, 153–162.

Mein, R. (1961). A study of the oral vocabularies of severely subnormal patients. *Journal of Mental Deficiency Research., 5*, 52–62.

Menyuk, P. (1969). *Sentences children use*. Cambridge, MA: MIT Press.

Miller, J. F. (1980). *Assessing language production in children: Experimental procedures*. Baltimore: University Park Press.

Miller, J. F. (1987). Language and communication characteristics of children with Down syndrome. In S. Pueschel, C. Tinghey, J. Rynders, A. Crocker, & C. Crutcher (Eds.), *New perspectives on Down syndrome* (pp. 233–262). Baltimore: Brookes Publishing.

Miller, J. F. (1988). The developmental asynchrony of language development in children with Down Syndrome. In L. Nadel (Ed.), *The psychobiology of Down syndrome* (pp. 167–198). Cambridge, MA: MIT Press.

Nadel, L. (1988). *The Psychobiology of Down Syndrome*. Cambridge, MA: MIT Press.

Nelson, K. (1973). Structure and strategy in learning to talk. *Monograph of the Society for Research in Child Development*, *38* (Serial 149).

Newport, E. (1981). Constraints on structure: Evidence from American Sign Language and language learning. In W. A. Collins (Ed.), *Aspects of the development of competence. Minnesota Symposia on Child Psychology* (pp. 93–124). Hillsdale, NJ: Lawrence Erlbaum Associates.

Newport, E. L. (1982). Task specificity in language learning? Evidence from speech perception and American Sign Language. In E. Wanner & L. R. Gleitman (Eds.), *Language acquisition: The state of the art.* (pp. 450–520). Cambridge, MA: Cambridge University Press.

Newport, E. L., Gleitman, H., & Gleitman, L. (1977). Mother, I'd rather do it myself: Some effects and noneffects of maternal speech style. In C. E. Snow & C. A. Ferguson (Eds.), *Talking to children: Language input and acquisition.* Cambridge MA: Cambridge University Press.

Pueschel, S. (1988). Visual and auditory processing in children with Down Syndrome. In L. Nadel (Ed.), *The psychobiology of Down syndrome* (pp. 199–216). Cambridge, MA: MIT Press.

Rescorla, L. (1989). The language development survey: A screening tool for delayed language in toddlers. *Journal of Speech and Hearing Disorders*, *54*, 587–599.

Rescorla, L. & Schwartz, E. (1990). Outcome of toddlers with specific expressive language delay. *Applied Psycholinguistics*, *11*, 393–408.

Ryan, J. (1975). Mental subnormality and language development. In E. Lenneberg & E. Lenneberg (Eds.), *Foundations of language development.* New York: Academic Press.

Sankoff, G., & Laberge, S. (1973). On the acquisition of native speakers by a language. *Kivung*, *6*, 32–47.

Scarborough, H. S. (1990). Measuring syntactic development: The Index of Productive Syntax. *Applied Psycholinguistics*, *11*, 1–22.

Scarborough, H. S., Rescorla, L., Tager-Flusberg, H., Fowler, A. E., & Sudhalter, V. (1991). The relation of utterance length to grammatical complexity in normal and language-disordered groups. *Applied Psycholinguistics*, *12*(1), 23–45.

Seagoe, M. V. (1965). Verbal development in a mongoloid. *Exceptional Children*, *31*, 269–273.

Semmel, M. I., & Dolley, D. G. (1971). Comprehension and imitation of sentences by Down's syndrome children as a function of transformational complexity. *American Journal of Mental Deficiency*, *75*, 739–745.

Share, J., Koch, R., Webb, A., & Graliker, B. (1964). The longitudinal development of infants and young children with Down's Syndrome (mongolism). *American Journal of Mental Deficiency*, *68*, 685.

Shipley, E., Smith, C., & Gleitman, L. (1969). A study in the acquisition of language: Free responses to commands. *Language*, *45*, 322–342.

Slobin, D. I. (1980). The repeated path between transparency and opacity in language. In U. Bellugi & M. Studdert-Kennedy (Eds.), *Signed and spoken language: Biological constraints on linguistic form.* (pp. 229–243). Dahlem Konferenzem, Weinheim: Verlag Chemie GmbH.

Thal, D., Bates, E., & Bellugi, U. (1989). Language and cognition in two children with Williams syndrome. *Journal of Speech and Hearing Research*, *32*, 489–500.

Varnhagen, C. K., Das, J. P., & Varnhagen, S. (1987). Neurological and visual memory span: Cognitive processing by TMR individuals with Down syndrome and other etiologies. *American Journal of Mental Deficiency*, *91*(4), 398–405.

Wisniewsk, K. E., Miezejeski, C. M., & Hill, A. L. (1988). Neurological and psychological status of individuals with Down syndrome. In L. Nadel (Ed.), *The psychobiology of Down syndrome* (pp. 315–343). Cambridge, MA: MIT Press.

6 A Case Study of Dissociations Between Language and Cognition

Richard Cromer
MRC Cognitive Development Unit

It is with some trepidation that I undertake the writing of this chapter on an unusual case of dissociation between language and intellectual abilities. The case concerns a condition often referred to as *chatterbox syndrome* or *cocktail-party syndrome*. However, for any of the claims to make sense at all, it must first be established that the individual not only talks excessively, but does so in a fluent fashion, using, at the very least, syntactic forms appropriately. The few times I have presented this material at conferences or in university departments, I have been able to show selected portions of interviews with the woman discussed herein on videotape. No one who has seen these has failed to be overwhelmed by the fluency of speech, its appropriateness, its complex syntactic forms, its correct use of semantic constraints, the extensive vocabulary, and the extraordinary skill with which the speaker uses normal pragmatic devices. The problem is how to convey this in written form. I use some extracts of the recorded spontaneous speech, although this is a poor substitute for being able to hear and view the individual.

In recent years, one of the more controversial issues in the acquisition of language has been the extent to which general cognitive development plays a part in that acquisition. One generally accepted notion has been the hypothesis of cognitive prerequisites for language, in which it is claimed that young children cannot even begin to acquire aspects of language until particular cognitive developments have occurred. This position was strongly advocated by the Piagetian school of development (for arguments pro and con, see Piattelli-Palmarini, 1980). This position has been questioned by linguists and some psycholinguists who see language, or some aspects of language, as being modular and, therefore, possibly encapsulated from more general cognitive functioning. A close examination of cases where a dissociation exists between language and more general cognitive functioning—where excellent language ability exists despite severe mental retardation and disability—could be very revealing. At the very least, close inspection of these processes may tell us which more general processes, if any, are necessary for language acquisition to proceed.

Furthermore, an examination of language itself in such cases may shed light on what may be modular in what is broadly called *language*. For example, does modularity apply only to the core syntax? Or does it apply to the language system in a broader sense, as in Shallice's (1988) notion of "isolable subsystems" seen from a neurological point of view, in which modularity is defined by which aspects of language are impaired by specific neurological damage? Or is modularity narrower even than the syntax itself, as seems to be the case in Fodor's (1983) discussion of modularity? At the present time, different researchers mean very different things by the term *modularity*, both in its scope and in its theoretical foundations (e.g., total encapsulation or not, etc.). Cases in which language has developed normally in relative "isolation" from general cognitive abilities may help to sharpen our definitions.

One interesting condition in which these issues can be studied is called chatterbox syndrome or cocktail-party syndrome. In addition to internal hydrocephaly, some children suffering from spina bifida have been reported by clinicians to talk excessively. It has often been claimed that the language of these children, if they are mentally retarded, is lacking in content. Early studies (e.g., Taylor, 1959) described these children in their preschool years as shining in their verbal fluency: "Most of them have an impressive vocabulary of 'big' words . . . Some have a tendency to talk like grown-ups" (p. 219). Hadenius, Hagberg, Hyttnas-Bensch, and Sjogren (1962), in a study of 23 hydrocephalic children, found 6 in whom mental retardation was observed along with "a peculiar contrast between a good ability to learn words and talk, and not knowing what they are talking about" (p. 118). They went on to describe these children as loving to chatter but thinking illogically, and they coined the term *cocktail-party syndrome* for the condition. Ingram and Naughton (1962) described 16 cerebral palsy patients with arrested hydrocephalus, 9 of whom fit this description. Their parents had often commented on the disparity between what the child could do and what he or she could say. Ingram and Naughton described the children as "chatterboxes," "excessively talkative," or "bletherers"; the term *chatterbox syndrome* has also come to be used to describe these hyperverbal children.

Tew (1979) studied 49 cases of spina bifida children born in South Wales between 1964 and 1966. A child was classified as showing cocktail-party syndrome only if he or she met stringent criteria that Tew set. Tew found that 20 of the 49 (40.8%) met his criteria. These 20 children were then compared to the remaining 29 spina bifida, non-cocktail-party-syndrome children, as well as to a group of normal controls of normal intelligence (mean IQ = 106), matched for sex, place in family, social class, and area of residence. The intriguing finding was that cocktail-party syndrome was diagnostically indicative of low intelligence. The interesting differences are between the two subgroups of spina bifida children. Those children classified as evidencing cocktail party syndrome scored between 26 and 32 IQ points lower than the other spina bifida children on all three measures of IQ (verbal, performance, and full scale).

These are the kinds of studies that have been reported on this unusual phenomenon, and it seemed worth pursuing investigations of such individuals in the light of more recent linguistic theory. If we now turn to the case which is referred to here as *D. H.*, we find two questions that must be raised and answered before the case can be assessed in terms of what it might or might not show about modularity:

1. Are the cognitive and intellectual abilities so limited?
2. Is the language really so startlingly advanced, or is it some sort of artifact (long-term echolalia, etc.)?

Only when these two issues have been dealt with adequately can the problems about modularity be addressed.

INTELLECTUAL ABILITIES

It is certainly the case that D. H. performed poorly on all the standardized tests that were administered. Here, mention is made of well-known standardized tests that have been given over the past years, although the pattern for a variety of other tests we have administered is identically poor. Her WISC-R (Wechsler, 1974) showed a verbal IQ of only 57, a performance score which was below any scalable level, and a full-scale IQ of 44. To give a feeling of what such performance means, D. H. cannot put three pictures in an order that tells a simple "story." On tests of information, although, she could tell us which finger was the thumb, that bacon comes from the pig, and, with difficulty, the seasons of the year; this was about the limit of her knowledge. (This contrasts dramatically with the "impression" D. H. gives when one is engaged in conversation with her.) Her scores on simple arithmetic problems were very poor, although she did get one or two of the simplest items correct. Attempts to put simple jigsaw-like pieces together to form a simple object (object assembly subtest) ended in complete failure. She showed no ability to encode simple designs on a pattern of blocks. She was unable to carry out adequately a task in which numbers are to be replaced with a standard set of symbols printed in full view. Her digit span scores were poor. Digit span is usually taken by psychologists and neurologists as a simple short-term memory test. The individual must repeat back digits read out at a standard rate. D. H.'s limits were four digits forward and only two digits backward.

It should be noted that on all of these tasks, D. H. was happily engaged with the experimenters and gave the appearance of someone who felt as though she wasn't doing too badly. On the other hand, it should also be noted that when problems were beyond her ability, she would cheerily say, "I don't know that one; I really don't know that one."

On a variety of other standardized developmental tests, D. H. performed equally poorly. For example, she was almost unscorable on the Columbia Mental Maturity Scale, which requires choosing the odd one out among a series of either three or five drawings (Burgemeister, Blum, & Lorge, 1972). She could not perform even at the most basic level on the Wisconsin Card Sorting task (Heaton, 1981).

Our worry at this point, considering the impression D. H. gives of being much brighter than these tests indicate, is that some other explanation for her apparently low intelligence were possible—for example, that she has some inability to perform on standardized tests where one must "stand back" and contemplate the test items in a reflective manner. However, further testing and observations led us to believe that this is not the case.

We decided to administer a new type of intelligence test that does not require this kind of reflectivity. In our research unit, Mike Anderson had been developing a version of what is called an *inspection time task* (Anderson, 1988). In this version, the subject watches a video monitor. A space creature appears for a very brief interval. It has antennae that are either identical in length or different in length. The subject's task is merely to state (by pressing an appropriate button) whether the antennae were the same or different in size. Note that all subjects can perform perfectly on the task given a long enough inspection time. It is only when the time of the appearance on the screen (inspection time) is decreased that errors begin to occur, and one can adjust this until the subject is showing chance performance. In other words, this task is a measure of perceptual uptake, an index of neural efficiency. Such a measure is particularly useful with retarded children because neural efficiency is the foundation of later intelligent behavior.

Anderson took his equipment to the hospital school where D. H. was currently in attendance. Once again, she performed at the most retarded levels; she showed no evidence of increased intelligent behavior even on a task that required no reflectivity. Furthermore, she showed poor performance on a task that measures neural efficiency.

It has been noted that D. H. can perform a number of tasks that require "reflectivity." For example, she performed normally or nearly normally on some tasks that were not directly testing intellectual abilities. Examples include a hierarchical drawing task in which the subject must draw a figure in a preordained hierarchical order—a task some aphasic children find impossible (Cromer, 1983). We also found that she performed in a reasonable way on Shallice's *Cognitive Estimates Test* (Shallice, personal communication), where strange questions are asked, such as "How much does a pint of milk weigh," or "How many slices are there in a loaf of bread?" Some brain-damaged patients give bizarre answers to these questions. D. H.'s answers were all normal and acceptable.

D. H. could easily do word association tasks (cf. Pietro & Goldfarb, 1985), although her answers were like a younger child with mainly syntagmatic, rather than paradigmatic, replies. Finally, she was able to perform appropriately on the *other minds* task. This is a task developed by Wimmer and Perner (1983) in which the person must give evidence of understanding that other minds can have false beliefs. This is successfully accomplished by normal 4-year-olds, but is failed by a majority of autistic children with a mental age of 9 (Baron-Cohen, Leslie, & Frith, 1985).

There is evidence, therefore, that D. H. can perform tasks that require reflectivity but do not require traditional intellectual content. But there is an even more compelling reason to feel that she really is intellectually impaired; this is simply the evidence of her everyday activities. When we began to study her abilities at the age of 14 (and it is still the case), she had no ability to read or write in spite of intensive teaching at the school. Her ability with numbers is poor, and she has been deemed unable to handle a bank account. Piagetian conservation tests show her to be a nonconserver. Furthermore, Sue Carey administered a number of tests of the understanding of animacy (see Carey, 1985). D. H. performs at the level of a 4- or 5-year-old. In other words, all of the evidence points to someone who is functioning in everyday life situations at the retarded level.

We started by asking two questions:

1. Are her intellectual abilities really so impaired?
2. Is her language really so good?

To the first of these, we can answer that her intellectual abilities are severely impaired. Now we must turn to the second question: Just how good are her language abilities?

In spontaneous conversation, her language appears to be normal. A short sample from some of the transcripts demonstrates this (see Table 6.1).

TABLE 6.1
Two Samples from Transcripts of D. H. in Conversation with R. C.

D. H.	*R. C.*
	Ah, I see. So there's a whole story there. She might fall in. If she fell in the water, what would happen then?
Well, she . . . if she . . . if she was a good swimmer, she could probably swim to safety.	
	Uh-hmm.
But . . . and also she's got a life jacket on.	
	Right.
So that would save her.	
	Right.
Like I fell in . . . I'm a guide you see and we went to . . . We go to this river to do canoeing and I fell in the river once.	
	Ah.
That wasn't funny; that was frightening. I said I'd never go . . . I said I'd never go canoeing again, and I still go canoeing now. And that's 3 years later that was. But my Dad's got a canoe and we go canoeing. I threw my Dad in once. Me and my brother threw him in together.	
	Uh-hmm.
That was funny, that was.	
	Would you like to see another picture?
	So how long have you been here then?
Yes.	
	Uh-huh.
Two and a half years.	
And Dad's getting fed up with moving around. He thinks it's time that I settle down — to school, which is fair enough. To him, it . . . he feels it's going to ruin my whole life if I don't settle down sometime.	
	Uh-huh.

TABLE 6.1 *(Continued)*

D. H.	R. C.
So I'm gonna have to, at some point, settle down, somewhere,	
	Uh-huh.
somehow. Mum didn't mind me moving about, but Dad objected to it because he knew it was bothering me and it was bothering my school work.	
	Um-hmm.
And now I'm (getting on) like a house on fire he doesn't want to destroy it. He said I'm not going to destroy this for her, she can just keep going.	
	Uh-huh.
I love to move around with my Dad because of his work.	
	Um-hmm.
But he's feels if he keeps on doing that to me, I'm never gonna get anywhere.	
	Um-hmm.
Which is fair enough. I've got friends here.	

LANGUAGE ABILITIES

It is often said that children with this dissociation between language and intellectual abilities indeed show good language ability. But this ability is rarely documented. More often than not, this means that standardized language-test scores are superior to nonverbal performance. My opinion is that this is just not good enough. If the syndrome is to have any meaning, it must be that the language of these children is normal and not merely slightly raised when compared with other nonverbal test performances.

D. H.'s performance on various language tests is not startlingly good. On the Northwestern Syntax Screening Test (Lee, 1971), she registered a score that gave her the equivalent of a mental age of 5;6. On the Test of Reception of Grammar (TROG) (Bishop, 1982), her mental age, if scored as the test directs, would be just above 4 years. Although she failed items—at which point the testing should have stopped—we continued because we were also interested in specific responses, which are discussed later. Giving her the maximum score obtained from this procedure still yielded only a mental age of just over 5 years.

Her vocabulary, which always seems fresh and inventive, was assessed by the British Picture Vocabulary Scale (BPVS) (Dunn, Dunn, & Whetton, 1982). Here she did somewhat better, scoring a mental age equivalent of 9;5 — which, incidentally, given her chronological age, would be the performance expected for someone with an IQ of 60.

What is one to make of such scores in a highly verbal and cooperative subject? Perhaps these children really are not good at language after all. Yet they speak fluently, using complex language with relative clauses, complement clauses, passives, and so on. Can it be that these tests are not really measuring language or at least tapping the language resources of the individuals being tested? One thing common to all of these tests is the need to contemplate a situation (say a picture) and then to make some judgment on a verbal statement about it. Perhaps it makes too deliberate a strain on specific attentional processes. Sigrid Lipka and I, therefore, decided to adapt a technique that got around this problem. It is based on Tyler and Marslen-Wilson's so-called *on-line processing task* (Marslen-Wilson & Tyler, 1980; Tyler, 1981).

The idea behind this task is that the subject's attention is entirely called away from what is really being examined. The technique involves using a changing "target" word; the subject presses a button as rapidly as possible on hearing the word. An example might be, "The beans are ready for planting." or "What we wanted were the peas." The subject is told just before each sentence which target word to listen for — "beans" in the first case, and "peas" in the second. It is, therefore, a very easy task. But how many readers noticed that beans was in an active sentence, whereas peas was in a sentence that involved a relative clause? We, in fact, used a much less detailed task than specific sentence type. Rather, we used three overall types of sentences. *Normal* sentences give both syntactic and semantic support for the expectation of what words may be coming up. By contrast, *anomalous* sentences, in which particular nouns or verbs have been arbitrarily replaced, provide only syntactic support. Finally, *scrambled* sentences provided neither semantic nor syntactic support. Eventually, we constructed 18 sentences. To control for position, sentence type, and so forth, we needed to make three sets of these sentences.

In a normal experiment, three groups of subjects could each be assigned to one of the conditions. But D. H. is a single subject, and she must act as her own control. Therefore, we had to test her on each condition. We did this at approximately 3-month intervals. For controls, we used 10 intellectually normal children, matched to D. H. on mental age on the British Picture Vocabulary Test.

The predictions were that normal sentences would produce the fastest responses, anomalous slower, and scrambled the slowest of all. Our preliminary results for the control group are:

Normal: 310.9 msec
Anomalous: 389.3 msec
Scrambled: 487.3 msec

Whereas the control group performed in the predicted fashion, D. H.'s results were "all over the place," and no meaningful pattern could be discerned. If D. H.'s abilities, as measured by this test, do not even include being able to benefit from the structure of sentences as opposed to nonsentences, then are her language abilities in everyday life an illusion? We still have reasons for believing that this is not the case.

The ability to do the so-called on-line processing task as we designed it may require additional skills that had inherent difficulties for D. H. The task requires "split attention," – hearing the sentence yet having to make a motor response. Perhaps this placed an additional burden on D. H. that did not exist for the intellectually normal children.

There may be even greater problems for trying to assess D. H.'s language by traditional language tests. Traditional measures used by developmental psychologists and neuropsychologists do not really measure those aspects of language that may be modular in the deeper and more modern linguistic sense. Take, for example, "passive" sentences. It is one thing to know that it is a passive sentence in the sense that one knows its grammatical structure. But it is another thing to know how to assign the roles of the nouns. What most tests examine is whether the individual is able to get the role assignment correct, but they never directly (or indirectly) test whether the structure of passives as such is understood. I am reminded of Luria's patient Zazetsky in *The Man with a Shattered World* (Luria, 1972) who, when asked "Is a fly bigger than an elephant?," replied that he knew that flies were small and elephants were large, but that he could not tell which was which when put this way in language (in other words, requiring the assignment of roles to the nouns).

Linebarger, Schwartz, and Saffran (1983) made a similar discovery for so-called agrammatic aphasic patients. They found that, given grammatical and ungrammatical forms of sentences to judge for grammaticality, these patients performed well, whereas they had performed poorly on traditional language measures. In other words, knowing whether particular double-object sentences or passive sentences are grammatical or not is very different from role assignments tested by most traditional language tests. Taking this lead, we decided to design our own specific grammatical judgments test for D. H. and to see what that might show about her language abilities.

We used six types of sentences. Three of these were sentence types on which D. H. performed correctly on standardized language tests: (a) prepositions, (b) singular/plural agreement, and (c) tense markers. Three other sentence types were those on which she performed poorly on the same standardized tests: (d) passives, (e) relative clauses, and (f) double-object constructions. We then constructed two grammatical and two ungrammatical sentences for each of these sentence types, for a total of 24 items.

There are tremendous problems concerned with making ungrammatical sentences ungrammatical. They must be "reasonable," so as not to be rejected because they seem patently absurd. They must also have a "reason" for their ungrammaticality. We did not find a totally adequate solution to these problems, but we tried to motivate the ungrammatical sentences linguistically. So we violated word order in the case of passives and in the use of prepositions. In double-object constructions, we violated selection restrictions on the verb. With relative clauses we filled in the gap so that there were too many role assignments.

D. H. was told that a friend of ours could not yet speak English. We had noted some of the things he said; could she tell us whether that was something you could or could not say in English? She had no trouble with this instruction and cooperated fully. A warm-up item (*The grass is green* vs. *Grass green the is*) ensured that she understood the task.

An example of two sentences each (grammatical and ungrammatical) are given here for each of the six sentence types:

- Prepositions: The tissue is in the box.
  The coat is the wardrobe in.
- Singular/Plural Agreement: The boy writes.
  The dogs barks.
- Tense Markers: The girl washed the dishes.
  The boy is climbed the mountain.
- Passives: The horse is pulled by the monkey.
  By the lady is kicked the man.
- Relative Clauses: John drove the car that I fixed.
  The lady that the girl paid the man held the oranges.
- Double-Object Constructions: The Queen gave the school the toys.
  The man donated the library the book.

The results were clear cut. D. H. gave basically correct grammatical judgments to all but the double-object sentences, all of which she found grammatical. (Some of these double-object constructions that violated selection restrictions were also found acceptable by some adults we informally tested.) She also corrected the ungrammatical sentences, saying, no, the way you said it "doesn't somehow fit," or "It should be 'The girl walks'," where the stimulus had been "The girl walk."

CONCLUSIONS

What can we conclude from our survey of D. H.'s intellectual and language abilities? We had already made the case that her intellectual abilities really are seriously impaired. Now we can further conclude that there is evidence from the grammatical judgment test that her grammar is as good as it looks in her fluent speech. But, then, we never seriously doubted this. Her speech was never echolalic, and her conversations are always engaged in style and in content with the person to whom she is speaking.

IMPLICATIONS

In a number of children, the syntactic module appears to be intact. In Down syndrome children, there is a delay but not a deficit in the basic grammar (see Fowler, 1984, and Fowler, Gleitman, & Gelman, 1985). Curtiss's case of Antony (Curtiss & Yamada, 1981) showed that his syntax was unimpaired but that aspects of his semantic system were odd.

In D. H., however, we observe excellence in all aspects of her language, not only in the syntax, but in the phonology, semantics, and even the nonlinguistic sphere of pragmatics, that is, in the use and coordination of those linguistic skills. Even if we leave aside Fodor's more narrow notion of modularity, and take Shallice's view of an "isolable subsystem," a view which is perhaps more neurologically useful, we are saddled with observations of a language system which appears to be too good, even for the wider notions of modularity.

One possibility is that the basic core grammar is a module (based on other converging evidence from linguistic theory), but that something else, perhaps some motivational or other unknown factor, allows the child to make use of this module and to elaborate those skills closely associated with its everyday use. It has certainly been noted that hyperverbal children of this type do not just possess good language. Rather, there seems to be a "press" to use language which leads to its chatterbox quality.

A similar problem appears in trying to interpret the behavior of individuals with savant syndrome. It would not be useful, either for understanding the individual or for shedding light on modularity, to cast the net too wide. We do not want to find ourselves in the perhaps absurd position of arguing for "calendar-calculation" modules, for example. Instead, we need to know if there is some core cognitive ability, preserved in some individuals, that is then elaborated, in savants syndrome for example, into a strange isolated skill. Perhaps something similar happens with hyperverbal individuals with chatterbox syndrome. It could be that they have a well-developed modular core grammar and, through very high motivation, subsequently elaborate that ability into the skillful use of all aspects of language that we see in cases like D. H.

REFERENCES

Anderson, M. (1988). Inspection time, information processing, and the development of intelligence. *British Journal of Developmental Psychology, 6*, 43–57.

Baron-Cohen, S., Leslie, A. M., & Frith, U. (1985). Does the autistic child have a "theory of mind"? *Cognition, 21*, 37–46.

Bishop, D. V. M. (1982). *T. R. O. G. Test for reception of grammar.* Abingdon, Oxon: Thomas Leach Ltd.

Burgemeister, B. B., Blum, L. H., & Lorge, I. (1972). *Columbia Mental Maturity Scale.* New York: Harcourt Brace Jovanovich, Inc.

Carey, S. (1985). *Conceptual change in childhood.* Cambridge, MA: MIT Press.

Cromer, R. F. (1983). Hierarchical planning disability in the drawings and constructions of a special group of severely aphasic children. *Brain and Cognition, 2*, 144–164.

Curtiss, S., & Yamada, J. (1981). Selectively intact grammatical development in a retarded child. *UCLA working papers in Cognitive Linguistics, 3*, 61–91.

Dunn, L. M., Dunn, L. M., & Whetton, C. (1982). *The British Picture Vocabulary Scale.* Windsor: NFER - Nelson.

Fodor, J. A. (1983). *The modularity of mind.* Cambridge, MA: MIT Press.

Fowler, A. (1984). *Language acquisition of Down syndrome children: Production and comprehension.* Unpublished doctoral dissertation, University of Pennsylvania, Philadelphia.

Fowler, A., Gleitman, L., & Gelman, R. (1985). *The acquisition of syntax by a Down syndrome child: A longitudinal study.* Paper presented at the meeting of the Society for Research in Child Development, Toronto, Canada.

Hadenius, A.-M., Hagberg, B., Hyttnas-Bensch, K., & Sjogren, I. (1962). The natural prognosis of infantile hydrocephalus. *Acta Paediatrica, 51*, 117–118.

Heaton, R. K. (1981). *Wisconsin Card Sorting Test Manual.* Odessa, FL: Psychological Assessment Resources, Inc.

Ingram, T. T. S., & Naughton, J. A. (1962). Pediatric and psychological aspects of cerebral palsy associated with hydrocephalus. *Developmental Medicine and Child Neurology, 4*, 287–292.

Lee, L. L. (1971). *Northwestern Syntax Screening Test.* Evanston, IL: Northwestern University Press.

Linebarger, M. C., Schwartz, M. F., & Saffran, E. M. (1983). Sensitivity to grammatical structure in so-called agrammatic aphasics. *Cognition, 13*, 361–392.

Luria, A. R. (1972). *The man with a shattered world.* New York: Basic Books.

Marslen-Wilson, W. D., & Tyler, L. K. (1980). The temporal structure of spoken language understanding. *Cognition, 8*, 1–71.

Piattelli-Palmarini, M. (Ed.). (1980). *Language and learning. The debate between Jean Piaget and Noam Chomsky.* London: Routledge & Kegan Paul.

Pietro, M. J. S., & Goldfarb, R. (1985). Characteristic patterns of word association responses in institutionalized elderly with and without senile dementia. *Brain and Language, 26*, 230–243.

Shallice, T. (1988). *From neuropsychology to mental structure.* Cambridge, England: Cambridge University Press.

Taylor, E. M. (1959). *Psychological appraisal of children with cerebral defects*. Cambridge, MA: Harvard University Press.

Tew, B. (1979). The "cocktail party syndrome" in children with hydrocephalus and spina bifida. *British Journal of Disorders of Communication, 14*, 89–101.

Tyler, L. K. (1981). Syntactic and interpretative factors in the development of language comprehension. In W. Deutsch (Ed.), *The child's construction of language* (pp. 149–181). London: Academic Press.

Wechsler, D. (1974). *Wechsler Intelligence Scale - Children* (rev. ed.). Windsor: NFER.

Wimmer, H., & Perner, J. (1983). Beliefs about beliefs: Representation and constraining function of wrong beliefs in young children's understanding of deception. *Cognition, 13*, 103–128.

7
Exceptional Cases of Language Development in Mental Retardation: The Relative Autonomy of Language as a Cognitive System

Jean A. Rondal
University of Liège, Belgium

It has long been considered that language and nonlanguage cognition interact closely, both in development and in mature functioning. The exact nature and extent of this interaction, however, is still the object of much controversy in psychological and psycholinguistic literature. In what follows, I restrict myself to dealing with whether (and, if yes, how) language depends on other aspects of cognition and general cognitive processes, leaving aside the other face of the problem—that is, the role of language in the treatment of nonlinguistic information and in the organization of individual knowledge. There is no question that language is a cognitive system. It is likely, therefore, that is shares some information and mechanisms with other cognitive subsystems. The question is: To what extent is the language function specific in the information it uses and the mechanisms it relies on?

There have been several general answers to this question in the last decades. They are relatively well known and need not be fully exposed here. In several books and articles, Piaget has presented his conception of the relationship between language and cognition or, to use his preferred terms, language and intellectual operations (see e.g., Piaget, 1963, 1970). To put it briefly, intellectual operations, in so far as they result from the interiorization of actions and from their external coordination followed by their mental coordination, remain for a long developmental time independent of language. Conversely, it is language that depends on intellectual development for its construction. The capacity to represent depends on the same knowledge structure that permits the construction of the known object. This representative capacity gradually emerges in the second half of the sensory-motor period (12–18 months of age). It can be observed in the symbolic play of the child and it increases the child's capacity for mental imagery and language. Language is only a product of a more general representational function. The pregrammatical semantic and lexical developments are directly dependent on early cognitive development, as Piaget argued. This was further sustained by authors such as Sinclair-De Zwart (1973) and Edwards (1973). It is necessary, however, to introduce a distinction between the mechanisms or processes that underlie our specific thoughts and the contents or concepts of these thoughts. It is no controversial issue that language encodes particular concepts. The Piagetian hypothesis further posits that particular nonlinguistic cognitive mechanisms are causally involved in the acquisition and functioning of the grammatical system.

Recent studies conducted in the Piagetian or non-Piagetian traditions do not support such a position (see Cromer, 1987, for a review and a discussion). The acquisition of particular cognitive skills (e.g., sensory-motor intelligence, logical decentration) and, of course, specific concepts precedes or is contemporaneous with the acquisition of particular linguistic abilities (e.g., first multiword utterances, reversible passives comprehension and production), but no clear causal relationship was ever demonstrated. There is also a good deal of evidence against this notion (see Cromer, 1987, for a summary).

In clear contrast with Piaget's point of view stands Chomsky's claim that human languages are made possible through the existence of a specific language faculty owing nothing to other cognitive functions (Chomsky, 1966, 1968, 1981). This view, or a related one, has been enlarged into a general modular theory by Fodor (1983). According to Fodor, a basic functional taxonomy of psychological processes can be established that distinguishes between transducers, input systems, and central processors. The transducers or sensory organs provide modality-specific immediate representations of proximal stimulus configurations. Input analyzers have, as their premises, representations of proximal stimulus configurations and, as their conclusions, representations of the character and distribution of distant objects. Fodor argued that language is basically an input system. As such, it is an "informationally encapsulated subsystem of the brain" composed of subroutines serving special objectives. A module is said to be informationally encapsulated to the extent that its data processing is limited to lower-level data (i.e., input from the transducers) and background information stored in the module itself or having arrived there as a result of the system's previous functioning. Fodorian modules have additional properties that need not be exposed here (e.g., domain specificity, mandatory character of the modus operandi, fastness, computational autonomy, limited permeability to central access). One of the major problems with considering language as a Fodorian module (see Marshall, 1984, and Shallice, 1984, for more detail on these problems as well as for other criticisms) has to do with meaning. As an encapsulated system (i.e., closed to any information outside itself), it is not clear how the module could properly handle the semantico-syntactic and logical forms. Nor is it obvious in this respect how one could account for the numerous data attesting to the semantic and pragmatic effects on word identification and sentence comprehension.

Chomsky (1980) supplied a significant distinction going beyond the general modular "language organ" and solving some of the contradictions involved in considering language as a Fodorian module. Chomsky suggested distinguishing between what he called the conceptual and the computational components of the language system. The first component embraces semantics and pragmatics and may be interconnected with nonlinguistic cognitive capacities. The second component involves syntax and phonology. It is said to constitute a truly autonomous processing mechanism. If we follow this distinction, we should look at the language organization as a set of modular devices, some non-Fodorian, with cognitive antecedents and correlates, and others more Fodorian, basically independent of nonlinguistic cognitive functioning.

Bickerton's *language bioprogram hypothesis* (Bickerton, 1981, 1984) is compatible with Chomsky's current stance. Generalizing to the problem of language acquisition from his detailed studies of the processes of creole formation, Bickerton argued that there exists an innately given bioprogram providing a skeletal model of language, which the child, guided by input from the target language, converts into the target language. This skeletal model consists of a restricted set of categories (limited number of constituents, such as sentences, nouns, verbs, and modifiers of nouns and verbs) and processes (single transformational rule, Chomsky's *Move α*; Chomsky, 1981).[1] It is said to impose a formal structure on the output of the conceptual component.

It has proved extremely difficult and hazardous to try disentangling the various determinants of language construction in the normally developing child, for these determinants interact with each other in subtle ways, sometimes over short periods of time. That is one of the reasons why a number of scholars in developmental psycholinguistics have recently turned their attention to mentally retarded children and adolescents.[2] These

---

[1]Even if Bickerton's language bioprogram hypothesis is compatible with Chomsky's distinction between conceptual and computational components of language, it should be stressed that the hypothesis itself, being nonparametric, is alternative to Chomsky's view of universal grammar, according to which all possible core grammars are somehow latent in the mind.

[2]A most important exception in this perspective is, of course, the seminal work of Lenneberg (Lenneberg, 1967; Lenneberg, Nichols, & Rosenberger, 1964), suggesting that language development follows a maturational timetable more prevalent than general cognitive disability itself for determining the course of this development.

subjects, by definition, exhibit delayed and incomplete intellectual development. Such situations may rightly be considered as supplying invoked (i.e., natural) experiments, allowing in principle to specify by default the role of nonlinguistic cognitive factors in language development. This endeavor is not exempt from difficulties, for:

1. Mental retardation is usually accompanied by organic, psychological, and existential difficulties, whose particular influences on linguistic development and functioning are not easy to assess and to keep separated from so-called truly intellectual influences.

2. There are delicate problems when it comes to matching mentally retarded and normally developing children to compare their respective rates and realizations in language acquisition.

Nevertheless, the literature on language acquisition in mentally retarded children is instructive. It attests to the modular nature of the language system with development in several components of language phonology, lexical and structural semantics, pragmatics, grammatical morphology and syntax, presents decalages, and dissociations going much beyond what can be observed in normal subjects and, once development has come to a stop, largely differing in degree of incompleteness from component to component and from subject to subject. Interesting relationships can be established between mental development and language development, for example, using psychometric measures of level of mental development such as mental age (MA). From reviews of the specialized literature (Rondal, 1984, 1988a; see also Cromer, 1988, for a review of corresponding data and Miller, 1988, for a summary and a discussion of a series of original data on Down syndrome children consistent with the present analysis), it would appear that important decalages are the rule rather than the exception between mental age (MA) expectations (reflecting the development in nonretarded subjects) and the actual realizations of the retarded subjects as to the phonological grammatical, morphological, and syntactic aspects of language development, whereas development in areas such as semantics and pragmatics tends to follow closely and in more direct proportion to the growth in mental age. The existence of such decalages and dissociations seems to fit with the Chomskyan distinction between the conceptual and computational components of the language system and with the indication that the latter are independent of the nonlinguistic cognitive capacities. I believe that the data on language development in the mentally retarded population reflect Chomsky's distinction. However, prudence should be exercised because of the caveats involved in the psychometric assessment of mental development. As noted by Baumeister (1967) and as I have discussed elsewhere (Rondal, 1985), MA is a rough and global index of mental development mixing in the same score a number of distinct capabilities, some clearly pertaining to the cognitive organization (judging from current preoccupations in cognitive psychology), some others not or not clearly so. Also, as MA is a composite measure, there are a number of different ways to obtain the same MA. These problems cloud, to a certain extent, the interpretation of the data. In order to ascertain the interpretation that I have proposed, it is necessary to broaden the research relating language and cognitive development in mentally retarded subjects using specific, well-defined, and separate measures of nonlinguistic cognitive capacities. Such data are largely missing at the present time.

Recently, a small number of highly interesting cases of dissociations between language and cognition were presented in the literature on mental retardation. Bellugi, Marks, Bihrle, and Sabo (1988) documented the cases of several adolescents with Williams syndrome who exhibited unusual linguistic capabilities for their level of mental retardation. The subjects, aged 11, 15, and 16 years at the time of the study, were still functioning at Piaget's preoperational stage of cognitive development. The language of the three subjects proved complex and often grammatically correct although not quite at chronological age levels. MLU's (in number of morphemes) calculated in a storytelling task reached 8.6 for one subject, 10 for the second one, and 13.1 for the third one. This latter subject's productive language was truly remarkable, including full passives, embedded relative clauses, conditionals, and, at times, multiple embeddings. The syntax was mostly correct except for occasional errors of overgeneralization of morphology and pronoun usage. The three children demonstrated comprehension of full reversible passives, affirmative and negative comparative and equative relational expressions, and other complex linguistic structures. Clearly, these Williams syndrome subjects were functioning linguistically at a level far beyond the one that would be expected on the basis of their general cognitive ability. Curtiss and Yamada (1981) reported the case of a retarded child operating at the 2-year level on nonlanguage test but exhibiting a relatively high level in expressive syntax. Anderson and Spain (1977) reported a study of 145 spina bifida children at 6 years. Among these, 40% showed hyperverbal characteristics to an important degree. These subjects were typically female, had lower IQs, and presented considerably higher verbal than performance skills. They used complex syntax but were often semantically inaccurate. They also produced a much higher rate of ready-made or cliché phrases than a group of nonretarded children matched for verbal IQ on the WPPSI test.

Seagoe (1965) documented much higher than average written language development in a Down syndrome male, IQ about 60 (etiological subcategory of Down syndrome not reported). Unfortunately, she did not supply any information on the speech of her subject. By the age of 11, this subject was keeping a written record of the numerous travels he was making with his family and he continued to do so until he was 43. The text excerpts supplied by Seagoe sound rather normal with a nice diversity of vocabulary, correct use of formal classes, and sentence and paragraph grammatical and semantic organization. I computed MLU (in morphemes) on one of the texts written by Seagoe's subject at age 21. MLU reached 16.75, which is quite remarkable by all standards even if written speech tends to be longer than oral speech. Several sentences were composed of coordinated or subordinated clauses. Few syntactic errors were committed. They entailed omission of obligating clause contituents.

A few years ago, I had the good fortune to discover in the Liège area the case of Françoise, a Down syndrome female adult with apparent quasi-normal language functioning. The case seemed intriguing enough that I decided to study it in detail. The study is virtually completed now and will be published in book form by Cambridge University Press (Rondal, in press). Only limited portions of the work are presented here.

Françoise was 33 to 34 years old at the time of the study. She was born in 1955. Down syndrome was diagnosed when she was 3-years-old. The karyotype revealed a genotype 47, XX, + free 21 in each of the metaphases studied (standard trisomy 21). The socioeconomic level of the family is upper middle class. Françoise made her first attempts at walking unassisted at around 2 years of age. The only word that she was able to pronounce at age 4 was /to/ for *couteau* (knife). No specific information is available on her receptive language ability at the time. At $4\frac{1}{2}$ years, she started language reeducation twice a week at the speech clinic of the University of Liège. She was taught to speak and to write by a team of speech pathologists. At 6 years and a few months, following a failed attempt at integration in a primary school for normally developing children, Françoise started attending a special school for moderately and severely mentally retarded children. After 10 years in that school, she had access to a secondary school for mentally retarded adolescents. At the time of the study, she was living in her home with her parents, frequenting an Occupational Center for adults with Down syndrome twice weekly. She was exempt from most of the organic problems affecting Down syndrome children in substantial proportions (i.e., cardiac malformations, pneumovascular difficulties, gastroduodenal problems, etc.).

Françoise was subjected to a large number of tests and various evaluation procedures over a period of 2 years. For assessing productive speech, members of my research team recorded 3 hours of Françoise's conversational speech in free interaction.[3] Portions of this corpus were analyzed using Halliday's *Functional Grammar* (1985) as technical reference. Halli-

---

[3] I am particularly indebted to Jean Françoise Bachelet for carrying out this part of the work.

day's grammar was adapted and completed for French using Dubois and Dubois-Charlier's *Elements de Linguistique Française* (1970) as a guiding reference. The assessment of receptive speech was made using homemade tasks adapted from my psycholinguistic studies with normally developing children, devised to evaluate the comprehension of active and passive declarative sentences, the comprehension of relative clauses, temporal and causal subordinate clauses, and the comprehension of pronominal coreference. Additionally, standardized tests were used to assess productive, receptive, and definitional lexical capabilities.[4] Françoise's cerebral specialization for language was tested using dichotic listening and dual task procedures. The nonlinguistic examination evaluated Françoise's functioning on a number of cognitive tasks: (a) short-term memory, (b) memory learning and selective recall, (c) visuographic capability, (d) visual discrimination and structuration, (e) computational capability, and (f) attention. In addition, she was given the verbal and the nonverbal subscale of the WAIS.

Françoise's 3 hours of conversational speech were transcribed verbatim and segmented into utterances. For segmenting, the procedure explained in Rondal, Bachelet, and Pérée (1986) was used. Mean length of utterance (MLU) was computed using the procedure defined in Rondal et al. (1986). This procedure differs from Brown's (1973) only in that ours counts as separate units the words and the bound grammatical morphemes added to the words, whereas Brown's does not. His procedure was intended primarily to quantify gross linguistic evolution in the young child. Ours applies to later language functioning, which justifies the modification introduced in the counting procedure. Françoise's MLU count yielded an index of 12.24 (standard deviation 9.65). No table exists for interpreting MLU values in adults, although 12 or so is sometimes cursorily referred to as the average value for conversational nonnarrative speech. Françoise's speech, therefore, conforms in mean length to the one usually observed in normal adults placed in corresponding functional contexts.

Sound articulation is perfectly normal. Her speech is fluent and normally intonated. Tonic and stress accents are correctly distributed (in French, the tonic accent falls on the last articulated syllable of the word or, more exactly, of the phonetical group, as some—mostly monosyllabic—words are not stressed). As to syntax, the sentences are mostly complete (except for the conventional ellipses appearing in exclamations, answers, recasts, and anticipations which were fully understandable in the conversational context and therefore denote mastery over conversational processes). The sentences are of the subject–verb–object or subject–verb–attribute type.

---

[4]I am indebted to Dr. J. J. Deltour, Mr. J. P. Broonen, Mr. J. M. Grailet, and Mrs. M. Monseur for administrating these tests as well as some nonlanguage tests and the WAIS, to be mentioned further.

They are properly constructed: Conventional French word order is followed with no exception. Declarative, interrogative (wh- and yes–no subtypes), imperative, emphatic, and exclamative sentences are used either affirmatively or negatively, in the latter case with the negative elements properly located in the sentence's sequential structure. Reflective constructions are not infrequent and correctly formed (e.g., *Je me suis dit. . .*). Full syntactic passives are very rarely used. They are rarely used in French in common conversation because of the prevalence of alternative constructions (e.g., active constructions introduced by the collective pronoun *on*, reflexive verbs). So-called lexical passives, more frequent in French, are common in Françoise's corpus (e.g., *quelqu'un est venu, être marié, être coiffé comme tout le monde*). Coordinated as well as subordinated as well as subordinated clauses are used. Among the latter ones, we observed nominal subordinates (subject, object, completive), relative subordinates, and circumstantial subordinates (temporal, comparative, causal, consequential, and conditional ones). Simple and, at times, multiple embedding may be observed. Tense agreement between main and subordinate clauses is properly marked. The various sentence subunits (noun phrase, verb phrase, prepositional phrase, adjectival and adverbial phrases) are correctly formed. Some are quite complex with the use of coordination, determiners, modifers, and embedded or chained relative clauses.

As to lexicosyntax and morphosyntax, the grammatically obligatory free and bound morphemes are correctly used without exception. Articles are properly marked for number, gender, and for the delicate contrast between specific and nonspecific reference (e.g., *the bike I have* vs. *a bike I saw*). Prearticles (absolute and relative quantifiers) are used and correctly placed before articles, preceded by the preposition *de* in the case of the relative quantifiers (e.g., *tous les hommes, beaucoup de romanichels*). Postarticles (cardinal and numeral) are also used and properly located following articles (e.g., *on a été tous les deux*). Personal pronouns are correctly marked for number, gender, person, and case, and they are properly positioned with respect to verbs. Pronominal coreference is clear with occasional exceptions. At times, coreference is respecified in text (e.g., *il mon beau frère a . . .*). In a few occasions, pleonastic uses of personal pronouns are noticed (e.g., *mon frère il habite . . .*). Possessive pronouns and adjectives are correctly marked for person, gender (of thing possessed), number (of things possessed and of possessors). Epithets are correctly marked for number and gender where applicable. Demonstrative pronouns and adjectives are correctly used with respect to number, gender, and proximal–distal contrast. This, together with the proper use of personal and possessive pronouns, attests to Françoise's mastery over the deixis function of language. Relative and interrogative pronouns and adjectives are correctly marked for number, gender, and case (where applicable). The presence of some of the most usual indefinite pronouns and adjectives, expressing either absolute or relative quantitative (e.g., *chaque, quelque*) or qualitative value (e.g., *même, autre*) is attested in the corpus. Lastly, verbs are correctly inflected in mood, tense, aspect, number, and person including the French polite plurals. Auxiliaries and modals are properly used except for occasional errors of auxiliary selection — fairly common in the Belgian/French-speaking community (e.g., *j'aurais passé en 4è.année* instead of the correct *je serais passée en 4è.année*, as action verbs normally take the *être* auxiliary).

The preceding characterized normal or quasinormal productive grammatical functioning of Françoise is corroborated by her results in a number of specific psycholinguistic tasks devised to assess advanced receptive capabilities. Reversible as well as nonreversible relative clauses introduced by the relative pronoun *qui* or *que* are correctly understood whether they are embedded or derived on the right side of the main clause. Causal subordinate clauses introduced by the conjunctive locution *parce que* are correctly understood whether the subordinate clause precedes or follows the main clause. Temporal subordinate clauses are correctly understood whether the clause order matches the order in which the referred events happened, are happening, or will happen. The mechanism of coreference in the case of anaphonic personal pronouns also proved to be mastered. Françoise appears to make systematic use of the number and gender correspondence between pronoun and noun to establish anaphonic coreference (e.g., *La secrétaire joue au tennis avec le professeur. Il vous téléphonera demain.*). In ambiguous cases, she seems to resort to a minimum distance principle to ground coreference (e.g., *Le maçon verra son directeur. Il téléphonera ensuite. Marc parle avec Robert. La boulangère lui apportera le pain.*). In sentences (actually paragraphs) of the latter type, it can be questioned whether the minimum distance principle is the most natural strategy. In such cases, I would be tempted, together with some others (e.g., Grober, Beardsley, & Caramazza, 1978), to consider that a parallel function strategy constitutes a higher order heuristic. This strategy consists of considering that the thematic organization of the first sentence will be maintained in the second one. If the pronoun functions as a theme in the second sentence, it will refer to the noun theme in the first sentence, and similarly for the rheme function (on the theme–rheme distinction, see Halliday, 1985). However, in a large scale study conducted with French-speaking adolescents and adults (Rondal, Leyen, Bredart, & Pérée, 1984), it was demonstrated that the dominant heuristic in ambiguous cases (only active sentences were used) was select the theme or grammatical subject of the first sentence as coreferent for the pronoun of the second sentence whether the pronoun functions grammatically as subject or as object. The tendency to choose subject or thematic dominance significantly increased with the age of the subjects.

Françoise does not appear to use either the parallel function or the dominant-theme strategy. Rather, she relies on a purely sequential and positional heuristic.

Comprehension of declarative affirmative active and passive sentences was also experimentally investigated. Active and passive sentences systematically varying in plausibility and plausible reversibility were given. Active and passive designating requests were used to elicit the interpretive responses (see Rondal, Thibaut, & Cession, in press, for more detail on the procedure as well as for normative data relating to French). Françoise proved capable of correctly interpreting 61 out of 64 sentences (the 3 errors may be attributed to distraction). Most remarkably, she could correctly identify the underlying grammatical subject or the underlying grammatical object in irrealis sentences with low-transitivity verbs (see Hopper & Thompson, 1980; e.g., *Le livre est imaginé par la boîte.*), therefore, with no pragmatic and semantic help, and even irrealis sentences that would turn realis were they reversed (e.g., *Le monsieur est imaginé par le livre.*), therefore going against pragmatic interpretive tendency.

Françoise's truly remarkable phonological and grammatical capacity is in sharp contrast with what is known of the same capacities in regular moderately and severely mentally retarded persons including the other Down syndrome subjects. With respect to these persons, it is well documented that phonological development is fairly difficult and remains incomplete (see Dodd & Leahy, 1989, for a review). The estimates of the incidence of speech defects vary from 25% (Burt, 1937) to 95% (Schlanger & Gottsleben, 1957), according to the criteria used and the population tested. The Down syndrome population is particularly prone to disordered phonology (Schlanger & Gottsleben, 1957; Zisk & Bialer, 1967). Down syndrome subjects exhibit more numerous articulation errors than MA-matched mentally retarded subjects of other etiologies (Rondal, Lambert, & Sohier, 1980). Some authors maintain that the articulation errors of Down syndrome subjects are, for the greater part, identical to the error patterns observed in young normal children, supporting the view that misarticulations in Down syndrome is mainly the result of delayed and then incomplete speech development (e.g., Van Borsel, 1988), whereas other authors insist that at least some of the Down syndrome subjects exhibit deviant errors (i.e., types of speech errors and inconsistencies not usually found in normal development; see Dodd, 1976). Grammatical development is also markedly reduced in moderately and severely mentally retarded subjects and particularly in Down syndrome persons (see Rondal, 1985, 1988b, for reviews of this abundant literature). Rondal (1978) found Down syndrome children aged about 10 years to have a mean MLU of 2.84 (standard deviation .14) computed in interactive free-play activities. Rondal, Lambert, and Sohier (1980, 1981) obtained MLU values centering around 3.40 (standard deviation .95) in the free conversation of Down syndrome children, aged 11 years 6 months in mean value. The mean MLU of Down syndrome adults (mean age, 26 years) studied by Rondal and Lambert (1983) was close to 6.00. For corresponding, but slightly more severe, MLU data concerning 11 Down syndrome children and adolescents, see Fowler (1988). The language of these subjects is, and usually remains over time, telegraphic in the sense of Brown (1973) (i.e., it is seriously lacking in functors [prepositions, articles, auxiliaries, pronouns, and conjunctions], and there exists clear evidence that these formal classes are poorly understood when they are at all; Bartel, Bryen, & Keehn, 1973, reported similar results with moderately and severely mentally retarded subjects from etiologies other than Down syndrome). Word ordering, however, is mostly correct. This double observation (i.e., correct word order together with a marked deficit in function words) closely parallels the situation usually described in aphasic agrammatism (cf. Grodzinsky, 1990). Grammatical morphological marking (nominal as well as verbal) remains poor and fairly inconsistent even in Down syndrome adults (Rondal & Lambert, 1983). Most importantly with relation to the present case, moderately and severely mentally retarded children rarely use subordination and do not understand it in the absence of pragmatic and situational facilitative effects. As a rule, they do not understand pronominal coreference mechanisms or passivization (Rondal, Cession, & Vincent, 1988).

We return to Françoise's corpus and consider the lexicon used. Although lexical usage seem to be generally correct, there are occasional mistakes: incomplete locutions, for example *y a*, *y avait*, instead of the correct form *il y a*, *il y avait*; incorrect adverbial derivations *drôl' dement* instead of *drôlement*; incorrect expressions, for example *habillé comme l'as de pique* instead of *habillé à l'as de pique*, *il m'faut déjà toutes les plumes pour voler* instead of *il m'faut déjà toutes mes plumes pour voler*; incorrect word forms, for example *décrapitude* instead of *décrépitude*. Françoise was also given the TVAP (Test de Vocabulaire actif et passif) — form F, 5 to 8 years, the TRT (Test des Relations Topologiques), the vocabulary task of the Test Battery used at the University of Liège for the assessment of aphasia, and the vocabulary subtest of the WAIS.[4] The picture denomination and pointing scores are indicative of a lexical development that is retarded and relatively weak, particularly in what concerns the locative expressions. On the word definition tasks, Françoise scored below the mean (WAIS Vocabulary subtest standard score: 7; population mean: 10; standard deviation: 3). She supplied imprecise or false definitions for terms such as *grouper*, *réparer*, *portion*, *cl; croûture*, *empoigner*, *aumône*, *tanière*, *instruire*, *fade*, *persévérant*, *monopole*.

The most striking limitation in Françoise's conversational speech is at the level of discourse organization. A basic theme–rheme organization is respected throughout the clauses and the usual given/new information structure is applied with no exception. But although discourse taken at the level of the speech turns and the paragraphs is grossly coherent, logically speaking, it is clear that the text often lacks in cohesion. According to Halliday (1985), text cohesion, a characteristic distinct from the thematic and information structures of the clauses, depends on making explicit the external relationships between individual clauses or groups of clauses. This realization is considered not to depend on grammatical structure. Combining to make up the textual component are the following four processes: (a) (inner)reference (an element introduced at one place in text can be taken as a reference point for something that follows), (b) ellipsis, (c) conjuction (explicitly stating the semantic relation holding between clauses or groups of clauses), and (d)lexical cohesion (choice of words: repetition of same words, use of related words, to support semantic continuity). As it appears, this is the conjuction process that is partially defective in Francoise's speech. She uses a number of conjunctive forms (e.g., *et*, *alors*, *mais*, *donc*), often located at the beginning of the utterances; but these forms do not really explicate a semantic relationship holding between clauses or utterances. They seem to be loose sequential connectors. Many utterances contain several repetitions of the same word, locution, or phrase. Stereotyped (idiomatic) expressions are placed here and there in the utterances (*comme vous voyez, si j'peux dire, pour vous l'dire honnêtement*, etc.). It seems to go by speech turn. When she starts using one such stereotyped expression, she continues using it for the rest of the speech turn, as if the first use had had a momentary self-priming effect. Also, she seems to have a tendency to alternate ideas pairwise i.e., to express one idea, turn then to a connected one, return to the first idea, and then continue with the second one; all that with limited explicit marking of the semantic relationship between the two ideas. These characteristics attest to a difficulty with text planning. In this respect, the stereotyped fillers that she uses may be the functional equivalent of the hesitation pauses identified by Goldman-Eisler (1968) and assumed to correspond to moments of planning for the discourse ahead.

Françoise nonlinguistic capacities are in marked contrast to her grammatical achievement. Her nonverbal IQ on the WAIS is 60 (verbal IQ: 67), with low to very low standard scores in the spatial subtests (object assembly, completing images, cubes), arithmetic, and memory for numbers (she recalls four digits in order and three digits in reverse order). Without exception, Françoise performance on the nonlinguistic tests (Rendement Mnéique de Rey, Bushke's Test of Selective Recall, Figure complexe de Rey, Figures enchevêtrées de Poppelreuter, etc.) — which cannot be fully described here for lack of space — is compatible with the average performance of other Down syndrome subjects (see Gibson, 1981, for example), which means that it is severely underdeveloped and problematic.[5] In possible relationship with the stereotypic use of idiomatic expresions in discourse, as previously mentioned, it could be indicated that Françoise presents a difficulty to inhibit ongoing automatic processes on Stroop tasks.

In summary, the cases reviewed and particularly the one of Françoise, studied in much detail, clearly reveal a dissociation between language components: phonology and syntax (encompassing lexico- and morphosyntax) on the one hand and lexicon and discourse organization (pragmatics), on the other hand. This dissociation corresponds to Chomsky's (1980) distinction between computational and concepted aspects of language. It also seems clear, in the exceptional cases alluded to and presented, that these computational components function in fair independence with respect to the limited nonverbal cognitive capacities exhibited. In contrast, the conceptual components of language in these subjects rather directly reflect their cognitive limitations. It is reasonable to assume that these conceptual components depend on nonverbal cognition for their development and/or that they are directly related to nonverbal cognition in their modus operandi. The data reviewed here are fairly consistent with a modular approach to the study of mind. What is the exact type of modularity theory for language may still be a premature question. One may want to risk, however, that a Fodorian conception (Fodor, 1983) is too molar (i.e., it does not establish sufficient distinctions between the modular properties of the various language subsystems) and leads to too strict a separation between language and the central systems. The basic language organization seems to call for at least two major related modules, a computational one and a conceptual one, each one subdivided into or made of likely autonomous units or submodules (minimally phonology and syntax in the first case and lexicon, general semantic, and discursive organization in the second case). Perhaps it would be better, terminologically and conceptually, to talk less of modules and more of functionally isolable language subsystems (following Shallice's suggestion, 1984).

Adopting the previously mentioned modular or subsystemic approach, how is one to explain the exceptional cases of language functioning reported

---

[5]Although it would be risky to establish too direct a relationship between Down syndrome and acquired aphasia, it is interesting to mention Caplan and Hildebrandt's (1988) suggestions that syntactic structures break down when the brain is damaged because of specific impairments in the parsing process and a decrease in the extent of computational space devoted to that function. But, as indicated in the case of one of the aphasic patients studied by these authors, it seems that parsing per se can be intact despite a severe short-term memory impairment, which suggests that the memory buffering utilized in parsing is specific to the syntactic submodule. Françoise's mediocre short-term memory capacity, coupled with her excellent syntactic processing, supplies yet another instance of external evidence in favor of the cognitive specificity of syntax.

passives, replacing missing pronouns, judgments of word interrelationships in sentences, use of temporal connectives such as *when, after, before*, etc.). Therefore, there may be purely syntactic operations that the right brain is not able to sustain under the usual circumstances. One will also recall, in connection with this, Curtiss' (1977) study of a severely deprived girl, referred to as Genie. After being discovered at the age of $13\frac{1}{2}$ years, Genie went on to acquire some language but her speech and her grammar remained abnormal. Dichotic listenting tests suggested that her receptive language was strongly lateralized to her right hemisphere.

We submitted Françoise, as well as a group of 24 other Down syndrome adults (aged between 21 and 36 years), to a dichotic listening task and a dual task procedure. The results for the 24 other Down syndrome subjects are in agreement with the indication in the literature, with some degree of individual variation (i.e., a left-ear/right-hemisphere advantage for speech perception, a left-hemisphere superiority for speech production). Françoise data, on the contrary, attest to homegeneous and clearly marked left-hemisphere dominance for speech perception and production. Admittedly, these data cannot be completely trusted in the present state of knowledge on the role of the two cerebral hemispheres in the intricate language functions and in the present state of limited technical sophistication. I will take them, tentatively at least, as supporting what seems to be a logical interpretive necessity (i.e., considering that for some mysterious reason Françoise's specific brain areas containing the computational mechanisms of language or allowing them to develop were spared in the pathological ontogenesis caused by the exceeding chromosomic material present in all individuals with standard trisomy 21).[6]

Why, then, would Françoise not have developed language within the normal time boundaries? Perhaps for the same reason, mutatis mutandis, that normal children do not develop language in the strict (grammatical) sense before 2 or 3 years. The general organic condition of Françoise probably delayed a few additional years for her linguistic maturational process. It may be that the computational component of language needs triggering from the conceptual component to be set to work and/or needs the raw material (first words, first multiword utterances) supplied by this component to start organizing it.

It might be argued against this interpretation that, after all, if Françoise's mental age is about 5 or 6 years, her language is simply compatible with what we know of her general intellectual capacity.[7] Along the same line of

---

[6]At this point, suspecting a possible error in the karyotype effectuated on Françoise's cells years ago and the possibility that she could actually be of the mosaic type, I had a new karyotype made. It yielded the same result as the original one.

[7]Ernst Moerk, personal communication, October 22, 1989.

speech sounds and related verbal material in tests of dichotic listening. Rather, they demonstrate a marked tendency for left-ear/right-hemisphere superiority in speech perception. Dual-task studies supply relevant data for analyzing cerebral dominance for speech production. According to the available data, Down syndrome individuals seems to depend on their left hemisphere for speech production (in the same way that normal people do). Elliott et al. (1987) speculated that the language problems of Down syndrome persons may be at least partially related to a dissociation between cerebral areas responsible for speech perception and production. Accordingly, this dissociation may cause difficulties or delays of communication between functional systems that normally overlap. If, as currently held, the left cerebral hemisphere is primarily a sequential analyzer and if the cortical mechanisms for speech reception are located within the right hemisphere in Down syndrome persons, it could be added that certain functions in these people are remote from the neural apparatus best equipped to handle these functions. Curiously, however, in three reported studies (Hartley, 1981; Pipe, 1983; Zekulin-Hartley, 1982) involving mentally retarded subjects of etiologies other than Down syndrome (etiologies unfortunately not reported) with comparable mental ages, no reversed cerebral dominance for speech perception was ascertained. The reversed dominance of Down syndrome individuals, therefore, might not be a function of mental retardation per se but rather a function of the specific genetic syndrome. Because retarded children with and without Down syndrome usually exhibit similar language problems at corresponding levels of retardation, this finding, if confirmed, would considerably vitiate the present argument and caution, once more, against trying to relate too directly specific brain structures and language behaviors. The problem, generally speaking, appears to be extremely complex. It should be kept in mind that common left handedness accounts for roughly 10% of the general population in a variety of cultures (Goodman, 1987). A substantial minority of lefthanders either have their language lateralized to the right hemisphere or have bilateral language representation (Bradshaw & Nettleton, 1983), without exhibiting language difficulties, developmental or otherwise. Most probably, it is only when language lateralization if forced to the right hemisphere by damage to the left hemisphere that language problems exist. Dennis and Whitaker (1976, 1977) reported case studies of children possessing only a right or a left hemisphere. Surgical removal of one brain half antedated the beginning of speech. By 9 or 10 years, different configurations of language skill developed in the isolated hemispheres: Phonemic and semantic abilities were similarly developed but genuine syntactic competence had been asymmetrically acquired. Subjects with right brain halves only remained deficient in understanding auditory language, especially when meaning interpretation depends on syntactic analysis (e.g., tag questions, reversible

in the literature together with Françoise's case and, conversely, the regular states of language development observed in mental retardation syndromes?

A first general explanatory hypothesis, one could propose, is learning. According to such a hypothesis, the exceptional cases documented would be subjects exposed to highly efficient language remediation programs who reacted most appropriately to such programs. This hypothesis must be rejected for the following reasons. It is not known that remediation programs applied to severely and moderately mentally retarded children have met with outstanding success in teaching phonology and grammar to these children. At the end of a recent thorough review of the literature on intervention for children with language and communication disorders, noted specialists such as Snyder-McLean and McLean (1987) acknowledged that intervention can be effective in modifying the course and impact of those disorders but that it is difficult to go beyond this global conclusion because so many unresolved methodological and evaluative problems remain in remediation work and because few of the published intervention studies provide data regarding the maintenance or generalization of treatment effects to the real-world communicative contexts in which supposedly acquired skills must ultimately be used by children. In the case of Françoise, for whom severe language retardation is evidenced until at least 5 or 6 years, the regular logopedic intervention took place more than 25 years ago, a time at which little was known about the developmental language disorders or the early intervention techniques applicable in such cases. Assuming that language intervention can be effective for teaching grammar, how could it be explained then that the cases considered in this chapter, as well as in some other recent papers, are exceptional? If learning were a valid explanation for these cases, there should be thousands of exceptional cases of language development among the mental retardation population who receive systematic language intervention (a numerous group of children in developed countries). Clearly, this is not the case. At best, it could be considered that the learning experience may be fully effective with some (unfortunately rare) children because these children are exceptional among their mentally retarded peers to begin with, which sets us on another explanatory course.

I have no data base to speculate on the intrinsic exceptionality of the language cases reported by Bellugi (1988) and others, but in the case of Françoise, it is probably worth mentioning that her cerebral organization for language corresponds to what may be observed in nonretarded people, which does not appear to be the case for other Down syndrome subjects.

A dozen specialized studies of cerebral specialization for language stimulus in Down syndrome using dichotic listening and dual task techniques have been reported in the literature (see Elliott, Weeks, & Elliott, 1987, for a review and a discussion). It appears that Down syndrome individuals do not exhibit typical right-ear/left-hemisphere dominance for

reasoning, one might add that the average language realizations of the nonexceptional mentally retarded subjects are also compatible with the 4 or 5 year mental-age level of development that constitutes the realistic upper level of mental evolution in these persons (see Gibson, 1981, for Down syndrome). Let me finish with a few words to explain why I believe that this is not a convincing counterargument. As previously demonstrated, Françoise's productive and, above all, receptive grammatical functioning is well beyong the 5 or 6 year level of normal language development. It is true, however, that her language conceptual development is compatible with her level of mental development. But this dissociation is precisely part of the argument developed in the preceding paragraphs. As to the nonexceptional mentally retarded subjects, it is known and was previously indicated, that their phonological and grammatical developments most often fall short of their mental developmental level as evaluated by the mental-age measure (to the extent that this measure means anything precise and may be trusted), whereas their language conceptual development is fairly predictible on a mental-age basis. These two indications are suggestive of a clear dissociation between computational and conceptual components of the language system and of the relative autonomy of the computational component from nonlinguistic cognition.

REFERENCES

Anderson, E., & Spain, B. (1977). *The child with spina bifida*. London: Methuen.

Bartel, N., Bryen, D., & Keehn, S. (1973). Language comprehension in the moderately retarded child. *Exceptional Children, 39,*

Baumeister, A. (1967). Problems in comparative studies of mental retardates and normals. *American Journal of Mental Deficiency, 71,* 477–483.

Bellugi, U., Marks, S., Bihrle, A., & Sabo, H. (1988). Dissociation between language and cognitive functions in Williams syndrome. In D. Bishop & K. Mogford (Eds.), *Language development in exceptional circumstances* (pp. 132–149). Edinburgh: Churchill Livingstone.

Bickerton, D. (1981). *Roots of language*. Ann Arbor, MI: Karoma.

Bickerton, D. (1984). The language bioprogram hypothesis. *The Behavioral and Brain Sciences, 7,* 173–188, 212–218.

Bradshaw, J., & Nettleton, N. (1983). *Human cerebral asymmetry*. Englewood Cliffs, NJ: Prentice-Hall.

Brown, R. (1973). *A first language*. Cambridge, MA: Harvard University Press.

Burt, C. (1937). *The backward child*. London: University of London Press.

Caplan, D., & Hildebrandt, N. (1988). *Disorders of syntactic comprehension*. Cambridge, MA: MIT Press.

Chomsky, N. (1966). *Cartesian linguistics*. New York: Harper & Row.

Chomsky, N. (1968). *Language and mind*. New York: Harcourt, Brace, & World.

Chomsky, N. (1980). *Rules and representations*. New York: Columbia University Press.

Chomsky, N. (1981). *Lectures on government and binding*. Dordrecht, Holland: Foris.

Cromer, R. (1987). The cognition hypothesis revisited. In F. Kessel (Ed.), *The development of* language and language researchers. (pp. 223–248). Hillsdale, NJ: Lawrence Erlbaum Associates.

Cromer, R. (1988). Differentiating language and cognition. In R. Schiefelbusch & L. Lloyd (Eds.), *Language perspectives* (2nd ed.) (pp. 91–124). Austin TX: Proed.

Curtiss, S. (1977). *Genie : A psycholinguistic study of a modern-day "wild child"*. New York: Academic Press.

Curtiss, S., & Yamada, J. (1981). Selectively intact grammatical development in a retarded child. *ULCA working papers in Cognitive Linguistics, 3*, 61–91.

Dennis, M., & Whitaker, H. (1976). Language acquisition following hemidecortication: Linguistic superiority of the left over the right hemisphere. *Brain and Language, 3*, 404–433.

Dennis, M., & Whitaker, H. (1977). Hemispheric equipotentiality and language acquisition. In S. Segalowitz & F. Gruber (Eds.), *Language development and neurological theory* (pp. 93–106). New York: Academic Press.

Dodd, B. (1976). A comparison of the phonological systems of mental age matched normal, severely subnormal, and Down's syndrome children. *British Journal of Disorders of Communication, 11*, 27–42.

Dodd, B., & Leahy, J. (1989). Phonological disorders and mental handicap. In M. Beveridge & G. Conti-Ramsden (Eds.), *Language and communication in mentally handicapped people* (pp. 33–56). London: Chapman & Hall.

Dubois, J., & Dubois-Charlier, F. (1970). *Eléments de linguistique française* [Elements of french linguistic]. Paris: Larousse.

Edwards, D. (1973). Sensory-motor intelligence and semantic relations in early child grammar. *Cognition, 2*, 395–424.

Elliott, D., Weeks, D., & Elliott, C. (1987). Cerebral specialization in individuals with Down syndrome. *American Journal of Mental Retardation, 92*, 263–271.

Fodor, J. (1983). *The modularity of mind*. Cambridge, MA: MIT Press.

Fowler, A. (1988). Determinants of rate of language growth in children with Down syndrome. In L. Nadel (Ed.), *The psychobiology of Down syndrome* (pp. 217–245). Cambridge, MA: MIT Press.

Gibson, D. (1981). *Down's syndrome*. New York: Cambridge University Press.

Goldman-Eisler, F. (1968). *Psycholinguistics experiments in spontaneous speech*. New York: Academic Press.

Goodman, R. (1987). The developmental neurobiology of language. In W. Yule & M. Rutter (Eds.), *Language development and disorders*. (pp. 129–145). Oxford: Mac Keith Press.

Grober, E., Beardsley, W., & Caramazza, A. (1978). Parallel function strategy in pronoun assignment. *Cognition, 6*, 117–133.

Grodzinsky, Y. (1990). *Theoretical perspectives on language deficits*. Cambridge, MA: MIT Press.

Halliday, M. A. K. (1985). *An introduction to functional grammar*. London: Arnold.

Hartley, X. (1981). Lateralization of speech stimuli in young Down's syndrome children. *Cortex, 17*, 241–248.

Hopper, C., & Thompson, S. (1980). Transitivity in grammar and discourse. *Language, 56*, 251–299.

Lenneberg, E. (1967). *Biological foundations of language*. New York: Wiley.

Lenneberg, E., Nichols, I., & Rosenberger, E. (1964). Primitive stages of language development in mongolism. (Research Publications, 42, pp. 119–147). New York: Association for Research in Nervous and Mental Disease.

Marshall, J. (1984). Multiple perspectives on modularity. *Cognition, 17*, 209–242.

Miller, J. (1988). The developmental asynchrony of language development in children with Down syndrome. In L. Nadel (Ed.), *The psychobiology of Down syndrome* (pp. 167–198). Cambridge, MA: MIT Press.

Piaget, J. (1963). Language et opérations intellectuelles [Language and intellectual operations]. In Collectif, *Problèmes de Psycholinguistique* [Problems of psycholinguistics]. Paris: Presses Universitaires de France.

Piaget, J. (1970). *Piaget's theory.* In P. Mussen (Ed.), *Manual of child psychology* (Vol. 2, pp. 703–732). New York: Wiley.

Pipe, M. (1983). Dichotic-listening performance following auditory discrimination training in Down's syndrome and developmentally retarded children. *Cortex, 19,* 481–491.

Rondal, J. A. (1978). Maternal speech to normal and Down's syndrome children matched for mean length of utterance. In C. E. Meyers (Ed.), *Quality of life in severely and profoundly retarded people: Research foundations.* (pp. 193–266). Washington, DC: American Association on Mental Deficiency.

Rondal, J. A. (1984). Linguistic and prelinguistic development in moderate and severe mental retardation. In J. Dobbing, A. D. B. Clarke, J. A. Corbett, J. Hogg, & R. Robinson (Eds.), *Scientific studies in mental retardation* (pp. 323–345). London: The Royal Society of Medicine & The MacMillan Press.

Rondal, J. A. (1985). *Language et communication chez les handicapés mentaux* [Language and communication in the mentally handicapped]. Bruxelles: Mardaga.

Rondal, J. A. (1988a). *Down's syndrome.* In D. Bishop & K. Mogford (Eds.), *Language development in exceptional circumstances* (pp. 165–176). Edinburgh: Churchill Livingstone.

Rondal, J. A. (1988b). Language development in Down's syndrome: A life-span perspective. *International Journal of Behavioral Development, 11,* 21–36.

Rondal, J. A. (in press). *Exceptional language development in Down syndrome. A case study and its implications for the cognition- language issue.* New York: Cambridge University Press.

Rondal, J. A., Bachelet, J.-F., & Peree, F. (1986). Analyse du langage et des interactions verbales adulte–enfant [Language analysis and analysis of adult–child verbal interactions]. *Bulletin d'Audiophonologie, 5-6,* 507–535.

Rondal, J. A., Cession A., & Vincent, E. (1988). Comprehension des phrases déclaratives selon la voix et l'actionnalité du verbe chez un groupe d'adultes trisomiques 21 [Comprehension of declarative sentences according to voice and actionality of verb in a group of adults with trisomy 21]. Liège : Université de Liège, Laboratoire de Psycholinguistique.

Rondal, J. A., & Lambert, J. L. (1983). The speech of mentally retarded adults in a dyadic communication situation: Some formal and informative aspects. *Psychologica Belgica, 23,* 49–56.

Rondal, J. A., Lambert, J. L., & Sohier, C. (1980). Analyse des troubles articulatoires chez des enfants arriérés mentaux mongoliens et non mongoliens [Analysis of articulatory disorders in mentally retarded children with and without Trisomy 21]. *Bulletin d'Audiophonologie, 10,* 13–20.

Rondal, J. A., Lambert, J. L., & Sohier, C. (1981). Elicited verbal and nonverbal imitation in Down syndrome and other mentally retarded children. *Language and Speech, 24,* 245–254.

Rondal, J. A., Leyen, N., Bredart, S., & Pérée, F. (1984). Coréférence et stratégie des fonctions parallèles dans le cas des pronoms anaphoriques ambigus [Coreference and the strategy of parallel functions in the case of ambiguous anaphoric pronouns]. *Cahiers de Psychologie Cognitive, 4,* 151–170.

Rondal, J. A., Thibaut, J. P., & Cession, A. (in press). Transitivity effects on children's sentence comprehension. *European Journal of Cognitive Psychology.*

Schlanger, B., & Gottsleben, R. (1957). Analysis of speech defects among the institutionalized mentally retarded. *Journal of Speech and Hearing Disorders, 22,* 98–103.

Seagoe, M. (1965). Verbal development in a mongoloid. *Exceptional Children, 31,* 269–275.

Shallice, T. (1984). More functionally isolable subsystems but fewer modules? *Cognition, 17,* 243–251.

Sinclair-De Zwart, H. (1973). Language acquisition and cognitive development. In T. Moore

(Ed.), *Cognitive development and the acquisition of language.* (pp. 9–25). New York: Academic Press.

Snyder-McLean, L., & McLean, J. (1987). Effectiveness of early intervention for children with language and communication disorders. In M. Guralnick & F. Bennett (Eds.), *The effectiveness of early intervention for at-risk and handicapped children* (pp. 213–274). New York: Academic Press.

Van Borsel, J. (1988). An analysis of the speech of five Down's syndrome adolescents. *Journal of Communication Disorders, 21,* 409–422.

Zekulin-Hartley, X. (1982). Selective attention to dichotic input of retarded children. *Cortex, 18,* 311–316.

Zisk, H., & Bialer, I. (1967). Speech and language problems in mongolism: A review of the literature. *Journal of Speech and Hearing Disorders,* 32, 288–241.

8 Dissociations in Form and Function in the Acquisition of Language by Autistic Children

Helen Tager-Flusberg
University of Massachusetts

INTRODUCTION

Autism is a pervasive developmental disorder that is characterized by delays and deficits in language acquisition, the absence of imaginative behaviors such as pretence play, repetitive or stereotyped activities, and profound impairments in social functioning (APA, 1987; Cohen, Paul, & Volkmar, 1987). Indeed, these deficits in the domain of socialization—in forming social relationships, engaging in social interactions, and in acquiring culturally appropriate social behaviors—are generally considered to be primary features of autism (Baron-Cohen, 1988; Fein, Pennington, Markowitz, Braverman, & Waterhouse, 1986; Kanner, 1943). In this chapter, I consider how these social impairments might influence the acquisition of language in autistic children: To what extent and in what particular ways are the known deficits in language functioning related to the difficulties that autistic children experience when interacting with other people[1]? The data presented here suggest strongly that whereas deficits in social functioning do influence aspects of communicative or pragmatic functioning, they do not have any identifiable influence on the course of grammatical development. Furthermore, the language of autistic children indicates that the

---

[1]It is important to note that autistic children vary widely in their overall level of functioning and in IQ. Only about 25% of the population are higher functioning, falling within the normal range of intelligence. About half of all autistic children never develop productive language; therefore, this chapter focuses on a limited part of the broader population of children with autism—those who are higher functioning intellectually and who develop language.

acquisition of grammatical form is quite dissociated from the development of functional aspects of language.

Social Deficits in Autism

Kanner's earliest clinical descriptions of children with autism included a variety of social impairments, including lack of attention and affection toward other people, withdrawal from people, lack of eye contact, treating people like objects, and socially inappropriate behavior (Kanner, 1943). Wing and Gould (1979) identified three subtypes of social impairment: (a) aloofness, (b) passive interaction, and (c) active but odd interactions, which can be identified based on the number and types of interactions that autistic children make (Volkmar, Cohen, Bregman, Hooks, & Stevenson, 1989). Typically, autistic children progress as they get older, from the aloof to the passive to the active-but-odd category (Volkmar, 1987). However, even when other features of the syndrome abate, individuals once identified as autistic continue to exhibit significant social difficulties (Rumsey, Rapaport, & Sceery, 1985; Rutter, Greenfield, & Lockyer, 1967).

Younger autistic children are by no means completely unresponsive to others, although parents often report that as infants their autistic children failed to use eye contact, did not engage in typical reciprocal social games such as "peek-a-boo," tended to ignore the presence of people, did not seek comfort from adult caregivers, and appeared to lack attachment (Ornitz, Guthrie, & Farley, 1977; Volkmar, 1987). More recently, Klin (1988) also found that young autistic children do not show a preference for listening to their mothers' speech. Nevertheless, by the time autistic children are toddlers or preschoolers, they do show differential attachment to their mothers (Shapiro, Sherman, Calamari, & Koch, 1987; Sigman, Mundy, Ungerer, & Sherman, 1986; Sigman & Ungerer, 1984) and recognize themselves in a mirror (Dawson & McKissick, 1984; Neuman & Hill, 1978; Spiker & Ricks, 1984). These aspects of social awareness still exhibit considerable dysfunction. For example, the quality of autistic children's attachment behaviors is quite deviant (Mundy & Sigman, 1989a). In general, autistic children's interactions with others, and even their self-recognition behaviors, are marked by the absence or limited expression of affect (Hobson, 1989).

One of the most significant aspects of social impairment in autistic children is their limited ability to engage in joint attention. Indeed, deficits in joint attention are currently viewed to be among the first clear signs of autism in infants less than 1 year old (Mundy & Sigman, 1989b). Autistic children fail to share with others attention to objects using coordinated alternating eye gaze (i.e., referential looking) and pointing or other nonverbal gestures (Curcio, 1978; Landry & Loveland, 1988; Loveland &

Landry, 1986; Mundy, Sigman, Ungerer, & Sherman, 1986; Sigman et al., 1986; Wetherby & Prutting, 1984). The paucity of joint attention behavior persists in verbal autistic children who rarely use language to call attention to interesting objects or events (Tager-Flusberg, 1989a; Wetherby, 1986).

In summary, research and clinical observations of autistic children indicate that they have profound impairments in social behaviors that persist over time. Of particular interest to work in language development are the deficits in joint attention and in reciprocal or social game playing and the lack of preference for their mothers' speech.

The Social Foundations of Communication and Language

In the mid-1970s, as a reaction against nativism, a number of prominent theorists proposed that language development was rooted in early social interactions between infants and their mothers (e.g., Bruner, 1975, 1977; Snow, 1979). In a number of ways, this move away from nativist theories that viewed language as an autonomous aspect of the mind, paralleled cognitivist approaches to language acquisition. The impetus for the social perspective came primarily from the introduction of pragmatics to the study of language development (Bates, 1976), which led to a shift from an exclusive focus on formal and semantic aspects of language to an increased emphasis on communicative function and communicative context.

On this view, the social context of language acquisition was considered to be central to the ontogeny of communication even in the prelinguistic period. Gestures and vocalizations that signaled requests, reference (i.e., joint attention behaviors), or social ritual (e.g., waving goodbye) were viewed as developing out of the reciprocal interactions and games of early infancy. Bruner summarized, "Our emphasis . . . has been upon *social* processes that are shared by prelinguistic and linguistic communication. Certainly these processes (turn taking, role interchange, etc.) *do* remain invariant across the change into language and provide a centrally important source of continuity" (1983, p. 128). The idea that there is continuity between the prelinguistic and linguistic stages is seen as a major strength of this theoretical perspective. Snow (1979) took this notion of continuity one step further, arguing that there is also continuity between the one word and multiword utterance stage, and between semantic and syntactic levels of analysis, all of which are rooted in the social interactional context of language development.

The social interactionist view of language acquisition, in fact, encompasses a number of different constructs and proposals. There is no unitary perspective other than the central idea that social processes underlie at least some aspects of language development and that communication is the driving functional force of language development. A variety of social processes have been proposed, including:

1. The complex interactions such as game playing and other turn-taking sequences (or *intersubjectivity*) between mothers and babies that are viewed as the foundation for the infant's developing notion of communicative intent (e.g., Bruner, 1983; Ratner & Bruner, 1978; Snow, 1981), discourse rules, and, by virtue of putative *structural parallels*, other aspects of language including initial grammatical structures (Bruner, 1977).
2. Speech addressed to children that is often expressed in simplified form to facilitate and direct language acquisition (see Snow & Ferguson, 1977).[2]
3. Imitation as a significant process in the acquisition of various aspects of language, including communicative functions, vocabulary, and even grammar (e.g., Bohannon & Warren-Leubecker, 1989).
4. The functions of utterances that determine the acquisition of form.

In this chapter, not all aspects of the social interactionist perspective are addressed. A number of important critical reviews have been published (e.g., Bates, Bretherton, Beeghly-Smith, & McNew, 1982; Shatz, 1982) and indeed few sympathizers with this theoretical orientation would now argue that all of language acquisition can be subsumed by this account. Therefore, this is not the goal of this chapter; rather, the focus here is on the contribution that can be made by the study of autistic children to our understanding of the scope of, and limits on, the role played by social factors in the acquisition of language. In her critique of the social perspective, Shatz (1982) noted that this theoretical view has emphasized the role of external social factors in shaping the course of language development: that is, the role played by the mother, who is responsible for joint activities with her infant, providing "simplified" speech, and so forth. In contrast, by focusing on autistic children who are known to have profound social impairments, the discussion here shifts to the role of social factors as a within-child mechanism for acquiring language.

---

[2]There is considerable controversy about how to characterize the special character of speech addressed to children. It is by no means clear that "motherese" is, in fact, simpler according to any obvious metric (e.g., Gleitman, Newport, & Gleitman, 1984), and not all children in all cultures will be exposed to motherese as it is defined in our culture (cf. Heath, 1983; Ochs, 1988). Nevertheless, for the purposes of this chapter, we do not take on this issue because it emphasizes social influences external to the child. Similarly, the controversy over whether children have negative feedback available to help correct their grammars is also not considered (Brown & Hanlon, 1970; Demetras, Post, & Snow, 1986; Hirsh-Pasek, Treiman, & Schneiderman, 1984; Morgan & Travis, 1989).

LANGUAGE ACQUISITION IN AUTISM

Early Development of Communicative Function

Social impairments in autism are related to deficits in the acquisition of certain aspects of communicative function. During the prelinguistic period, autistic children make few communicative attempts, and these are limited to protoimperative gestures or vocalizations. Numerous studies have found that in nonverbal autistic children protodeclarative functions are strikingly absent (Curcio, 1978). When autistic children do begin to acquire language, they continue to produce a limited range of speech acts that are primarily geared toward obtaining desired objects or responding to their mothers' test questions (Ball, 1978; Mermelstein, 1983; Wetherby, 1986). Even among older, linguistically able autistic individuals, their utterances are limited; they rarely add new information to the ongoing topic of discourse (Anderson & Tager-Flusberg, 1988). One exception to this may be the excessive monologuing of some autistic individuals who can speak endlessly about their own pet hobby without regard to the attention or interest of the listener (Paul, 1987)[3].

The paucity of declarative functions in the communications or language of autistic children may well be related to their deficits in joint attention (Landry & Loveland, 1988). This suggests one interesting association between a significant social behavior (joint attention) and certain communicative functions (declaratives/informativeness) that emerges from the study of autistic children. However, it is important to note that this relationship is quite specific; there does not appear to be a global relationship between joint attention and the development of intentional communication, given that autistic children are unimpaired in their use of imperatives, requests, and responses.[4] This specific relationship between joint attention and declarative functions in language among autistic children confirms the kind of continuity between the prelinguistic stage and the early development of language suggested by Bruner (1983). Social dysfunction in infancy leaves an indelible mark on certain aspects of communicative functioning in the language of autistic children.

---

[3]Numerous other examples of autistic children's inability to take into account their listeners' needs are available in the clinical and empirical literature, However, much of this work is fairly unsystematic and lacks relevant control groups and, therefore, will not be reviewed in detail.

[4]It is interesting to note that despite deficits in joint attention (cf. Bruner, 1983), autistic children are unimpaired in the development of lexical semantics: Concepts and meanings that underlie the words they use are identical to those of control groups (Tager-Flusberg, 1985a, 1985b), and the course of lexical development is also similar to other groups of children (Tager-Flusberg et al., 1990).

Grammatical Development

The early literature on language in autistic children emphasized the atypical development of syntax and morphology in this population. Kanner (1946) discussed what he viewed as some of the deviant aspects of autistic children's language, especially the excessive echolalia, or imitation, and the unusual use of phrases (or "metaphorical" language), which suggested the absence of meaning.[5] A number of researchers have since argued that because autistic children rely so heavily on echolalia, they do not progress through the same stages of grammatical development; for example, their utterances do not show gradual increases in length and they appear not to analyze the structure of the utterances they produce (e.g., Prizant, 1983; Simon, 1975). If true, this suggests a very different pattern for the acquisition of syntax in children with autism; put another way, the processes by which they acquire grammar may not be the same as those for normally developing children, presumably because of their deficits in social functioning. Cross-sectional studies of the grammatical structure of autistic children's utterances suggest that these children's grammars are not different from those of control groups of normally developing and mentally retarded children (Bartolucci, Pierce, & Streiner, 1980; Howlin, 1984; Pierce & Bartolucci, 1977); however, these data do not tell us about developmental sequence or process and, therefore, do not directly address the issue.

We recently completed a longitudinal study of 6 higher functioning autistic boys who were all in the process of acquiring language (Tager-Flusberg et al., 1990). Spontaneous speech samples were collected at bimonthly intervals in the children's homes while they were interacting with their mothers. The visits, which lasted about 1 hr, were video- and audiotaped. Verbatim transcripts of the conversation, which included rich notes on the ongoing activity and context, were later prepared in the form of computer files. The autistic children were matched at the start of the study on chronological age and productive language level to six children (four boys and two girls) with Down syndrome. Thus, we could compare the autistic children to a nonautistic group of children who were also delayed in acquiring language, but who do not have similar social impairments, ensuring that any differences in developmental patterns found among the autistic children could not be attributed to delayed onset. Table 8.1 summarizes the main characteristics of the 12 children in the study, including information about their ages, nonverbal IQ scores, mean length

---

[5]Note, however, that research conducted with higher functioning autistic children does not support the view that the development of meaning is in any way aberrant (see Footnote 4).

TABLE 8.1
Subject Characteristics

Child	Age	IQ	MLU	Length of Time Followed	Number of Visits
Autistic:					
Stuart	3;4	61	1.17	15 mos.	8
Roger	3;9	105	2.31	22	10
Brett	5;8	108	3.74	22	10
Mark	7;7	75	1.46	26	13
Rick	4;7	94	1.73	22	11
Jack	6;9	91	3.03	25	12
Down Syndrome:					
Charlie	3;3	46	1.21	13 mos.	6
Kate	4;1	65	2.98	12	6
Penny	5;1	63	2.69	15	7
Martin	5;4	47	1.63	24	11
Billy	5;7	49	1.68	25	13
Jerry	6;9	54	2.86	24	11

of utterance (MLU) at the start of the study, and the length of time they were followed.

What kinds of changes over time occurred in MLU and in the use of different grammatical constructions? To answer this, we first prepared samples of 100 complete spontaneous utterances taken from each transcript, excluding imitations, repetitions, and routines. MLUs were computed on these samples using the Systematic Analysis of Language Transcripts (SALT) program (Miller & Chapman, 1985); The general findings were that, despite within-group variability in the rate of change, all the children whose MLUs were below 3.5[6] at the start of the study showed gradual increases in MLU, similar to the developmental patterns found for normal children (Brown, 1973; Miller & Chapman, 1981), and, more importantly, similar to what was found for our Down syndrome control subjects. Two of the six autistic boys and the two girls with Down syndrome exhibited rates of MLU change that were within normal limits, despite their delayed onset (Tager-Flusberg et al., 1990). These MLU data certainly contradict Simon's (1975) claim that autistic children do not show gradual increases in MLU. On the contrary, their MLU profiles were within the normal or developmentally delayed range and there was nothing particularly aberrant about the autistic children's developmental patterns.

MLU is a simple measure of length that is assumed, for English-speaking

---

[6]Because of the unreliability of MLU as an index of development beyond 4.0 (see Brown, 1973), it is not surprising that we did not find systematic increases for the children whose language was already quite advanced.

children, to reflect the addition of new grammatical constructions that are acquired in a systematic order by normal children (Brown, 1973). It may be, however, that autistic children do not acquire grammatical constructions in the same developmental order. To test this, we employed the Index of Productive Syntax (IPSyn), a measure developed recently by Scarborough (1990), which correlates highly with MLU but provides a more detailed picture about the grammatical content of a language sample. The measure consists of 56 items, divided into four categories: (a) noun phrase, (b) verb phrase, (c) question/negation, and (d) sentence structure. Within each category, the items (ranging from 11 to 20) are sequenced developmentally, based on current knowledge of the acquisition orders found in descriptive studies of language development.[7] For the purpose of this analysis, we noted for each sample the specific items within each category that were present, and then reviewed the resulting profiles, noting the maximum or highest level item scored in each category. Given that the items are arranged in order of emergence, a normal pattern of development would be to find systematic profiles, with the highest item present in each category increasing over time. For example, in the verb phrase category, developmentally early items include verb, participle or preposition, prepositional phrase, and copula; intermediate items include auxiliary verb, present progressive -*ing*, and present tense modal; later items include past tense modal, regular past tense -*ed*, and past tense auxiliary. A systematic profile would exhibit the presence of only the developmentally early items at lower MLUs, with the gradual addition of intermediate and then later items with corresponding increases in MLU. By and large, both the Down syndrome and autistic children showed highly systematic and similar-looking profiles on the IPSyn (see Tager-Flusberg et al., 1990, for more details). The autistic (and Down syndrome) children exhibited orderly development of grammatical constructions or features within each IPSyn category, which mirrored the sequence in which normal children acquire these same constructions.

These findings confirm that grammatical development in these autistic children does not show a deviant pattern, despite the fact that the children were quite impaired in their social development, including poor joint attention skills (Tager-Flusberg, 1989a). There appears to be no evidence, therefore, that social factors play a significant role in the acquisition of syntax (Bruner, 1975; Snow, 1979). Thus, our data suggest that there is a marked asynchrony, or discontinuity, between the development of commu-

---

[7]IPSyn is typically used to provide an overall score based on marking the presence of 0, 1, or 2 different examples for each of the items in the measure and awarding the corresponding number of points. Scores are then summed both within and across subscales to yield a total IPSyn score, which is highly correlated with MLU (Scarborough, 1990; Tager-Flusberg et al., 1990).

nicative function and the acquisition of grammar in autistic children (Tager-Flusberg, 1988). Social deficits significantly affect aspects of communicative function while sparing the grammatical components of language. This kind of asynchrony provides support for the idea that there is domain specificity in language acquisition and that at least some (but clearly not all) aspects of language are autonomous of other aspects of development. This notion is developed further in the next sections in which the acquisition of specific forms is analyzed in order to investigate more closely the relationship between the acquisition of form and function.

FORM AND FUNCTION RELATIONS
IN THE LANGUAGE OF AUTISTIC CHILDREN

The Development of Personal Pronouns

One prominent linguistic error that autistic children make, first noted in Kanner's original description of the syndrome (Kanner, 1943), is that they tend to refer to themselves as *you* and to their conversational partner as *I*. These kinds of pronoun reversal errors have been explained in a variety of ways. Some view them within a psychodynamic perspective (e.g., Bettelheim, 1967); others suggest that they are the by-product of echolalia coupled with limited comprehension (e.g., Bartak & Rutter, 1974; Fay & Schuler, 1980); a more recent hypothesis is that they reflect a lack of attention to the speech addressed to other people (Oshima-Takane & Benaroya, 1989; cf. Klin, 1988). Reversal errors have also been noted occasionally among other populations including normal children (Chiat, 1982; Schiff-Myers, 1983), deaf children learning sign language (Petitto, 1987), and blind children (Dunlea, 1989; Fraiberg, 1977). They are generally interpreted as evidence for a pragmatic difficulty in understanding shifting reference between the speaker and listener (Charney, 1980; Chiat, 1982), given that the primary function of first- and second-person pronouns is to denote these discourse roles. Whereas most normal, retarded, and other nonautistic children do not have difficulty with the pragmatic aspects of pronouns, a more typical error is in case marking, especially using the accusative (*me*) or possessive form (*my*) instead of the nominative, *I*. Budwig (1989) suggested that these case errors are very frequent during the period when children speak primarily about themselves.

One question that has not been addressed in the literature on pronoun development is the relationship between these two kinds of error patterns. Another way to put this would be to ask how the development of grammatical aspects of pronouns (i.e., case) might be related to the development of pragmatic aspects (i.e., discourse or speaker roles). To

TABLE 8.2
Pronoun Usage and Errors

	Autistic		Down Syndrome	
	N	%	N	%
Total Number of Pronouns	1,673		2,270	
Self	1,412	(84.4)	1,817	(80.0)
Other	261	(15.6)	453	(20.0)
Case Errors	2	(0.12)	28	(1.23)
Reversal Errors	220	(13.15)	0	(0.0)

answer this, we used the data from our longitudinal study of the autistic and Down syndrome children (Tager-Flusberg, 1990). All complete child utterances that included a first- or second-person pronoun were extracted from the transcripts using the search procedure in SALT (Miller & Chapman, 1985), but imitations, repetitions, idioms, and other routine utterances were excluded from further analysis. Each pronoun was then coded along three dimensions: (a) reference (self or other), (b) case (nominative, accusative/dative, possessive, reflexive), noting clearly when errors were made,[8] and (c) reversal error (e.g., reference to self as *you* or *your* or to mother as *I* or *me*). Only unambiguous examples were coded for reversal errors; the videotapes and transcripts were used to check for their presence, based on both nonverbal and verbal context.

In this chapter, the focus of the analyses is limited to the distribution of the main kinds of error patterns found in the two groups of children. Table 8.2 provides a summary of the total number of pronouns used by each group and the total number of case errors and reversal errors. The most striking feature of these data is the almost complete dissociation between the two types of errors. The Down syndrome children made no reversal errors — they never confused the linguistic marking of speaker and listener. However, five of the six Down syndrome children did make case marking errors.[9] These errors were all first-person errors; the majority (89%) involved using *me* or *my* for the nominative form, including the following examples:

1. My get it.
2. Me cool off.

---

[8]Note that elliptical responses to questions such as, "Who is a good boy?" "Me!" were not coded as errors.

[9]The only Down syndrome child who did not make any case errors was the youngest and least mature linguistically — Charlie. He only produced a total of nine pronouns in very limited linguistic contexts. It may be that personal pronouns were not yet a productive part of his linguistic system.

3. My can't tell you.
4. Me gonna play with Debbie Cox.
5. Do down me arm.

In contrast, the autistic children made a significant number of reversal errors: Over 13% of their pronouns confused the speaker and listener roles, and these errors were made by every one of the autistic children. However, it is important to note that in each sample, reversal errors were produced alongside correct pronoun usage. Reversal errors were distributed across all cases (but there were no examples of a pronoun that had both a case and a reversal error), and included errors of reference to both self and other, as in the following examples:

6. You want candy.
7. Hurt yourself.
8. I write.
9. Stan helped you.
10. Are you watching the video?
11. I'm wearing glasses.
12. Help you please.

These errors occurred at all MLU stages and, in fact, became more frequent as the children's language abilities increased, although by the end of the study, two of the autistic children had stopped making them. In contrast, the case marking errors among the Down syndrome children occurred primarily when MLU was between 1.5 and 3.0.

I have interpreted these pronoun-reversal errors as evidence that autistic children are confused about speaker/listener role relations (Tager-Flusberg, 1989a, 1990; see also Chiat, 1986; Hobson, 1990). Their problems in understanding discourse roles are related to their social deficits—specifically impaired social cognitive functioning. Autistic children have great difficulty understanding that different people have distinct conceptual perspectives—that people perceive, interpret, remember, and respond to situations in unique ways. This kind of conceptual perspective-taking ability is required in order to understand the different roles of speaker and listener (Loveland, 1984), and this is reflected in the way pronouns are used in ongoing discourse. Thus, we can trace the pronoun-reversal errors made by autistic children (and perhaps other children, too) to particular aspects of their social deficit.

On this account, functional aspects of personal pronouns are related to social factors, but this does not appear to hold for grammatical aspects, specifically, knowledge of the case system. Case-marking errors were quite rare among the autistic children (though perhaps no more so than among other populations of children) but were more frequent among the Down syndrome children who had no specific social impairments. The data in Table 8.2 point to a complete dissociation between reversal and case errors — that is, between errors denoting difficulty in function, and errors denoting difficulty in form. This supports, then, the view that form and function are not so clearly linked in the acquisition of language by autistic children.

The Development of Questions

There has been a considerable amount of descriptive research conducted on the development of questions in normal children. A clear picture has emerged from these studies on the sequence of development in both form and function as well as their interrelationships (e.g., Bloom, Merkin, & Wooten, 1982; Clancy, 1989; Erreich, 1984; James & Seebach, 1982; Vaidyanathan, 1988). Children's earliest questions rely on rising intonation, which are equivalent to simple yes/no questions, and fixed formulae, such as *What that*? Gradually over the course of several months or even years, children's *wh-* questions expand in semantic scope and content and begin to incorporate appropriate auxiliary or modal verbs. Finally, the subject and auxiliary (or copula) are inverted to result in fully formed questions. These questions serve a variety of functions. James and Seebach (1982) categorized questions asked by children aged between 2 and 5 into the following inclusive categories: (a) information seeking, (b) conversational, and (c) directive. They found that the majority of questions asked by 2- and 3-year-olds were information seeking; some were conversational. Only older preschoolers, however, asked a significant number of questions to direct the behavior of other people, especially to gain attention. More recently, Clancy (1989) and Vaidyanathan (1988), studying children acquiring Korean and Tamil, respectively, investigated form–function relations in children's questions. Their data suggested that children tend to use *wh-* forms to seek information, whereas yes–no forms are used for various conversational and directive functions.

The consistent developmental patterns for question production found among normal children provide a useful background against which we studied autistic children in order to address the issue of the relationship between form and function (Tager-Flusberg, 1989b). For this analysis, four language samples spanning 1 year of the longitudinal study were taken from each of the six autistic and six Down syndrome children. The SALT program was again used to extract all utterances that were marked by punctuation (based on rising intonation or appropriate syntax) as questions. Questions were then coded for *form* (primarily *wh-* or yes/no), noting whether an auxiliary verb (or copula) and subject–auxiliary inversion were present, and *function*, using the following categories: (a) information

TABLE 8.3
Percentage of Well-formed Formed Wh- and Yes/No Questions at Different MLU Stages

	Autistic		Down Syndrome	
	Wh-	Yes/No	Wh-	Yes/No
MLU Stage				
Stage I	7	0	8	0
Stage II	40	44	27	60
Stage III	89	4	55	11
Stage IV	100	57	82	25
Stage V	91	83	84	46

seeking — external (about objects or events) or internal (about psychological states), (b) test questions (the answer was known to the child), (c) requests, (d) direct attention, (e) agreement, and (f) clarification.[10]

Autistic children asked significantly fewer wh- questions than the Down syndrome children (a mean of 9.3 per 1,000 utterances, compared to 28.2 for the Down syndrome group). Table 8.3 provides information about the percentage of those yes/no and wh- questions that contained verbs that were well formed (defined, as those questions including auxiliary verbs, or a copula verb, and inversion), for each MLU stage. We can use these data to compare the acquisition of these grammatical aspects of question-asking in the two groups. We see from this table that there was a gradual increase in the percentage of wh- questions that were well formed for both groups. With the exception of a curious jump at Stage II, a similar pattern was obtained for yes/no questions. At Stage II, there were very few yes/no questions and those that included inversion of subject and auxiliary may simply have been routines. By and large, both groups showed a similar developmental profile, although it appears that at the later stages a somewhat higher proportion of the autistic children's questions were well-formed. These developmental profiles are not unlike those reported for normally developing children (e.g., Erreich, 1984), confirming that the acquisition of form is not deviant in autistic children.

The distribution of the children's questions into the main functional categories is shown in Table 8.4. Autistic children asked significantly fewer questions that sought information or that served the conversational func-

---

[10]About 15% of the autistic children's questions could not be easily classified according to pragmatic function because they were distinctly odd. Given the choice of verb, these utterances should have been made as statements rather than questions and, thus, involved an unusual kind of perspective error (e.g., When requesting help from his mother, one boy said, "Do I need help?"). These question errors are not considered in this chapter, but see Tager-Flusberg (1989a, 1989b).

TABLE 8.4

Mean Number (and Standard Deviation) of Questions in Each Pragmatic
Function Category for Autistic and Down Syndrome Groups

	Autistic		Down Syndrome	
Information-external	9.06	(11.37)*	17.28	(11.94)*
Information-internal	1.46	(5.03)	2.16	(3.07)
Test	4.18	(11.33)	3.24	(4.77)
Request	5.40	(8.78)	2.80	(4.52)
Attention	1.74	(6.09)	1.58	(3.64)
Agreement	3.23	(4.16)*	9.61	(11.45)*
Clarification	1.55	(2.68)**	6.04	(6.66)**

*$p < .05$.
**$p < .01$.

tions of agreement and clarification. This suggests that in interesting and
important ways autistic children's questions served somewhat different
functions than those asked by the Down syndrome children and that these
differences can be traced to their social impairments.

Table 8.5 shows the relationship between form and function by
indicating the percentage for each functional category that were in wh- or
yes/no form. Chi-square analyses were used to test for group differences.
We see from the table that exactly those functional categories that were
used significantly less frequently by the autistic children (information
seeking, agreement, and clarification) showed significantly different
form–function relationships.

Not only did the autistic children ask questions to serve somewhat
different functions, they also showed an unusual pattern of form–function
relationships for certain functional categories. Yet these functional differences did not influence in any discernible ways their acquisition of the

TABLE 8.5

Form and Function Relationships in Questions from Autistic and
Down Syndrome Children

	Autistic		Down Syndrome	
	Yes–No	Wh-	Yes–No	Wh-
Information-external	32[a]	68	11	89*
Information-internal	93	7	88	12**
Test	18	82	7	93
Request	98	2	100	0
Attention	100	0	100	0
Agreement	100	0	74	26*
Clarification	82	18	32	68*

[a]% of functional category in each syntactic form.
*$p < .01$.
**$p < .05$.

highly complex syntactic and morphological aspects of questions. Again, we find strong evidence from autistic children for the dissociation between the acquisition of form and the acquisition of function.

Summary

The previous sections illustrated how form and function can be quite asynchronous in the course of acquiring language. The example of personal pronouns utilized an error analysis, contrasting the relative frequency of case-marking and reversal errors. The former indicate systematic errors in acquiring one aspect of the formal system of personal pronouns and were relatively more frequent among the Down syndrome children. The latter suggest errors in acquiring a pragmatic feature of first- and second-person pronouns and were only found among the autistic children. The analysis focusing on the development of questions in these groups of children highlighted acquisition patterns for both form and function. As predicted, the autistic children showed a paucity in the relative frequency of certain pragmatic functions of questions, which also showed up in distinct form/function relationships. Yet, once again, we found that these differences did not affect the acquisition of form. In other analyses of these longitudinal data, we have confirmed this pattern of asynchrony of form and function in the language acquisition of autistic children. Examples include differences in the functions served by negation (Tager-Flusberg, 1989c; Tager-Flusberg & Keenan, 1987) and the past tense (Tager-Flusberg, 1989c), as well as asynchronous patterns of discourse development (Anderson & Tager-Flusberg, 1988).

CONCLUSIONS

The main focus of this chapter has been on the role played by social interaction in the acquisition of language. Some theorists have argued that the course of language development is largely determined by social factors, beginning in the infancy period (e.g., Bruner, 1975, 1977; Snow, 1979, 1981). The findings from autistic children reported here paint a somewhat different picture: Certain aspects of language development are profoundly impacted by the kinds of social impairments that are at the core of the autistic syndrome; at the same time, we find that other domains of language develop in a relatively normal fashion and, thus, appear to be largely independent of social influences.

Social deficits in autism—particularly the paucity of joint attention, problems in understanding people,[11] limited empathy and affective communication, lack of interest in social games, and difficulties in reciprocal social interactions—all have a profound impact on the development of particular communicative, pragmatic, and functional aspects of language. The language used by children with autism serves a more limited range of functions and shows significant impairment in certain areas of discourse, especially in speaker/listener relations. The data from autistic children confirm the views of those researchers who have emphasized the connection between social factors and aspects of communicative functioning.

On the other hand, it is also clear from the data presented here that autistic children are not impaired in their grammatical development. Thus far, research has not uncovered one area of deviance in the order of development or even in the process of development (Tager-Flusberg & Calkins, 1990) in the domains of syntax and morphology. This suggests that acquiring communicative competence and acquiring grammar are not integrated or continuous developmental processes in language acquisition. Nor can we conclude that the putative parallels in the structure of social interaction patterns and the structure of language (cf. Bruner, 1977) bear any relation to grammatical development. The most significant lesson that we have learned from looking at language development in autistic children is that grammar is quite autonomous of functional aspects of language—a truth that will come as no surprise to many linguists, but one that must still be learned by some developmental psychologists.

ACKNOWLEDGMENT

Preparation of this chapter was supported by a grant from the National Institute of Child Health and Human Development (1R01 HD 18833).

REFERENCES

American Psychiatric Association (1987). *Diagnostic and statistical manual of mental disorders*, (3rd ed., rev.). Washington, DC: Author.

Anderson, M., & Tager-Flusberg, H. (1988 June). *Conversations between mothers and children: A longitudinal study of autistic and Down syndrome children*. Paper presented at the Symposium for Research on Child Language Disorders, Madison, WI.

Ball, J. (1978). *A pragmatic analysis of autistic children's language with respect to aphasic and normal language development*. Unpublished doctoral dissertation, Melbourne University, Australia.

---

[11]Recently autistic children's social, communicative, and cognitive impairments have been interpreted as evidence for a core deficit in the acquisition of a "theory of mind" (e.g., Baron-Cohen, 1988; Baron-Cohen, Leslie, & Frith, 1985; Hobson, 1989). This proposal is attractive as it also has the potential for providing a unitary account of the language deficits in this population (Tager-Flusberg, 1989a).

Baron-Cohen, S. (1988). Social and pragmatic deficits in autism: Cognitive or affective? *Journal of Autism and Developmental Disorders, 18*, 379–401.

Baron-Cohen, S., Leslie, A. M., & Frith, U. (1985). Does the autistic child have a "theory of mind"? *Cognition, 21*, 37–46.

Bartak, L., & Rutter, M. (1974). The usage of personal pronouns by autistic children. *Journal of Autism and Childhood Schizophrenia, 4*, 217–222.

Bartolucci, G., Pierce, S., & Streiner, D. (1980). Cross-sectional studies of grammatical morphemes in autistic and mentally retarded children. *Journal of Autism and Developmental Disorders, 10*, 39–50.

Bates, E. (1976). *Language in context.* New York: Academic Press.

Bates, E., Bretherton, I., Beeghly-Smith, M., & McNew, S. (1982). Social bases of language development: A reassessment. In H. W. Reese & L. P. Lipsitt (Eds.), *Advances in child development and behavior* (Vol. 16, pp. 7–75). New York: Academic Press.

Bettelheim, B. (1967). *The empty fortress.* New York: The Free Press.

Bloom, L., Merkin, S., & Wooten, J. (1982). Wh- questions: Linguistic factors that contribute to the sequence of acquisition. *Child Development, 53*, 1084–1092.

Bohannon, J. N., & Warren-Leubecker, A. (1989). Theoretical approaches to language acquisition. In J. B. Gleason (Ed.), *The development of language.* Columbus, OH: Merrill.

Brown, R. (1973). *A first language.* Cambridge, MA: Harvard University Press.

Brown, R., & Hanlon, C. (1970). Derivational complexity and order of acquisition in child speech. In J. R. Hayes (Ed.), *Cognition and the development of language.*(pp. 11-53). New York: Wiley.

Bruner, J. S. (1975). From communication to language - a psychological perspective. *Cognition, 3*, 255–287.

Bruner, J. S. (1977). Early social interaction and language acquisition. In H. R. Schaffer (Ed.), *Studies in mother–infant interaction* (pp. 271-289). New York: Academic Press.

Bruner, J. S. (1983). *Child's talk.* New York: Norton.

Budwig, N. (1989). The linguistic marking of agentivity and control in child language. *Journal of Child Language 16*, 263–284.

Charney, R. (1980). Speech roles and the development of personal pronouns. *Journal of Child Language, 7*, 509–528.

Chiat, S. (1982). If I were you and you were me: The analysis of pronouns in a pronoun-reversing child. *Journal of Child Language, 9*, 359–379.

Chiat, S. (1986). Personal pronouns. In P. Fletcher & M. Garman (Eds.), *Language acquisition*, (2nd ed.), (pp. 339-355). New York: Cambridge University Press.

Clancy, P. (1989). Form and function in the acquisition of Korean wh- questions. *Journal of Child Language, 16*, 323–347.

Cohen, D. J., Paul, R., & Volkmar, F. (1987). Issues in classification of pervasive developmental disorders and associated conditions. In D. J. Cohen & A. M. Donnellan (Eds.), *Handbook of autism and pervasive developmental disorders* (pp. 20-40). New York: Wiley.

Curcio, F. (1978). Sensorimotor functioning and communication in mute autistic children. *Journal of Autism and Childhood Schizophrenia, 2*, 264–287.

Dawson, G., & McKissick, F. (1984). Self-recognition in autistic children. *Journal of Autism and Developmental Disorders, 14*, 383–394.

Demetras, M. J., Post, K. N., & Snow, C. E. (1986). Feedback to first language learners: The role of repetitions and clarification questions. *Journal of Child Language, 13*, 275–292.

Dunlea, A. (1989). *Vision and the emergence of meaning: Blind and sighted children's early language.* Cambridge: Cambridge University Press.

Erreich, A. (1984). Learning how to ask: Patterns of inversion in yes–no and wh-questions. *Journal of Child Language, 11*, 579–592.

Fay, W., & Schuler, A. L. (1980). *Emerging language in autistic children.* Baltimore, MD: University Park Press.

Fraiberg, S. (1977). *Insights from the blind*. New York: Basic Books.

Fein, D., Pennington, B., Markowitz, P., Braverman, M., & Waterhouse, L. (1986). Toward a neuropsychological model of infantile autism: Are the social deficits primary? *Journal of the American Academy of Child Psychiatry, 25*, 198–212.

Gleitman, L., Newport, E., & Gleitman, H. (1984). The current status of the motherese hypothesis. *Journal of Child Language, 11*, 43–79.

Heath, S. B. (1983). *Ways with words*. New York: Cambridge University Press.

Hirsh-Pasek, K., Treiman, R., & Schneiderman, M. (1984). Brown and Hanlon revisited: Mothers' sensitivity to ungrammatical forms. *Journal of Child Language, 11*, 81–88.

Hobson, R. P. (1989). Beyond cognition: A theory of autism. In G. Dawson (Ed.), *Autism: Nature, diagnosis, and treatment* (pp. 22–48). New York: Guilford.

Hobson, R. P. (1990). On the origins of self and the case of autism. *Development and Psychopathology, 2*, 163–181.

Howlin, P. (1984). The acquisition of grammatical morphemes in autistic children: A critique and replication of the findings of Bartolucci, Pierce, and Streiner, 1980. *Journal of Autism and Developmental Disorders, 14*, 127–136.

James, S., & Seebach, M. (1982). The pragmatic function of children's questions. *Journal of Speech and Hearing Research, 25*, 2–11.

Kanner, L. (1943). Autistic disturbances of affective contact. *Nervous Child, 2*, 217–250.

Kanner, L. (1946). Irrelevant and metaphorical language in early infantile autism. *American Journal of Psychiatry, 103*, 242–246.

Klin, A. (1988). *The emergence of self, symbolic functions, and early infantile autism*. Unpublished doctoral dissertation, University of London.

Landry, S., & Loveland, K. (1988). Communication behaviors in autism and developmental language delay. *Journal of Child Psychology and Psychiatry, 29*, 621–634.

Loveland, K. (1984). Learning about points of view: Spatial perspective and the acquisition of "I/you." *Journal of Child Language, 11*, 535–556.

Loveland, K., & Landry, S. (1986). Joint attention in autistic and language delayed children. *Journal of Autism and Developmental Disorders, 16*, 335–350.

Mermelestein, R. (1983, October). *The relationship between syntactical and pragmatic development in autistic, retarded, and normal children*. Paper presented at the Eight Annual Boston University Conference on Language Development, Boston, MA.

Miller, J., & Chapman, R. (1981). The relation between age and mean length of utterances in morphemes. *Journal of Speech and Hearing Research, 24*, 154–161.

Miller, J., & Chapman, R. (1985). *Systematic analysis of language transcripts: A user's guide*. Madison, WI: University of Wisconsin Language Analysis Laboratory.

Morgan, J. L., & Travis, L. (1989). Limits on negative information in language input. *Journal of Child Language, 16*, 531–552.

Mundy, P., & Sigman, M. (1989a). Specifying the nature of the social impairment in autism. In G. Dawson (Ed.), *Autism: Nature, diagnosis, and treatment* (pp. 3–21). New York: Guilford.

Mundy, P., & Sigman, M. (1989b). The theoretical implications of joint-attention deficits in autism. *Development and Psychopathology, 1*, 173–183.

Mundy, P., Sigman, M., Ungerer, J., & Sherman, T. (1986). Defining the social deficits of autism: The contribution of nonverbal communication measures. *Journal of Child Psychology and Psychiatry, 27*, 657–669.

Neumann, C., & Hill, S. (1978). Self-recognition and stimulus preference in autistic children. *Developmental Psychobiology, 11*, 571–578.

Ochs, E. (1988). *Culture and language development*. New York: Cambridge University Press.

Ornitz, E. M., Guthrie, D., & Farley, A. J. (1977). Early development of autistic children. *Journal of Autism and Childhood Schizophrenia, 7*, 207–229.

Oshima-Takane, Y., & Benaroya, D. (1989). An alternative view of pronominal errors in autistic children. *Journal of Autism and Developmental Disorders, 19,* 73–85.

Paul, R. (1987). Communication. In D. J. Cohen & A. M. Donnellan (Eds.), *Handbook of autism and pervasive developmental disorders* (pp. 61-84). New York: Wiley.

Petitto, L. (1987). On the acquisition of language and gestures: Evidence from the acquisition of personal pronouns in American Sign Language. *Cognition, 27,* 1–52.

Pierce, S., & Bartolucci, G. (1977). A syntactic investigation of verbal autistic, mentally retarded, and normal children. *Journal of Autism and Childhood Schizophrenia, 7,* 121–134.

Prizant, B. (1983). Language acquisition and communication behavior in autism: Toward an understanding of the "whole" of it. *Journal of Speech and Hearing Disorders, 48,* 296–307.

Ratner, N., & Bruner, J. S. (1978). Games, social exchange, and the acquisition of language. *Journal of Child Language, 5,* 391–401.

Rumsey, J., Rapaport, J. L., & Sceery, W. R. (1985). Autistic children as adults: Psychiatric, social, and behavioral outcomes. *Journal of the American Academy of Child Psychiatry, 24,* 465–473.

Rutter, M., Greenfield, D., & Lockyer, L. (1967). A five to fifteen year follow-up of infantile psychosis: Social and behavioral outcome. *British Journal of Psychiatry, 113,* 1183–1189.

Scarborough, H. (1990). Index of productive syntax. *Applied Psycholinguistics, 11,* 1–22.

Schiff-Myers, N. (1983). From pronoun reversals to correct pronoun usage: A case study of a normally developing child. *Journal of Speech and Hearing Disorders, 48,* 385–394.

Shapiro, T., Sherman, M., Calamari, G., & Koch, D. (1987). Attachment in autism and other developmental disorders. *Journal of the American Academy of Child and Adolescent Psychiatry, 26,* 480–484.

Shatz, M. (1982). On mechanisms of language acquisition: Can features of the communicative environment account for development? In L. Gleitman & E. Wanner (Eds.), *Language acquisition: The state of the art* (pp. 102-127). New York: Cambridge University Press.

Sigman, M., Mundy, P., Ungerer, J., & Sherman, T. (1986). Social interactions of autistic, mentally retarded, and normal children and their caregivers. *Journal of Child Psychology and Psychiatry, 27,* 647–656.

Sigman, M., & Ungerer, J. (1984). Attachment behaviors in autistic children. *Journal of Autism and Developmental Disorders, 14,* 231–244..

Simon, N. (1975). Echolalic speech in childhood autism: Consideration of possible underlying loci of brain damage. *Archives of General Psychiatry, 32,* 1439–1446.

Snow, C. E. (1979). The role of social interaction in language acquisition. In W. A. Collins (Ed.), *Children's language and communication - Minnesota Symposia on Child Psychology* (Vol. 12, pp. 157-182). Hillsdale, NJ: Lawrence Erlbaum Associates.

Snow, C. E. (1981). Social interaction and language acquisition. In P. Dale & D. Ingram (Eds.), *Child language: An international perspective* (pp. 195-214). Baltimore, MD: University Park Press.

Snow, C. E., & Ferguson, C. (1977). *Talking to children: Language input and acquisition.* New York: Cambridge University Press.

Spiker, D., & Ricks, M. (1984). Visual self-recognition in autistic children: Developmental relationships. *Child Development, 55,* 214–225.

Tager-Flusberg, H. (1985a). The conceptual basis for referential word meaning in children with autism. *Child Development, 56,* 1167–1178.

Tager-Flusberg, H. (1985b). Constraints on the representation of word meaning: Evidence from autistic and mentally retarded children. In S. A. Kuczaj & M. Barrett (Eds.), *The development of word meaning* (pp. 69-81). New York: Springer-Verlag.

Tager-Flusberg, H. (1988). On the nature of a language acquisition of disorder: The example of autism. In F. Kessel (Ed.), *The development of language and language researchers (essays in honor of Roger Brown)* (pp. 249-267). Hillsdale, NJ: Lawrence Erlbaum Associates.

Tager-Flusberg, H. (1989a, April). *An analysis of discourse ability and internal state lexicons in a longitudinal study of autistic children.* Paper presented at the Society for Research in Child Development, Kansas City, MO.

Tager-Flusberg, H. (1989b, March). *The development of questions in autistic and Down syndrome children.* Paper presented at the Gatlinburg Conference on Research and Theory in Mental Retardation, Gatlinburg, TN.

Tager-Flusberg, H. (1989c). A psycholinguistic perspective on language development in the autistic child. In G. Dawson (Ed.), *Autism: Nature, diagnosis, and treatment* (pp. 92–115). New York: Guilford.

Tager-Flusberg, H. (1990, June). *Understanding pronoun reversal errors in autistic children.* Paper presented at the Symposium for Research on Child Language Disorders, Madison, WI.

Tager-Flusberg, H., & Calkins, S. (1990). Does imitation facilitate the acquisition of grammar? Evidence from a study of autistic, Down's syndrome, and normal children. *Journal of Child Language, 17,* 591–606.

Tager-Flusberg, H., Calkins, S., Nolin, T., Baumberger, T., Anderson, M., & Chadwick-Dias, A. (1990). A longitudinal study of language acquisition in autistic and Down syndrome children. *Journal of Autism and Developmental Disorders, 20,* 1–21.

Tager-Flusberg, H., & Keenan, T. (1987, June). *The acquisition of negation in autistic and Down syndrome children.* Paper presented at the Symposium for Research on Child Language Disorders, Madison, WI.

Vaidyanathan, R. (1988). Development of forms and functions of interrogatives in children: A longitudinal study in Tamil. *Journal of Child Language, 15,* 533–549.

Volkmar, F. (1987). Social development. In D. J. Cohen & A. M. Donnellan (Eds.), *Handbook of autism and pervasive developmental disorders* (pp. 41–60). New York : Wiley.

Volkmar, F., Cohen, D. J., Bregman, J. D., Hooks, M. Y., & Stevenson, J. M. (1989). An examination of social typologies in autism. *Journal of the American Academy of Child and Adolescent Psychiatry, 28,* 82–86.

Wetherby, A. M. (1986). Ontogeny of communicative functions in autism. *Journal of Autism and Developmental Disorders, 16,* 295–316.

Wetherby, A. M., & Prutting, C. (1984). Profiles of communicative and cognitive-social abilities in autistic children. *Journal of Speech and Hearing Research, 27,* 364–377.

Wing, L., & Gould, J. (1979). Severe impairments of social interaction and associated abnormalities in children: Epidemiology and classification. *Journal of Autism and Developmental Disorders, 9,* 11–29.

9

The Interdependence of Social, Cognitive, and Linguistic Development: Evidence from a Visually Impaired Child

Ann M. Peters
University of Hawai'i

INTRODUCTION

The aim of this chapter is to present evidence of ways in which social, cognitive, and linguistic development can be mutually interdependent. Although the other chapters in this volume attest to the possibility that these strands can develop independently, we see here that the converse is also possible. In the case presented here, we see how the acquisition of language is grounded in opportunities for social interaction, whereas certain aspects of cognitive development, especially the child's ability to conceptualize the noncontiguous world and to plan his own activities, are intertwined with language learning.

An important question for researchers in child development has to do with the roles of various kinds of input in *both* cognitive and linguistic development, and an important challenge is to disentangle the influence of the verbal from the nonverbal channels as much as possible. The strategy to be used here is to look at the ways a child can utilize various kinds of information in the speech that he or she hears—the input. Input is important because children's earliest language use is necessarily based on the particulars of the language they hear. We note, however, that speech to children is not primarily aimed at providing data for language learning. Rather, it is embedded in a more general context of socialization in which the goals of caregivers include teaching their children how to act as acceptable members of their culture. A number of researchers have argued that it is social interaction that provides the impetus, the context, and a continuing support for the internalization and personal construction of culture, including language (e.g., Bruner, 1978, 1983; Cazden, 1983; Vygotsky, 1962, 1978). Although language is indeed an important channel for the communication, transfer, and internalization of information relevant to socialization, it is not the only one, because nonverbal modeling and interaction also serve in this capacity. Therefore, in seeking to determine the role of language use in the acquisition of the language system, one problem is how to disentangle the influence of the verbal from the nonverbal channels.

One approach to this challenge is to look at the language acquisition of blind children, for whom nonverbal information is less easily accessible. We can investigate the developmental context within which such children acquire their language by contrasting their language development with that of sighted children. In the process, we can look for insights about how social, cognitive, and linguistic development all affect each other. Let me motivate three questions that we can ask.

Blind children lack access to visual information about aspects of the environment that will be important for both cognitive and linguistic development. Not being able to see events as they occur means that they will have less available data, both for figuring out how the world works in general and for constructing the mapping between language and its referents. Furthermore, they are also unable to make use of common channels for social interaction, such as eye contact, direction of interlocutor's gaze, and interlocutor's body orientation. Therefore, it would not be surprising if these children came to rely especially heavily on their developing language skills as a source of information about events and people in their noncontiguous environment. These considerations lead to the first question:

1. How is the development of the linguistic system affected when language itself must bear a greater than normal burden as a channel for social and cognitive information?

To the extent that blind children do rely heavily on linguistic input for information about normally visible events, it seems possible that language may become an important source of data for areas of development that we traditionally think of as cognitive, such as classification (when learning of the linguistic form precedes discovery of the cognitive category) or planning of one's own activities (to be illustrated later). This leads us to the second question:

2. In what ways can language development be seen to influence cognitive development?

Finally, because for these children social interaction is restricted to touch or talk, desire for social interaction in nontouching situations could provide a strong motivation to learn to use language effectively. Hence our third question:

3. In what ways might the desire for social interaction foster special social and linguistic strategies that may in turn affect cognitive and linguistic development?

The observations presented in this chapter are drawn from an ongoing study of the language development of a single child named Seth. In the exploration of a new or complex area, a case study provides special advantages:

1. Longitudinal data allow the investigator to gain insights into the dynamics of how this particular child's language evolved.
2. Reducing the complexity of a project by narrowing the focus to a single subject can leave the researcher time and energy to investigate rich and unanticipated detail.
3. This extra "space" also allows room for the exploration of new methods for tracing and understanding what drives developmental changes.

Although immediate broad generalizations are not possible until more children have been studied, the wealth of insights gained from a case study can lead to formulation of questions for further research.

In the data from Seth we focus on specific activities in which he engages with his father and the development of language use within these activities. We see that it is indeed possible to discern clear interactions between social, cognitive, and linguistic development. The remainder of this chapter demonstrates how, guided by his father's verbal coaching, Seth learned to participate in joint activities such as being fed, talking on the telephone, finding his ball, going for walks, or building block towers, and how he simultaneously learned how to talk about these activities. We see that cognitively he learned to use their scriptlike sequencing and predictability to help him anticipate what was likely to happen next. He also used these properties to help guide his social interaction with his father and later to plan his own attempts to carry out some of the activities by himself. At the same time, each of these routines supported his acquisition of specific kinds of linguistic information, such as vocabulary (e.g., names of foods, farm animals, or items encountered in the park), semantic subnetworks (e.g., qualities such as good/bad, rough/smooth, hot/cold, or colors), and even particular grammatical constructions (e.g., locative constructions with verbal particles and prepositions).

BACKGROUND

Although Seth is visually impaired, he is neurologically intact in all other respects. He was born with hypoplasia of the optic nerve and was totally blind, with no pupillary response to light well into his first year. He subsequently developed some poor quality peripheral vision (assessed at 20/800 at 40 months) so that by 12 months he was able to avoid obstacles when crawling, and by 25 months he could grasp bright objects 1 or 2 inches in diameter and distinguish colors (Example 6c). Nevertheless, his ability to obtain visual information about the world does not yield very precise information: Details are available to him only when he is close enough to an object to put the outer corner of his left eye extremely close to it. Thus, he lacks access to the power of the visual system to gather information about the noncontiguous world and to make connections between physically separated objects and contexts (see Dunlea, 1989, and Andersen, Dunlea, & Kekelis, 1984, for discussion). Importantly for his early communicative development, he has never been able to use eye contact or shared gaze as a means of social interaction.

Data on the development of Seth's language between 15 and 48 months were collected by his father, Bob Wilson (referred to herein as BW), who was both Seth's primary caregiver and a graduate student in linguistics at the University of Hawai'i. During this period, Seth's parents were separated, then divorced. Although Seth did see his mother periodically, these data, which are in the form of 1 to 3 hr of audio tape per week and almost daily diary notes, consist almost entirely of father–son interactions at home or on outings. Seth also attended an Easter Seal program for handicapped children between the ages of 6 months and 4 years, but no tapes were made there. The observations presented here are based on transcriptions of tapes and diary notes made between 20 and 30 months.

Because Seth neither shows evidence of an isolation syndrome nor suffers from a cognitive deficit (except to the extent that lack of access to visual information qualifies as "isolation" or " cognitive deficit"), his case does not bear upon these issues. It is also not clear that his visual handicap affected his syntactic development in any significant way. On the one hand, we have found some interesting anomalies in his early morphosyntax, including unusual *wh-* questions (1a), the use of *whatta* as a question word (1b, 1c) (Peters, 1987; Wilson & Peters, 1988), and the use of *didja* as a past tense marker rather than a question former (1d, 1e) (Wilson, 1986). Examples of these anomalies include:

1a. What did I get lost at the?
1b. Whatta I'm doing?
1c. Whatta we're gonna buy?
1d. Didja help you drive. (= I helped Daddy drive.)
1e. Didja 'fraid the balloon. (= I was afraid of the balloon.)

On the other hand, Bickerton's (1990) study of the diary data from Seth, Hildegard Leopold, and Cheryl Brislin suggests that, in pace and general nature of his syntactic progress, Seth was quite comparable to the other two.

A look at development in other areas of language, however, such as ability to interact verbally (Peters, 1987), or morphological development (Peters & Menn, 1990), reveals many ways in which Seth's progress in these domains is closely intertwined with and strongly influenced by his social and cognitive development. I believe that this interdependence was stronger than is usually the case because of his limited access to information about the world "out there" (that part of the world which he could neither see nor touch at a given moment). The lack of a visual channel thus rendered him more dependent on speech, both as a source of information about the world and as a means of social interaction.

The situation in which visually guided interaction must be replaced by heavier reliance on language is more than a curiosity because it forms a natural control, allowing us to "factor out" communication in the visual domain and focus on the interplay between language use and language acquisition. Urwin, too, in her study of the interactions between parents and three otherwise normal blind children (1982, 1984; unfortunately only up to about 20 months), found heavy reliance on the vocal/verbal and tactile modes of interaction. She noted, "By the last quarter of the first year each of these infants would collaborate in and prolong vocal imitation sequences and quasi-dialogues. . . . Jerry, for example would keep in contact with his mother for as long as 20 minutes at a time while she got on with her housework in the next-door room" (1984, p. 149). We can view otherwise normal blind children such as Seth as limiting cases — children for whom language can be expected to play a maximal role in cognitive and social development. This is because it is primarily through this medium — even before they have acquired it as a formal system — that they will obtain much of the information in which their knowledge of the world will be grounded.

Lacking longitudinal data on everyday interactions between parents and other blind children of Seth's age, it is not possible to tell whether his father is more linguistically facilitative than other parents of such children, but what we find in this case is BW constantly giving Seth information about objects and their names and attributes (e.g., that *trees* have *bark* that can be *rough* or *smooth*, or that *flowers* go in a *vase* that is *pretty*). He also instructs Seth verbally and physically on how to do things that a sighted child would almost surely learn by observation. Both his coaching and Seth's subsequent increased mastery of such tasks are illustrated in the mealtime and ball-finding sequences in Examples 3 and 5, and the block-building sequences in Example 6. Furthermore, it is through speech, rather than by visual means such as eye contact or shared gaze, that Seth conducts most of his social interaction. The other side of this coin is that the contents of the "data base" which Seth will use to discover the formal structure of his language are particularly strongly influenced by the social and cognitive functions which language had to serve, both for Seth and for his caregiver. In particular, it seems that his heavy dependence on highly contextualized language use leads to an initially high proportion of formulaic phrases.

It is likely that a strong need for what language can accomplish may motivate a child to adopt a formulaic approach to language learning—a "pick it up and use it before you have had time to analyze it" strategy. This suggestion is consistent with reports of young school-age children learning a second language in an immersion setting where they must use their emerging language skills for social and cognitive ends as soon as possible (e.g., Tabors, 1987; Wong Fillmore, 1979). The tendency of researchers interested in formulaic speech (e.g., Nelson, 1973) has been to take a social perspective and to note that children who make use of speech formulas are motivated by a strong desire to interact socially. The perspective here is more functional: When circumstances beyond learners' control force them to use language before they have analyzed it, a formulaic strategy is a very natural one.

This drive to use language affects Seth's linguistic development in at least three ways:

1. Seth has in his father a caregiver who is willing and able to make a great deal of highly tailored, situation-specific language available to him—language that, as Seth internalizes it, can guide him through the activities inherent in the particular situation. (We see an illustration in Example 6.)

2. As already mentioned, the lack of constant visual input makes it difficult for Seth to generalize across contexts, and this, coupled with the context-specificity of his father's language, contributes to an early isolation of contexts from each other, in terms of both the physical activities and the language involved. Peters (1985) noted that a consequence of this was an apparent "compartmentalization" of the language in Seth's interactions when he was in the 20–28 month range. For instance, we have found that it

is possible to write "scripts" for activities such as mealtime, bathtime, walking in the park, or building block towers, and that each such script is distinctive in vocabulary, formulaic expressions, and even some syntactic constructions. (We see mealtime talk in Examples 2 and 3 and block building in Example 6.)

3. The tapes show that Seth is a child who is extremely eager to engage in social interaction with his father. From an early age he learned to use strategies such as imitation and subsequent memorization of context-appropriate formulaic expressions to promote and prolong such interaction. Other reports have shown how his heavy use of immediate and deferred imitation led to temporary usages on his part, which made sense within their contexts but were syntactically deviant from adult grammar (Peters, 1987; Wilson, 1986; Wilson & Peters, 1988). (These include the structures illustrated in Example 1. See also Hoban, 1986, for discussion of the quantity and functions of Seth's imitation and repetition.)

THE INTERTWINING OF SOCIAL
COGNITIVE, AND LINGUISTIC
DEVELOPMENTAL STRANDS

In this section, we see how Seth first imitated and later reproduced specific chunks of language, including whole scripts as well as sentence-length formulas, in predictable routine situations, gradually becoming able to produce more and more on his own. We also consider some possible effects of this developmental path on both his linguistic and cognitive development.

It has already been suggested that Seth and his father depended more than other parent–child pairs on language as a means of interaction. Evidence for this can be seen when we compare their mode of interaction with that of dyads involving sighted children. Starting when Seth was 24 months old, the tapes include a series of episodes in which Seth and his father (BW) collaborate in building block towers (see Peters, 1985, and Example 6). Both the input and Seth's ready absorption of it were extremely striking: BW was clearly relying heavily on language to help him scaffold Seth's developing block-building abilities, and Seth, in turn, was not only internalizing that language, but later using it to guide his own activities. We wondered if we might find similar language in dyads in which the child was sighted. My colleague, Betsy Brandt, collected tapes from two mother–son pairs in block-building situations, but she found that in neither case was there much situation-specific language—for both dyads, the physical and visual channels were preferred to the verbal.

In order to understand how the development of Seth's linguistic system was affected by his use of language to promote and prolong social interaction, we first need to know something about the input language he hears from his father. This is especially important because of Seth's heavy reliance on imitation.

BW's speech to Seth is characterized by heavy use of what Heath calls the *eventcast* — an extension of the idea of play-by-play sportscasting. Heath and Branscombe (1986) defined the eventcast as providing "a running narrative on events currently in the attention of teller and listeners. . . . A sportscaster's account of a game during play, a preplay of a travel plan, and a mother's explanation to a preverbal infant of what she is doing as she prepares a baby's bottle represent eventcasts" (p. 17). For example, as BW puts Seth in his highchair he says, "There's your tray — Let's bring you over here — an' I'll git . . . some milk 'n a cup."

We can develop Heath and Branscombe's (1986) notion a little farther by observing that, as he eventcasts for his child, a caregiver provides just that information about the event that he deems important for the child to pay attention to. Such language simultaneously serves at least three functions:

1. It highlights culturally important aspects of the activity.
2. It provides linguistic labels for the objects, attributes, and/or actions involved.
3. It models syntactic constructions useful for talking about the event.

In summary, it gives the child a script to use in thinking about, rehearsing, and carrying out this event or activity (e.g., by means of private speech or monologues). Thus, in order to eventcast an activity, the caregiver must have a sense of which culturally and cognitively appropriate aspects of the situation to highlight; that is, he must have done some sort of task analysis (whether conscious or not). Although not all caregivers eventcast — Heath and Branscombe described a culture in which they do not — Seth's father does a great deal of it. The relevance of these notions to the present volume lies in the observation that scripts can provide support for a child in (a) interpreting subevents as part of a larger whole, (b) predicting what is likely to happen next, (c) beginning to participate in the scripted activity, (d) planning his own actions within this context, and (e) taking on increasing responsibility for carrying the activity to completion. In Example 6, we see how Seth was able to internalize BW's eventcasting language and later make use of it to guide his own block-building activities.

A close examination of BW's speech shows that, in an effort to help his handicapped child function as normally as possible, he seems to have done a good deal of unconscious analysis of the various daily contexts in which Seth has to function. This is revealed by the fact that the language he gives Seth is very situation specific, consisting of information and commands designed to help Seth function as well as possible in each particular context.

This extremely task-specific nature of BW's speech may be one of the primary causes of the apparent compartmentalization of Seth's language learning mentioned earlier.[1] In his turn, Seth actively absorbs this language in the process of interacting with his father in context-governed ways.

Example 2a illustrates both BW's careful task-specific language and Seth's absorption of it. Here BW is concerned with developing Seth's independence in drinking juice from a cup. Because Seth cannot see the consequences of how he puts his cup down, he often sets it precariously on the edge of his table or tray. BW coaches Seth to push his cup back as he sets it down and Seth imitates (lines 10 and 12):

Example 2a.   Cup handling (20.3 months)[2]:
1. S: **n juice.**
2. BW: Go ahead, have some juice. (12 s)
3.   Oh, you drink so well.
4.   (10 s; sound of glass being set down)
5.   Push, push it a little. Uhm?
6.   Put the glass back up . . .
7.   give a little push.
8.   Push it back from the edge.
9.   Good.
10. S: **'mpuysh.**
11. BW: Empush it.
12. S: **'mpish it.**

Example 2b shows BW giving an even more explicit description a week later:

Example 2b.   Cup handling (21.0 months)
1. BW: Push it back.
2.   Push it back. See
3.   when you getcher juice . . .
4.   you put it back on the table
5.   while you push it back
6.   so it doesn't fall off the edge . . .
7.   That's so nice. (8 s)

---

[1]I would like to thank Vera John-Steiner for pointing this out.

[2]Ages are in months weeks. Transcriptions in / / are at a broad phonetic level. Where needed for clarity, glosses are given in parentheses. Whenever either Seth or BW immediately imitate/echo each other, this has been highlighted by vertically aligning the imitated portions of speech. The following symbols have been used:

'= glottal stop

.= falling intonation   ?= rising intonation

In many of the routine contexts on these tapes, the language has characteristics of a loose script in that many of the specific words or expressions are predictable and sometimes the sequence in which they occur as well. The context-specificity of BW's input has the effect that context can provide Seth with cues to inform him which of his scripts to draw on in a given situation. Although he first encounters this language through interaction with his father, it eventually becomes sufficiently internalized so that he can use it on his own. As already suggested, scripts simultaneously make available *cognitively* useful information about possible action sequences and *linguistically* useful information about relevant vocabulary, (formulaic) expressions and their acceptable variations (out of which linguistic patterns can be induced), and, in some cases, specific syntactic structures (such as the concentration of locative expressions found in their ball game, Example 5). The convergence of the linguistic, social, and cognitive developmental strands is therefore particularly evident in the context of these scripts.

There are several kinds of evidence that Seth is indeed acquiring the language of a particular routine:

1. He imitates his father, either immediately or a little while later (as we see in 2a).
2. He spontaneously produces the appropriate language at the relevant point in the script.
3. He produces some of the language as he monologues to himself while his father is otherwise occupied.

Example 3 gives examples of mealtime language. It illustrates both the scriptlike character of language in this context and spontaneous production and monologuing by Seth.

Example 3a shows some of BW's language as he feeds Seth at 20.3 months. Seth spontaneously imitates his father in lines 7 and 11, and BW elicits an imitation in lines 15–16:

Example 3a.   Mealtime at 20.3 months
1. BW: Let's get this all straight.
2.   Daddy will sit down
3.   and I'll feed you some of it.
4.   It'll be good.
5. S: /**piys**/. (please = yes)
6. BW: Good cereal.
7. S: /**n sioh**/.
8. BW: Uh huh.
9.   It's good.
10.   Has raisins in it and everything.

11. S: /ənsis/?
12.   (D starts some coffee, then gets back to feeding.)
13. BW: Is that good cereal?
14.   It's good.
15.   Say "good."
16. S: /guət/.

Example 3b is from a mealtime 3 weeks later. BW eventcasts in lines 11, 16, 21, 23–25. Seth is now able to spontaneously produce part of the script at the appropriate point in the routine (in lines 17–20 he anticipates the attaching of his tray):

Example 3b.   Mealtime at 21.2 months
  1. BW: Here lemme putcha in your high chair.
          (in lines 2–10 they playfully alternate saying "come on")
11. BW: Here ya go.
12.   Come on.
13. S: **Oatmeal?**
14. BW: Come.
15.   Come now.
16.   Come get in the high chair. (8 s)
17. S: **Push in tray.**
18.   **Push in tray.**
19.   **Push in tray.** (loud noise of BW putting tray on high chair)
20.   **Tray?**
21. BW: There's your tray?
22. S: **Tray?**
23. BW: There's your tray—
24.   Let's bring you over here—
25.   an' I'll git . . . some milk 'n a cup. (6 s)

During many of the feeding sessions, BW becomes preoccupied with cooking while Seth is held captive in his highchair. Seth often passes some of the time monologuing to himself. Example 3c shows two excerpts from monologues at 24 months that echo his father's language from earlier mealtime sessions. The first part clearly echos BW's language in Example 3a, including the elicited imitation (line 11). The second part reflects the frequent questions which BW asks Seth as he feeds him, as well as the meal-end ritual of wiping Seth's face with a paper towel and then having Seth "dump it in the rubbish."

Example 3c.   Mealtime at 24.0 months
  1. S: **Goo-od.**
  2.   **Goo-od.**   (7 s; BW scrambling eggs)
  3.   **'m.**

4.	**Bee good!**	(10 s; BW still cooking)
5.	**Please-**	
6.	**/mauwhuw/.**	(12 s)
7.	**Didja cookuh?**	("did you cook it?")
8.	**/tætsut/.**	(?)
9.	**Cook /tætsu/.**	(?)
10.	**Yeah.**	(creaky)
11.	**Say "yeah."**	

A little later — BW is still cooking:

12.	S:	**Me'eal.**	("oatmeal")
13.		**'kay?**	(15 s; BW chopping and scraping)
14.		**Wha' 're you jwingking.**	
15.		**What're you jringking.**	
16.		**Wamp me, yeah?**	("wipe me")
17.		**N doot da wubbish?**	
18.		**N doot da wubbish out?**	
19.		**Wamp me out.**	
20.		**N goot da wubbish out.**	

It is not surprising that as he tries to formulaically reproduce the language of a script, Seth is more accurate at the prosodically, and hence phonologically, more salient portions. This results in clearer renditions of the major lexical items, whereas small functor words tend first to appear as "filler syllables," which only gradually acquire the phonetic characteristics of their adult targets. A representative example is the development of the expression "talk on the phone" through our set of transcribed half-hours, as summarized in Example 4:

Example 4.   Filler syllables: Evolution of **"talk on the phone"**

22.0 months:		talk ə	phone	13
25.0 months:		talk **in**	telephone	4
		talk **on** ə	teleph-	1
		talk **ə**dl	telephone	1
26.3 months:	wan' *Daddy*	talk tə	telephone	1
27.1 months:		talk ə Ma **on da**	phone	1

(imitating "talk to Mommy on the phone")

At 22.0 months Seth produces the filler-form "talk ə phone" some 13 times. (On this tape, BW models the full form for him twice: "You wanna talk on the phone-" and "You talk on the phone?"; once he honors what Seth is able to do by eventcasting "You wanna talk-a-phone.") By 25.0 months, Seth is still not sure whether the middle bit contains *in* or *on* or something else: He says "talk in telephone" 4 times, "talk on ə telephone" once, and "talk ə dl telephone" once (on this tape BW only models full forms: *on your* once, *on the* twice). Subsequent to this, the expression nearly disappears from our transcriptions, although it resurfaces once at 26.3 months when Seth produces one instance of "wan' Daddy talk tə telephone" and again at 27.1 months, at which time he is able to imitate "talk to Mommy on the phone" with both *on* and *the* in place (see Peters & Menn, 1990, for a fuller discussion of the evolution of "fillers" into grammatical morphemes).

The way in which Seth's linguistic development is intertwined with his cognitive development can be seen if we look at the emergence of Seth's ability to comprehend verbal particles and prepositions in the context of looking for his ball.[3] Here we can trace progress in his ability to both understand his father's language and guide his own actions. The context is that when Seth was about 24 months old his father started showing him how to play with a ball. Although Seth quickly learned to throw the ball, he could not see where it had gone. BW, tiring of running after it, began coaching Seth to find it himself, using locatives such as *back, by, behind, under, around, in.*

Example 5a shows a relatively early instance of BW engaging in this kind of coaching. He tries using **by** and **back** to describe both where the ball is (turns 2 and 4) and where Seth should go (turn 6). When it becomes apparent that his verbal instructions are not leading Seth to the ball, BW gets up and physically shows Seth where to look (turns 14–18). We see that Seth already knows that a possible strategy is to look in his room (turn 1). Once the ball has been located, Seth verbally coaches himself to "go get it," reinforced by BW (turns 19–20).

Example 5a.   Ball retrieval at 24.3 months[4]
1. S: Look[k] **in** your room.
2. BW: It went **in** the bedroom **by** your rocker.
         It went **by** your little rockin' chair.
3. S: wə̃ **by**   rock ə chair.
4. BW: Way **back** in the corner.
5. S: ⌠ No?   ⌡ (looking for ball)
6. BW: ⌊ Go **back**-⌋   Go **back by** your rockin' chair. Go **back** – (3 s)
         It's there. Go **back** – No no!
         Go – go – Go **by** your rockin' chair. **Back** –
         Go *way* **back** byhin' the closet. (changing **by** to **behind**)
         By your rockin' chair. You'll find it.
         Your ball is **back** there.
7. S: Ball?
8. BW: Yes, it's there.
         Keep goin' **back behind**jer rockin' chair. (4 s)

---

[3]I would like to thank Gigi Glover for her assistance and insights in the analysis of the ball-finding episodes.

[4]In this set of examples, BW's particles and prepositions are highlighted. Contrastive stress is also indicated in italics.

9. S: No?
10. BW: Yes it is. It is really there.
11. S: ə̃ get it. (softly)
12. BW: Hmm? It's there.
13. S: It dere.
14. BW: I see where it is. Come on. Come on.
15. S: Wan' find 'em.
16. BW: Look
17. S: ⎰ Yeah.   ⎱
18. BW: ⎱ It's right ⎰ **behind**jer rockin' chair. See?
            Back here? Come **aroun' back. Back** here. Come **back** here.
            See— There it is. Right there.
            Ooh. Feel the wind blow.
19. S: Well go get it! (getting the ball)
20. BW: Go get it? Good for you.

A month later, Seth seems more able to follow his father's directions and retrieves the ball relatively quickly.

Example 5b.   Ball retrieval at 25.3 months
1. BW: Where did it go.
2. S: Where'd   it go.
3. BW: Can you see it?
4. S: Can   see it?
5. BW: It didn't go **over** there.
         Look **behind** Daddy.
6. S: əhind Daddy.
7. BW: Look **behind** *Daddy.*
8. S: Look by   *Daddy.*
         /ima nau?/ Let's try.
9. BW: Try **over on** *this* end now.
         Look **up behind** Daddy's *head.*
         Look   **behind** Daddy's *head.*
         Oh, you see it?
10. S: /ə koi/head.
11. BW: Good you found it.

Although Seth demonstrates some comprehension of *behind* in Example 5b, he still has more to learn. In reviewing the transcript of the next episode, recorded a week later, BW explained that at this time *behind* only referred to one side of the bed. In Example 5c we see another instance of combined verbal and physical input aimed at extending the concept. Here, Seth has thrown the ball in one direction but has gone looking in another.

Example 5c.   Ball retrieval at 26.0 months
1. BW: Oh, it went **behind** Daddy's bed.

2. S: 'hind Daddy's bed
3. BW: Not *that* side. Come. Let me show ya.
      Come on. Show ya. (coaxing S in direction of ball)
      Not **over** *there*. That ball went **back — behind** *here*.
      Behind the bed.
4. S: 'hind the bed. (reaches behind BW's head, on top of bed)
5. BW: Not *on* it.
      Not **behind** *Daddy*.
      It's **behind** the *bed*, see?
      Back there? You got it now?

Two successful retrievals from 27.1 show Seth developing good comprehension of *by*, *around*, and *back*.

Example 5d.   Ball retrieval at 27.1 months
  1. S: Where's za ball.
  2. BW: The ball is **by** Daddy's desk. (enunciating distinctly)
  3. S: No.
  4. BW: Yeah. It's **by** Daddy's chair.
        By the desk and **by** the chair.
        See it yet? Walk **around** the chair.
        Walk **around** the chair, can you?
        Oh, 'kay, ya gonna crawl **under**. (4 s)
        There it is.
  5. S: Now I can throw it.
  6.   Where's za ball.
  7. BW: Bird, it went **back by** the file— **by** Daddy's file cabinet.
  8. S: File cabinet?
  9. BW: Yeah, go **back** there, see?
 10. S: See?
 11. BW: See, **by** the clock. Daddy's file cabinet is **by** the clock.
 12. S: By da clock. (S gets the ball)
 13. BW: Yeah.

A month later, at 28.1, we see how Seth is now able not only to understand the situation from BW's verbal description, but to extend it conceptually. As we see in Example 6, at the same time as he has been learning to retrieve his ball he has been learning to build block towers and to knock them down with a big cardboard mailing tube. In Example 5e his ball has landed on top of the fan. When BW remarks that maybe Seth could knock it down (turn 3), it seems that Seth makes a connection with the block-building script (see example 6c, lines 4 and 6) and goes to get his tube. BW's turns 6 and 7 suggest that he has not made this connection himself and is surprised at Seth's actions. Here, then, Seth not only understands the situation from his father's verbal description but is also able to generalize beyond the immediate script.

Example 5e.   Ball retrieval at 28.1 months

1. BW: Oh, it didn' come **down**.
         It's **up on top of** the fan.
         Can you find it?
2. S: Find it?
3. BW: You hafta go **behind** the fan and look **up** there high.
         An' maybe you can knock it **down**.
4. S: Knock it down, Dad.
5. BW: ⎧What? What Bird?⎫
6. S: ⎩Knock it down. ⎭
       ⎧Knock it down.⎫
7. BW: ⎩You went—   ⎭ You went an' got the cardboard tube.
         So ya could knock it **down**. Good fer you. (eventcasting)

Another kind of evidence for the intertwining of Seth's cognitive and linguistic development is the way in which he becomes able to use script language to guide himself through an activity. The block-building episodes already mentioned illustrate how quickly Seth was able to pick up language introduced in a new, cognitively challenging context. We see how he immediately begins to imitate (6a) and then to try to use bits of the modeled language to control tower-building interactions with his father (6b), and how 2 months later he is able to use it for self-guidance and planning of tower building by himself (6c).

The first block-building episode on the tapes occurs when Seth is 24.3 months old. At first, BW describes the activity as "building a house," but then he switches to "building a tower," a label they use consistently from then on. (This and other linguistic evidence suggests that this is the first time they engage in this activity.) They build and knock down eight towers one after another, take a break, and then build several more. Example 6a shows BW's language as they work on the second tower. BW is already encouraging Seth to try to use the new language he has provided during the building of the first tower (lines 6,8–9), and Seth is trying to imitate him (lines 10, 12, 17, 19).

Example 6a.   Tower building at 24.3 months; tower #2
 1. S: *Dank* **you**.   (handing block to BW so he'll build some more)
 2. BW: Okay.
 3.   Thank you.   (taking it)
 4. S: **'m put ət back?**   (wants BW to build another tower)
 5. BW: 'Kay—where ya want me ta put it back,
 6.   in the bloc—in the box? (trying to elicit new language)
 7. S: **No?**
 8. BW: D'ya want me ta put it up on—
 9.   D'ya want me ta build it *up*?

10. S: /hə kɔ **wi nəp**/?
11. BW: Okay, Daddy'll build it up. There.
12. S: **Buil'i'lup.**
13. BW: Daddy's makin' a *tower*.   (3 sec)
14.   Daddy's makin' a *tower* out of these blocks,
15.   it's high.
16.   See how high?
17. S: **High!**
18. BW: If you *push* it it will fall down.
19. S: **fa *down*.**
20. BW: You c'd *kick* it with your foot 'n it'll fall down. (S does)
21. S: **Oh—**   (blocks crash down)
22. BW: Fall down.   (more block noises)

Moving now to the language used as they build their 11th tower (after taking their break), we find Seth already trying out a new construction, both spontaneously (lines 1–2), and with BW's encouragement (line 19), as well as imitating (lines 12, 16, 20, 26–28) ("*a* one" = "other one").

Example 6b.   Tower building at 24.3 months; tower #11
 1. S: **m put da *a* one na top.**   (5 s; breathing, stacking)
 2.   **Put da *a* one.**   (clunks)
 3.   **Hewp me!**
 4.   ⎰ **eey!** ⎱
 5. BW:⎱ Okay. ⎰   (clunks)
 6.   Okay.   (clunks)
 7.   Put the blue one up there—   (stacking)
 8.   An'le's put the—   (clunks)
 9.   Daddy can't grab that, that's so slick.
10.   Put the yellow one up there.
11. S: **Hewp me.**
12.   ⎰ **hewp me m** ⎱ **put da *a* one ut deyow.** ("up there")
13. BW:⎱ Okay. ⎰
14.   Okay—
15.   I help you put the other one up there.
16. S: **m put da *a* one ut deya?**
17. S: **Dank you**   (handing block to BW)
18. BW: Okay—
19.   You want ⎰ me ta—   ⎱
20. S: ⎱ **put da *a* one?**⎰
21. BW: Okay, here it goes.
22.   I gonna put it way up high.
23.   Oh ⎰ look.⎱
24. S: ⎱ **xx** ⎰
25. BW: Daddy made a high tower.
26. S: **Tower!**

27.   **Ni'   tower.**
28.   **High tower!**
29. BW: High tower.

Two months later, when Seth is 26.3 months old, they engage in another long sequence of tower building (only short episodes having been recorded in the interim). By now Seth is much more in control, having learned how to stack the blocks physically as well as the appropriate language to use as he does so. After they build eight towers BW tells Seth, "This time I want **you** to build the tower. By yourself." Seth accepts the challenge, and after some more negotiation he starts building, talking to himself as he works. Such a monologue would be interesting enough because it illustrates Seth's ability to use language for planning his own activities. But it is more than a monologue: His intonation suggests two "voices"—one higher pitched than the other. The lower pitched voice sounds more competent and in control—perhaps it is a "Daddy voice." (This voice is shown in boldface.) What is the mumbly, whiney, higher pitched voice? It seems to be an "incompetent Seth" who is not quite sure how to proceed and who needs the reassuring guidance of his father's voice. These voices interweave as follows: In lines 3 and 5 the confident voice announces Seth's intention to build a tower and knock it down. In lines 4, 8, and 10 it reinforces and reassures him; in lines 9 and 16 it eventcasts that he has found and added blue and red blocks. On the other hand, in lines 11, 14, and 17, the less sure voice says it wants to add blue, yellow, and red blocks and receives reassurance in line 12.

Example 6c.   Seth's tower-building monologue at 26.3 months; tower #9

1. **I wan' kick it.**   (softly)
2. I want—I wanta finish—   (mushy)
3. **I wanna build the tower 'n knock it down.**   (emphatic)
4. **Okay!**   (brightly)
5. **I wanted ta build th' tower 'n knock it down.** (clearly)
6. me doo!   (mushy)
7. wawawan niww Bird.   (mushy, high)
8. **Build one by *self***   **(low, clear)**
9. **a put the *blue* one.**
10. **num by self.**
11. Put—I can put the blue one by self.   (high, whiney)
12. **Eeyeah.**   (agreeing)
13. **This tower.**   (low, clear)
14. I wanna put the lellow one.   (higher)
15. **Oh.**
16. **So put the red one by self.**   (lower)
17. Dis a red one.   (higher)

The evolution of a "competent Seth voice" out of an externally guiding "Daddy voice" clearly illustrates development in a situation in which the need for language as a social and cognitive tool structured the learning situation so that being able to *use* the language was primary. This, in turn, paved the way for the acquisition of the underlying formal system.

CONCLUSIONS

The examples we have just seen illustrate ways in which Seth's visual impairment augmented the influences of social interaction and specificity of context on the way his language developed. They suggest that we will not really understand language acquisition until we know how it both affects and is affected by concurrent social, cognitive, and biological development. Although researchers have traditionally separated these areas in order to make them more tractable, a broader view encompassing as many relevant strands as possible is periodically necessary. (For further discussion see Barber & Peters, 1992.)

The reader may ask how much we can conclude from this one case. Is Seth unique? To what extent is his developmental picture a result of his blindness? Or of his father's strongly interactive style? To address these questions, we need to ask which aspects of Seth's development are crucial to the present thesis that social, linguistic, and cognitive development are intertwined. I see three key elements: (a) Seth's reliance on routines as a means of simultaneously enhancing social interaction, comprehension of linguistic input, and acquisition of information and expectations about how the world works, (b) his heavy use of imitation as a strategy that simultaneously promotes both social interaction and language use, and (c) his transformation of language learned in routine situations into private speech that he can use to guide his thinking and activities.

These three elements are not unique to Seth's case or even to blind children. An important body of recent research based on the proposals of Vygotsky (1962, 1978) provides evidence for them in normal children as well. Briefly, the simultaneous importance of routines to social, linguistic, and cognitive development is addressed by Bruner (1978), Cazden (1983), Miller (1982), Ninio and Bruner (1978), Ratner and Bruner (1978), and Watson-Gegeo and Gegeo (1986). The use of imitation as a vehicle for language learning is discussed by Bloom, Hood, and Lightbown (1974), Moerk and Moerk (1979), and Snow (1981), and as a simultaneous vehicle for socialization by Schieffelin (1979) and Watson-Gegeo and Gegeo (1986). Finally, research on the development of private speech as a means of cognitive self-guidance is reported by Berk and Garvin (1984), Fuson (1979), and John-Steiner and Tattar (1983).

Although most of the chapters in this volume present clear evidence for the dissociation of language and cognition, Seth's case suggests that it is not necessarily the case that such dissociation occurs. Rather, we see here how development in each of these three areas can be fostered by development in the others. It is important to remember that the human organism may have available to it more than one possible route for development — that it may be more flexible and better able to operate within a wider range of variability than we might conclude solely from the rest of this volume.

For all children, some aspects of language acquisition are heavily influenced by progress in other developmental dimensions. In particular, the time at which a child first begins to produce speech is affected by biological, social, and cognitive development.[5]

On the biological front, the complexity of human linguistic systems suggests that a human child must carry some degree of preprogramming for learning the language of the environment. On the other hand, the fact that human languages are not totally wired in (as contrasted with the calls of many species of birds or monkeys), but are arbitrary and socially negotiable in many ways, makes it clear that important functional physiological connections must be established postnatally. Moreover, the time at which speech emerges is affected by development in the neurophysiological ability to perceive, remember, and (re)produce language in appropriate circumstances.

Socially, linguistic development is tied to a growing desire to interact with others in increasingly complex ways and the realization that speech is one means for achieving this.

Relevant cognitive developments include the ability to learn which chunks of remembered language are appropriate in which circumstances, and the realization that linguistic labels are useful for organizational activities such as making plans, or classifying objects, activities, or attributes. Moreover, children will actively internalize caregiver-provided guidance for new activities so that they can direct their own participation (John-Steiner & Tattar, 1993).

As for linguistic development, Vygotsky (1962) pointed out the dynamic and irreversible effect which the emergence of language has on other strands of development. It is language *use* that paves the way for linguistic analysis and the child's construction of his or her own linguistic system. In this view,

---

[5]I am following Vygotsky (1962) in calling the earliest language-like productions "speech." They do not qualify as "language" since they are not yet part of an integrated system. Rather, they are separate — or only very partially connected — items. See Peters (1986) for a discussion of the transition from "item learning" to "system building," and Barber and Peters (1992) for discussion of the cross-catalysis of different developmental strands.

the desire to use language for social and cognitive ends motivates the child to remember useful language which then becomes available for analysis.

These same three developmental dimensions also play roles in determining which chunks of speech a particular child will first attempt to produce.[6] For instance, those aspects of input speech which are perceptually salient (e.g., chunks which are stressed or occur frequently or predictably) are more likely to be remembered (Slobin, 1985). Participation in social interaction and the development of means for greeting, requesting, or participating in entertaining interactive activities (Halliday, 1973) can be expected to lead a child to identify and try to (re)produce language that will be useful in achieving those goals. Cognitively, these chunks of speech must be both of rememberable size and useful to the child in anticipating or planning activities and/or in categorizing or otherwise cognitively organizing the world. Seth's absorption of the language for building block towers is a particularly nice example, showing the mutual influence of all of these strands.

Not only do biological, social, and cognitive development influence the growth of language, but language itself turns back to affect them in irreversible ways, building neural pathways, strengthening social bonds, and promoting more complex cognitive organization. Biologically, experience affects neurological development in at least two ways:

1. Early in development, the repeated use of a neurological pathway, whether, it be motor, perceptual, or associative, affects neurological structure by determining which dendrites are preserved and which are lost ("pruned") and by determining which pathways are eventually myelinated for faster, more efficient processing (e.g., Simonds & Scheibel, 1989).

2. Later on, learning effects, including automatization, may also affect neural structure, though not so radically. This means that a child's cumulative experience with trying to process language renders his neural pathways for doing so more efficient, both for processing language he has already learned and for dealing with new language.

Socially, a child may begin to produce speech in a routine such as object naming in order to interact with his caregiver (for examples, see Ratner & Bruner, 1978; Wilson & Peters, 1988). The very act of participating in such activities also leads to acquisition of labels for new cognitive categories, a growing ability to categorize new objects, the acquisition of new vocabu-

---

[6]The term *chunk* is meant to be neutral with respect to size. It may consist of a single syllable (*hi* or *ba*), a multisyllable word (*daddy*), or a whole adult phrase (*look-at-that!*). See Peters (1983) for discussion.

lary, and increases in resources for social interaction. The term *circular causality* (Yates, 1982) is useful for describing this kind of situation in which use of and development in each of several systems ratchets each of the others in nonreversibly additive ways.

The kind of interdependence of social, cognitive, and linguistic development illustrated here also raises several sets of questions for future research. The first set concerns the effect of routine contexts on the early acquisition of language for sighted children. Under what circumstances do they, too, rely on context as a support for their emerging language? Griffiths (1986) showed how the production of first words occurs in routines. Is only open class vocabulary involved? To what extent can context facilitate the emergence of closed class words? If this does happen, does semantic content play a role so that only the acquisition of those closed class words with the greatest semantic content, such as locatives, are so affected? This last question is suggested by the fact that Seth's learning of locative prepositions took place largely in the context of learning to find his ball (under the bed, in the clothes basket, behind the dresser)—a context in which these prepositions have a particularly high functional load.

Secondly, remarkably little systematic exploration has been done on the effect of context on the acquisition of general, productive grammars. Under what circumstances does it prevent or encourage development? When a particular syntactic construction is first acquired within the confines of a particular situation, is it also confined to a single or very narrow range of forms? Under what circumstances does context allow for a construction to be generalized? Peters (1983) pointed out that when expressions are frozen, like nursery rhymes, songs, or the pledge of allegiance, there is little chance for them to be incorporated in a more general grammar. This is why errors of misperception or analysis of such expressions often persist for a long time. One prediction is that the existence of several contexts in which a given construction occurs would facilitate generalization. For instance, Seth learned *off* and *on* in at least three different situations: turning the taperecorder on or off, turning the bath water on or off, and having his clothes put on or off. Besides singularity versus multiplicity, what other attributes of context might affect generalization?

If it turns out that the course of development of a particular grammatical construction is indeed sensitive to the kinds of contexts in which it is first encountered, we may have a kind of sensitivity to initial conditions in which some situations would facilitate and others would limit grammatical development. Finding contrasting sets of such situations would help us understand the dynamic process of grammatical development. We also need to know the limits of such sensitivity: To what degree are children's developing linguistic systems *not* sensitive to context?

Finally, the possibility of the influence of context on grammatical development raises new questions about the nature and effects of input speech. For instance, what is the relation between the earliest kinds of grammatical constructions acquired and caregiver speech aimed at teaching and socializing a child? Are any of these early constructions traceable to linguistically encoded task analyses such as those presented by Seth's father? Seth's learning of prepositions in the context of learning to find his ball suggests that such influences may be demonstrable if looked for.

The dissociation evidence suggests that the human organism is provided with a kind of fail-safe, in that when one developmental strand is impaired the others may be robust enough to carry on in its absence. Seth's case, on the other hand, suggests that when all strands are developing normally, we may expect to find them cross-catalyzing each other's growth. Perhaps the most significant aspect of this case, then, is the way it illustrates how strong this interaction *can* be, showing us an important path that is open to children, even though it may not be one that it is always taken. We are reminded to continue to be open to the possibility that there may be a multiplicity of developmental paths available to the human organism.

ACKNOWLEDGMENTS

Preparation of the original form of this chapter was supported by the MIT Center for Cognitive Science under a grant from the A.P. Sloan Foundation's program in Cognitive Science. I would also like to thank Helen Tager-Flusberg for helpful comments on the present form of the chapter and Eileen Cain, Robert Hsu, Vera John-Steiner, Ray Moody, and Catherine Snow for feedback on earlier versions. Transcription of the Seth data was made possible by NSF grant BNS-8418272.

REFERENCES

Andersen, E. S., Dunlea, A., & Kekelis, L. (1984). Blind children's language: Resolving some differences. *Journal of Child Language, 11* (3), 645–664.

Barber, E. J. W., & Peters, A. M. W. (1992). Ontogeny and phylogeny: What child language and archaeology have to say to each other. In J. A. Hawkins & M. Gell-Mann (Eds.), *The evolution of human languages, SFI studies in the sciences of complexity*, (pp. 305–352). Redwood City, CA: Addison-Wesley.

Berk, L. E., & Garvin, R. A. (1984). Development of private speech among low-income Appalachian children. *Developmental Psychology, 20* (2), 271–286.

Bickerton, D. (1990). *Syntactic development: The mind just does it.* Unpublished manuscript, University of Hawai'i, Honolulu.

Bloom, L., Hood, L., & Lightbown, P. (1974). Imitation in language development: If, when, and why. *Cognitive Psychology, 6,* 380–420.

Bruner, J. S. (1978). The role of dialogue in language acquisition. In A. Sinclair, R. J. Jarvella, & W. J. M. Levelt (Eds.), *The child's conception of language* (pp. 241–256). New York: Springer-Verlag.

Bruner, J. S. (1983). *Child's talk: Learning to use language*. New York: Norton.

Cazden, C. B. (1983). Peekaboo as an instructional model: Discourse development at home and at school. In B. Bain (Ed.), *The sociogenesis of language and human conduct* (pp. 33–58). New York: Plenum.

Dunlea, A. (1989). *Vision and the emergence of meaning*. New York: Cambridge University Press.

Fuson, K. C. (1979). The development of self-regulating aspects of speech: A review. In G. Zivin (Ed.), *The development of self-regulation through private speech*(pp. 135–217). New York: Wiley.

Griffiths, P. (1986). Early vocabulary. In P. Fletcher & M. Garman (Eds.), *Language acquisition* (2nd ed., pp. 279–306). New York: Cambridge University Press.

Halliday, M. (1973). Relevant models of language. In M. A. K. Halliday (Ed.), *Explorations in the functions of language*. London: Edward Arnold.

Heath, S. B., & Branscombe, A. (1986). The book as narrative prop in language acquisition. In B. B. Schieffelin & P. Gilmore (Eds.), *The acquisition of literacy: Ethnographic perspectives* (pp. 16–34). Norwood, NJ: Ablex.

Hoban, E. (1986). *The promise of animal language research*. Unpublished doctoral dissertation, University of Hawai'i, Honolulu.

John-Steiner, V. & Tattar, P. (1983). An interactionist model of language development. In B. Bain (Ed.), *The sociogenesis of language and human conduct*(pp. 79–97). New York: Plenum.

Miller, P. J. (1982). *Amy, Wendy, and Beth: Language learning in South Baltimore*. Austin: University of Texas Press.

Moerk, E., & Moerk, C. (1979). Quotations, imitations, and generalizations. *International Journal of Behavioral Development, 2*, 43–72.

Nelson, K. (1973). Structure and strategy in learning to talk. *Monographs of the Society for Research in Child Development, 149* (38, Nos. 1–2).

Ninio, A., & Bruner, J. S. (1978). The achievement and antecedents of labeling. *Journal of Child Language, 5*, 1–15.

Peters, A. M. (1983). *The units of language acquisition*. Monographs in Applied Psycholinguistics. New York: Cambridge University Press.

Peters, A. M. (1985, October). *Routines as loci for language development*. Paper presented at the Boston University Conference on Language Development, Boston, MA.

Peters, A. M. (1986). Early syntax. In P. Fletcher & M. Garman (Eds.), *Language acquisition* (2nd ed., pp. 307–325). New York: Cambridge University Press.

Peters, A. M. (1987). The role of imitation in the developing syntax of a blind child. *Text, 7*, 289–311.

Peters, A. M., & Menn, L. (1990). *The microstructure of morphological development: Variation across children and across languages*. (ICS Tech. Rep. No. 90–19). University of Colorado, Boulder, CO.

Ratner, N., & Bruner, J. S. (1978). Games, social exchange, and the acquisition of language. *Journal of Child Language, 5*, 391–401.

Schieffelin, B. B. (1979). Getting it together: An ethnographic study of the development of communicative competence. In E. Ochs & B. B. Schieffelin (Eds.), *Developmental pragmatics* (pp. 73–108). New York: Academic Press.

Simonds, R. J., & Scheibel, A. B. (1989). The postnatal development of the motor speech area. *Brain and Language, 37*, 42–58.

Slobin, D. I. (1985). Cross-linguistic evidence for the language-making capacity. In D. I. Slobin (Ed.), *The crosslinguistic study of language acquisition* (Vol. 2, pp. 1157–1256). Hillsdale, NJ: Lawrence Erlbaum Associates.

Snow, C. E. (1981). The uses of imitation. *Journal of Child Language, 8*, 205–212.

Tabors, P. (1987). *Development of communicative competence by second language learners in a nursery school classroom: An ethnolinguisitic study*. Unpublished doctoral dissertation, Harvard University, Cambridge, MA.

Urwin, C. (1982). The contribution of nonvisual communication systems and language to knowing oneself. In M. Beveridge (Ed.), *Children thinking through language* (pp. 99–128). London: Edward Arnold.

Urwin, C. (1984). Dialogue and cognitive functioning in the early language development of three blind children. In A. E. Mills (Ed.), *Language acquisition in the blind child* (pp. 142–161). San Diego: College-Hill Press.

Vygotsky, L. S. (1962). *Thought and language*. Cambridge, MA: MIT Press.

Vygotsky, L. S. (1978). *Mind in society: The development of higher psychological processes*. Cambridge, MA: Harvard University Press.

Watson-Gegeo, K. A., & Gegeo, D. W. (1986). Calling out and repeating: Two key routines in Kwara'ae children's language socialization. In B. B. Schiefflin & E. Ochs (Eds.), *Language socialization across cultures* (pp. 17–50). New York: Cambridge University Press.

Wilson, B. (1986). *The emergence of the semantics of tense and aspect in the language of a visually impaired child*. Unpublished doctoral dissertation, University of Hawai'i, Honolulu.

Wilson, B., & Peters, A. M. (1988). What are you cooking on a hot?: A 3-year-old blind child's "violation" of universal constraints on constituent movement. *Language, 64,* 249–273.

Wong Fillmore, L. (1979). Individual differences in second language acquisition. In C. J. Fillmore, D. Kempler, & W. S-Y. Wang (Eds.), *Individual differences in language ability and language behavior,* (pp. 203–241). New York: Academic Press.

Yates, F. E.(1982). Outline of a physical theory of physiological systems. *Canadian Journal of Physiological Pharmacology, 60,* 217–248.

Author Index

Numbers in *italics* indicate pages on which complete references appear.

221

Subject Index